THE TURBULENT SEA

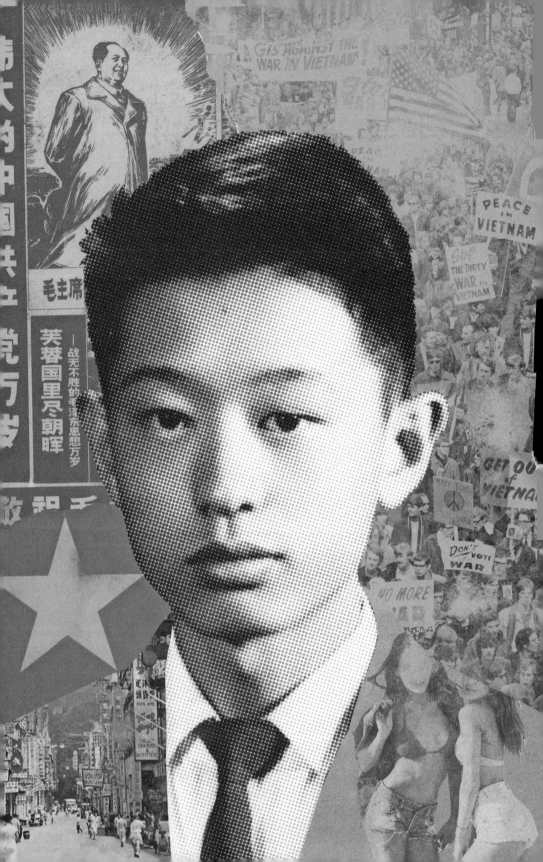

THE TURBULENT SEA

PASSAGE TO A NEW WORLD

Charles N. Li

Regan Arts.

To Kate, Rachel, Gabriel
my family, my love and my inspiration

CONTENTS

THE 1960S WERE MY FORMATIVE YEARS.

In 1961, I arrived in the United States, naïve, starry-eyed, looking like a scrawny teenager even though I was already twenty-one. Beginning with my flight to America, powerful events throughout the decade hit me like an endless tsunami, wave after wave, sweeping away my past, cutting me loose from all my tethers, and unbeknownst to me, transforming me into a person I could never have foreseen becoming.

It may be lamentable that I grew up in a pitiless, unforgiving China and a brutal British colony, Hong Kong, only to land in an America that was on the cusp of being torn apart in a soul-searching transformation. But World War II, the Chinese civil war, totalitarianism in China, colonialism in Hong Kong, and the tumultuous 1960s in America educated me in ways no institutional curriculum could possibly have done. Grief and hardship notwithstanding, the wars, the poverty, the oppression, the broken family, the turmoil during the first thirty years of my life laid bare the human condition for me to ponder and taught me lessons that were at once edifying, provocative and challenging.

The turmoil in America's 1960s began with a new socio-political and environmental awareness among many Americans. This awareness was initiated by the debunking of the "affluent society"' in Michael Harrington's *The Other America: Poverty in the United States*, the invigoration of the civil rights movement under the leadership of Martin Luther King Jr., and a chilling clarion call on the human degradation of planet earth by Rachel Carson's "Silent Spring" in the *New Yorker*. The revelation and exposure of the dark side of the United States shocked the conscience of many Americans. Many of the prospering American middle class, who had trusted the American institutions wholeheartedly since World War II, began to question their government's moral authority. But that was merely the beginning, the tip of the iceberg of the turbulence in the 1960s.

Then came the Vietnam War and the antiwar movement, a juggernaut alongside the concomitant repudiation of established norms by the new "baby boomer" generation that was coming of age. Young Americans raged against the war, demanded equality and justice for all, agitated for political reform, fueled the feminist movement, rebelled against environmental destruction, trashed values dear to the heart of their elders, and sought alternative lifestyles in their existential quandaries. Tension and conflict mounted in the United States. Confrontations between dissidents and the authorities dominated American life. The assassinations of John F. Kennedy, Martin Luther King Jr. and Robert Kennedy further exacerbated the turbulence.

I used the metaphor of the open sea for the title of my memoir exploring the first two decades of my life, *The Bitter Sea: Coming of Age in a China before Mao*. The metaphor remains valid in my American experience during the 1960s, which constituted the third decade of my life. Hence, the title of this volume, *The Turbulent Sea: Passage to a New World*.

Part One of this book recounts my experience of leaving Hong Kong and pursuing formal education at Bowdoin College, Stanford University and, finally, UC Berkeley.

Part Two narrates the stories of five remarkable individuals, Yuha, Keith, Anatole, Rudy, and Francelle, who played vital roles in my intellectual, political, psychological and professional development. It was not their intention to influence me, change my values, mold my personality, or impose a particular worldview on me. Nevertheless, my belated growing-up during my twenties was shaped and forged by my interactions with them. The stories about them, while providing some snapshots of the time in an academic environment, reveal what happened in America and what transpired in my head in the 1960s. But I was, by no means, aware of my mental processes or my intellectual progression.

The last person in Part Two, David, an old friend from Hong Kong, had a chance meeting with me one evening in Berkeley toward the end of the decade. Our interaction, inadvertently, induced me to embark on a new pursuit, a pursuit that has reconnected me to the culture and civilization in which I spent the first two decades of my existence.

This book could not have been written without the emotional and psychological support of my family—Kate, Rachel and Gabriel. Their love and encouragement are invaluable.

Many friends helped me as I wrote this book. Anna and Petar Kokotovich, Roger Friedland, Jeff Saltzman and Peter Saltzman offered constructive criticism. David Sprecher provided positive feedback. Laura Kalman and Kate Metropolis went to great lengths to shepherd the narrative into maturity. They read an early draft, raised insightful questions and pointed out my lapses into grammatical as well as narrative quagmire. Kate Metropolis edited several versions of the manuscript, caught unidiomatic expressions along the way and improved my writing skill.

Years ago, Judith Regan, through repeated prodding, coaxed me into creative writing. Creative writing has always fascinated me, but I lacked the confidence to plunge in. Now, writing and reading have become a daily routine, injecting vigor and validation in my life. Thanks to her, I look forward to that routine every morning. As usual, her editorial comments and suggestions on an earlier draft of this book were illuminating. Without them, my effort to write this book could not have come to fruition.

PART ONE

LEAVING HONG KONG

IT WAS SEPTEMBER 7, 1961. A TWA (TRANS WORLD AIRLINE) plane, its four propeller engines roaring, hurtled through the cumulus clouds as it climbed into the sky. Hong Kong, with all of its bustling activities and densely packed low-rise buildings, shrouded in a thin cocoon of soot and smog, was receding fast. Soon it shrank into a nondescript speck in the South China Sea. As the plane leveled, its roar shifted into a steady drone, the cumulus clouds vanished, and at a distance, the pale blue sky met the glittering, deep blue sea in an arc that looked to me like nature's artful design of a hidden entrance to an infinite void.

"An infinite void?" The self-monitor system in my brain screamed, even though I was choking with emotions. I began to worry that the perception of an infinite void could lead to infinite loneliness, an ailment of fear and despair that had haunted me from time to time. Whenever the ailment descended on me, I felt as if I had been cast into the dark matter of outer space: silent, lifeless and amorphous.

My very first bout of infinite loneliness occurred in 1951, when Father, after lashing out at me physically, announced that I wasn't his son because his offspring could not possibly be as impertinent, ill-mannered and ugly as I was. The physical punishment was not remotely as devastating as his announcement that I wasn't his son, and therefore, I didn't belong to his family. It was tantamount to a pending death sentence because, in 1951, a homeless child in Hong Kong was unlikely to survive. The possibility of being cast out of a home produced a crippling fear in me. That fear, coupled with the knowledge that there was no place for me in this world, brought on infinite loneliness. Even today, I can still feel that suffocating despondency at the time when I stared into the open space after escaping into the mountains of Hong Kong's New Territories, which remained pristine and unspoiled.

By the time I was eighteen years of age, after having suffered infinite loneliness repeatedly, I had developed a way of combating it:

Run as if the devil were behind, closing the gap.

In the New Territories, I ran until my legs started cramping and my chest felt as if it was going to explode. Then, I stopped, holding onto a tree or leaning against a boulder to avoid collapsing. As soon as my shaky legs were strong enough to support my weight, I bent over while moaning and sucking air like a bellow. Once the savage pounding of my heart subsided and the cramp-inducing flood of lactic acid in my legs receded, I resumed running. This two-stage cycle of therapeutic combat against infinite loneliness was repeated until utter exhaustion had obliterated all my emotions. Then, dragging myself to my living quarters, I collapsed in my bed, semi-comatose for a while, and fell asleep in sweat-drenched clothing.

On my journey to the United States, I wanted to avoid infinite loneliness at all costs. But an airplane was not a place to run. In order to ward off the onset of that deadly ailment, I began to mount a mental defense, questioning myself and reminiscing about my life in Hong Kong.

"Has the fear of stepping into the unknown induced this pessimistic image of an infinite void?" I wondered.

"Yes," I sighed and reluctantly admitted that leaving the only world and culture familiar to me was unsettling and frightening. Hong Kong, a brutal and unforgiving British colony in the 1950s, was not a place that I treasured. After 1949, millions of Chinese refugees poured into Hong Kong from China to escape the communists. At the time, Hong Kong was an economically backward British colony, far from becoming a glittering tourist attraction and international financial center. Its only nascent industry involved garment and textile production, created by immigrant entrepreneurs from Shanghai. The Chinese people living in Hong Kong did not even qualify as second-class citizens. In fact, calling them citizens was an exaggeration. They were stateless colonial subjects, under the thumb of Brits, who went there to enrich themselves and enhance the royal coffers as the era of European colonialism was coming to an end. The People's Republic of China did not consider the people of Hong Kong citizens and refused to extend any protection or grant any rights to them. They didn't qualify for Chinese passports. Nor were they entitled to British passports. Everyone's preoccupation in Hong Kong during the 1950s was physical survival: finding food and shelter. In fact, the expression for seeking employment in the local Cantonese language, "won-sei," literally means "looking for food."

Stressed by their struggle for survival, Hong Kong people became obsessed with financial security, a goal that was psychologically unattainable even for those few who had amassed a fortune. The rich remained insecure because in the back of their minds, they knew that their wealth could vanish into thin air at any moment due to an unforeseen political change. An individual had no protection against political upheaval or the unscrupulous machination of a government agency. The fear of destitution and abject penury haunted the Chinese people for nearly one hundred years until the Communists came to power. During the first 40 years of their reign, before the reintroduction of a harnessed free enterprise and guided capitalism, the Communists relegated wealth to the dustbin. Everyone in China, except the communist cadres, lived at a subsistence level. But the Communists had their own distinctive ways of terrorizing people. Chairman Mao, for instance, favored the mobilization of mobs to vanquish what he perceived as his opposition or rivals, beginning with the Land Reform Movement, the Rectification Campaign, the Anti-Rightist Campaign, and ending with the so-called Cultural Revolution.

Burdened with irremediable insecurity, a Chinese resident's life in Hong Kong was reduced to an endless process of calculating who had gained or lost, and how much, in every human interaction. Even a normally altruistic act of giving a gift to someone who was not a member of the family or one's close-knit social group became a calculated undertaking. The giver chose the gift in order to achieve the maximal impact it might have on the recipient to reciprocate, and the recipient assessed the gift and the relationship, trying to figure out an optimal response at minimal cost. Every behavior, every thought, every action of a colonial subject in Hong Kong depended on his/her computation of financial loss and gain. Chasing money not only dominated everyday life, it constituted the core of a person's mental activity.

Even a popular riot was triggered by money. In 1956, the colonial government raised the bus fare from what was equivalent to 2 U.S. cents to 4 U.S. cents. A protest ensued. In no time, the protest morphed into a massive riot that endured for three days. The British government responded by deploying the Gurkha regiment of its colonial army, who were natives of Nepal. Armed with semi-automatic weapons and their signature knife, a curved blade for lopping off the head of an enemy in hand-to-hand combat, the Gurkha guarded the affluent neighborhoods where the Brits, Europeans and some wealthy Chinese lived. The rest of Hong Kong became an open city, at the mercy of the rampaging and plundering mobs.

The day the riot started, a mob in Kowloon intercepted a limousine carrying the Consul General of Switzerland and his wife, who were returning to the city from an excursion in the New Territories. The rioters, venting their anger and hatred against the British colonial overlords, did not recognize any distinction between the British and the Swiss, or, for that matter, the distinction between the British and most other Caucasians. The Consul General and his wife were dragged out of their limo and beaten to death. It became a major international incident that preoccupied the Hong Kong police and media for weeks.

In the mid-1950s, I was an acerbic teenager attending a Chinese high school. People's obsession with money already made me cringe. In my biology class, after a weeklong session on neuroanatomy, I announced that I had made a new discovery. When my classmates went quiet and focused their attention on me, I claimed that the brain of Hong Kong people, aside from the phylogenetically primitive components that maintained bodily function, had evolved into a unique organ consisting of only two parts:

"A limbic region engendering basic emotions like fear, anger, sadness, joy, and a calculator for computing monetary gains and losses in daily activities and interactions."

Some of my classmates broke into laughter; others sat stone-faced. My teacher was not amused. He immediately sent me to the Dean of Students, who meted out my punishment by ordering me to stand against the wall outside of his office for one hour, in plain view of all students in the school.

In contradiction to my abhorrence of the colonialists and my desire to escape Hong Kong's physical and psychological confinement, I felt jolted and depressed when the TWA plane took off from Kai-De airport, as if I were undergoing an amputation. An intangible but significant part of me had been cut off, relegated to the past, destined for the recess of fickle memory. For the first time, I began to understand why freedom could be traumatic to a prisoner after years of incarceration in a penal colony he hated. Freedom meant losing a familiar culture and environment, no matter how abominable that environment might be.

The day before my departure, I bade farewell to my girlfriend, Kim, an athletic young woman with brown hair, almond eyes and a sensuous mouth, like a succulent cherry, inviting kisses. We became acquainted with each other in a track meet where I won the 100-meter sprint, and she triumphed in women's broad jump. A few months later, she became my "girlfriend" because we held hands when we walked together. Holding hands was the limit of physical contact between girlfriend and boyfriend in those days among Chinese of my age. It provided a comforting, reassuring and sometimes even arousing link between the couple, while demonstrating to the world that they had agreed, without ever mentioning a matrimonial vow, to become husband and wife someday when circumstances permitted them to take such a step forward in life.

The farewell was excruciating.

With tears streaming down her cheeks, Kim presented me a heavy, dark green sweater, which she had knit with her own hands at night after work during the week before my departure. She whispered, in a trembling voice, that she knit the sweater because she wanted to keep me warm in the cold winter of America. That was all she said as she held on tightly to both of my hands while we stood facing each other outside of her family's apartment. I was breathless with excitement and sadness. Excitement because I was experiencing love, something I had been yearning for since my childhood in a broken and dysfunctional family, sadness because of the brevity of that experience imposed by the circumstance. Paradoxically I also felt a serenity and contentment that I had never known before, as if that brief flash of love, ephemeral as it might be, had momentarily melted away all the bitterness and anger in my life.

Instinct urged me to embrace her, kiss her, caress her and never let go of her. While straining to contain those bursting desires, I also felt dreadfully guilty for having decided not to spend my last evening in Hong Kong with her, even though I desperately wished to do so. But prudence and fear of the consequence of passion had curtailed my wish. I had chosen the safe alternative of spending my last evening in Hong Kong with my two closest loyal companions. We were devoted brothers to each other. That evening, after a late farewell dinner of our usual meager meal at a street vendor, we walked briskly, in grief-stricken silence, around the Victoria peak of Hong Kong overlooking the harbor on one side and the open sea on the other side. We walked and walked, paying no attention to time, until the sun rose, which reminded me that I had to say goodbye to my mother in her Christian seminary on my way to the Kai-De airport. During the night, my friends and I were so distraught that none of us felt the impact of pounding the cement for hours and none of us knew what to say.

Three downcast bosom friends, too proud to shed tears, yet too sad to utter a word, marched endlessly in the darkness, as if we were trying to escape a looming apocalypse.

For fifteen months before my departure, my two best friends and I had shared a cramped, dilapidated room adjacent to a reeking communal bathroom and shower on the same floor of a stark and ugly concrete building. Each room in the building housed a group of tenants, and the landlord didn't care how many people shared a room as long as he received the rent on time. The calculator in his brain always maximized the rent he could collect according to the demand and supply of the market. The rent he charged fluctuated from month to month. Most of the fluctuations trended upward, but the increase was never high enough to cause the tenants to leave en masse.

Sleeping on beat-up mattresses laid on the concrete floor, my friends and I had forged a life by sharing everything, including the money each of us earned by tutoring children of rich families who withered in the ruthless competition of their secondary schools. Tutoring those rich kids enabled us to eke out a living in that harsh and pitiless British colony. Each of us yearned to establish a family, to feel the warmth and comfort of belonging to some loved ones. But without a college education, a profession and a stable income, establishing a family was beyond our reach. While struggling to survive, we did our best to create a kind of surrogate family for each other. Yes, we bonded as if we were each other's security blanket.

Devoted friendship in Chinese culture implied a level of closeness that would be unimaginable in Western culture. Close friends, like members of a traditional Chinese family, viewed privacy and personal distance, both physical and psychological, as a barrier in their relationships. Members of a close-knit, bonded social group identified with each other and shared everything: their thoughts, feelings and material possessions. Most importantly, they depended on each other and were proud of that dependence.

As youngsters in Hong Kong, my friends and I had learned that Europe and America were lonely places where individualism ruled supreme. We didn't understand "individualism," neither did we seek to understand it. In our mind, it was some highfalutin cover term for a selfish and self-centered existence. Westerners, we learned, did not bond with anyone in the way we understood bondedness in human relationships. They needed to keep a distance from each other even if they belonged to the same family. Once, we heard that a young Englishman took a loan from his parents to pay for his postgraduate education at the University of Hong Kong. To us, that represented the most ludicrous and outlandish practice. In our world, parents had the authority to refuse funding an offspring's pursuit for some reason, whatever it might be. But they would never consider giving a loan to an offspring. If they deemed an offspring's monetary need justified, as it was in the case of educational expenses, they would take a loan themselves to meet the need of the offspring. To the Chinese mind, a loan was a business transaction among unrelated people. It had no place in a close-knit relationship.

As my friends and I walked the night before my departure, we were painfully aware that our brotherly and mutually dependent bond, which conferred to each of us a measure of security and some sense of belonging, would soon be broken for good. My friends would miss my companionship, and I would have to struggle against infinite loneliness in America.

Of course, my friends were happy for me because I was on the threshold of a new life in America that was supposed to be promising and rewarding in terms of conventional success—but they couldn't help regretting the end of our shared life buoyed by a heartfelt camaraderie and brotherhood.

Neither could I!

A new life, made possible by a scholarship from the World University Service funded by the U.S. State Department, implied the termination of an old life that was penurious and hazardous but compensated by fellowship, loyalty and mutual devotion. It would be highly unlikely that we would meet again. Like all young residents of Hong Kong who dared to dream, we aspired to a life without discrimination, a life brimming with opportunities for advancement in a society anchored on freedom and meritocracy. But fate picked only one of us to pursue that goal.

During our long, brisk walk, I couldn't refrain from fantasizing how wonderful it would be if the three of us could go to America together, backing each other up, exploring the unknown as a team, helping one another succeed, and avoiding the curse of infinite loneliness that confronted literally every Chinese immigrant in the Western world.

We didn't know much about America. Our rosy image of the United States as a land of wealth, freedom and opportunity grew out of our naivete and distorted information from *LIFE Magazine* and *LOOK Magazine*. Like everyone else in Hong Kong, we believed that the United States was the land of promise. Even though my friends didn't say a word about their wish to go to America with me, they were, in all likelihood, indulging in the same fantasy as I was when we marched tirelessly and silently around the Victoria Peak that night.

Now, sitting in a window seat in the TWA plane and staring at the arc where the sea and the sky met, the prospect of succumbing to infinite loneliness continued to haunt me. In order to alleviate my fear, I reassured myself,

"No, I am NOT entering a 'void,' I'm heading toward Meiguo."

Meiguo is the Chinese word for "America." The first syllable, *mei*, means "beautiful," and the second syllable, *guo*, means "country."

"So, you are going to the 'beautiful country,' huh?" The prefrontal lobe of my brain monitored me mercilessly, not allowing me to escape into fantasy. "You'd better make sure that you excel, whatever you do!"

That sort of admonition usually comes from a Tiger Mom or a stern father, part and parcel of parenthood prevalent among Chinese families. Even though my mother, detached and aloof, was never a Tiger Mom to me, and I had little experience with normal family life, I could not escape the influence of the Chinese cultural norm of seeking success at all cost, that is, conventional success gauged by wealth and prestige. Indeed, I embraced it as the centerpiece of my life.

Most people of a nation that has been war-torn, demoralized and destitute for more than a century, like China, suffer from endless anxiety. Preoccupied with survival, they find it difficult to understand that striving to be a wholesome and compassionate human being capable of seeking joy and happiness might be more important than conventional success during our transient existence on earth. Generations of deprivation, abject poverty and European dominance in China promoted the mentality that the meaning of life rested exclusively with the pursuit of fame and wealth, regardless of the toll and consequences. In such an environment, it is common for people, especially young males in a male chauvinistic culture, to suffer from debilitating anxiety, often bordering on being pathological, resulting in warped personality or stunted psychological development. Yet "Tiger parents" would probably snicker with utter contempt if they learned of Tennessee Williams' discourse on the dehumanizing trappings of wealth and success in his essay, "The Catastrophe of Success," published as a journalistic piece after *The Glass Menagerie* became a huge hit on Broadway. When I mentioned the essay to one of my siblings in our old age, decades after we had settled comfortably in the United States, he laughed and reprised,

"That's ridiculous! Who is this Tennessee Williams? He probably suffered from delusions."

When I mentioned that Williams was a great writer, he mused:

"Well, artists can be weird. What else matters in life if it is not money? You need money to buy everything."

I wanted to retort, "Well, life is much more than every THING money can buy!" Those words were at the tip of my tongue, but I held back. It wouldn't change his opinion and might very well provoke his hostility.

As I was trying to look ahead into my life while sitting in the airplane carrying me to the United States, I felt the crippling anxiety generated by the desire for success, the success in the pursuit of money and prestige that was imprinted on me. My mind began to wonder,

"What will become of me in America?"

"Will I excel?"

"Am I going to be rejected again as I was cast away in China after graduating from high school in Hong Kong?"

"Am I smart enough to compete for an advanced degree in America?"

Of course, I didn't have a clue about the answers to those questions. The only available venue for mitigating my anxiety was to remind myself that my failure in China wasn't my fault.

Just three years earlier, I failed to gain access to a university education in China. The Chinese communists rejected me because they considered my father a major counterrevolutionary. The policy of the Communist government in the 1950s prohibited a son or daughter of a counterrevolutionary from receiving a university education. The destiny of the offspring of counterrevolutionaries was life-long hard labor. It didn't matter if the offspring was not a counterrevolutionary, and it didn't matter if the offspring was capable, intelligent and hard-working. Even though this Chinese policy was common knowledge in Hong Kong, I took a chance by returning to China after high school, partly because I had no other opportunity of getting a university education and partly because my father encouraged me to go back.

In the Confucian civilization, a father's wish, even if it was expressed as an encouragement, not an explicit command, exerted immense pressure on a son to accede to that wish. A teenage son was expected to obey. My father, after he was convicted as a collaborator with the Japanese at the end of the Second World War and escaped to Hong Kong as the Communists defeated Chiang Kai-shek's Nationalist government in the mainland, continued to dream of a political comeback. If I returned to China, I would serve as a probe, a litmus test, for him to assess the Communists' attitude toward him.

Despite my effort to ward off infinite loneliness on the airplane, grief, melancholy and fear engulfed me—grief for leaving my friends in Hong Kong; melancholy for being alone, cut off from all social connections and familiar cultural norms; fear, the worst and the most debilitating of all emotions, because I was on the brink of stepping into an alien world.

"What will happen to my friends? Will we ever eat those cheap 'rice bowls' again, squatting in front of a street vendor, like we did most days in the industrial district of Hong Kong?" I wondered.

It was comforting to think about eating, which was always pleasurable when one was hungry, even if the food consisted of nothing special. In Hong Kong, my friends and I were hungry all the time. We assumed that it was a normal condition of youth, not something that deserved special attention. In 1958, at the beginning of the Chinese famine brought on by Chairman Mao's Great Leap Forward campaign that killed tens of millions of people, I felt a different kind of hunger. It was relentless, disabling and painful, insistent on monopolizing my attention, no matter what I did or how I tried to distract myself. Of course, that was starvation, not just the need for better nutrition. For the Great Leap Forward Campaign in 1958, Chairman Mao mobilized all 660 million people in China to abandon their daily duties in order to make steel in their backyards. Students stopped learning, teachers stopped teaching, bureaucrats stopped doing their office work, farmers stopped growing food, industrial workers stopped manufacturing products, technicians and engineers stopped practicing their trades. In less than one year, 660 million people depleted the nation's grain reserve. Famine ensued. Every week, the authority reduced everyone's rice ration. At a thought-reform school in southern China where I, as the son of a counterrevolutionary, was undergoing political education and ideological rehabilitation, my daily caloric intake consisted of two bowls of low-grade, rough rice. No protein, no vegetables. That was starvation. In starvation, the tactic of mind-over-body didn't work. The needs of the body rendered the mind irrelevant. It was not just the stomach that was cramping. The brain screamed for food. One became angry, despondent and inching toward insanity.

In Hong Kong, my friends and I were merely undernourished, not starving. With rare exceptions when we splurged on payday or some other occasion for a good meal, we ate twice a day: once in the evening, once in late morning. Our food might be lacking in quality and nutrition because we couldn't afford anything better. But it didn't matter. What mattered was that my stomach did not cramp, my brain didn't scream for food, and wolfing down two or three bowls of steamed rice covered with some salty vegetables stir-fried with a sprinkle of shredded pork felt heavenly.

But the thought of eating led me back to yearning for my friends, who were always my companions at meals, and the yearning for my friends brought on melancholia. I made a conscious effort to stop that train of thought.

As I was struggling to clear my mind and overcome fear, the thin air of the cabin paired with the steady drone of the airplane engines began to sap my energy. In no time, my brain was shutting down, and I slipped into a slumber for the long flight.

ANCHORAGE, ALASKA

WHEN THE PLANE LANDED IN ANCHORAGE, ALASKA, AFTER refueling in Tokyo, the flight crew instructed all passengers to deplane in order to go through immigration and customs inspection.

At the immigration checkpoint, a thickset uniformed officer, all shoulders, sitting in a kiosk, looked at my papers: a letter from the U.S. State Department certifying that I had been granted a full scholarship including room and board to attend Bowdoin College in the state of Maine, a J-1 student visa issued by the U.S. Consulate in Hong Kong, and my Hong Kong identity card.

"Where is your passport?" the immigration officer barked.

"I don't have one," I replied haltingly but matter-of-factly.

"What do you mean you don't have one?" The officer didn't like my answer and stared at me with steely eyes. "What's your nationality?"

"I guess I am Chinese."

He looked me over carefully for a moment, decided that I wasn't being flippant or disrespectful, and asked, "Why don't you have a Chinese passport?"

"I don't because China, I mean the People's Republic of China or Communist China, does not consider me a citizen."

"What about Taiwan, the other China?"

"I have never been there. I spent the last three years in Hong Kong."

"Are all Hong Kong people stateless like you?" he asked.

"No, the compradors have British passports, a special category of British passport that doesn't allow them to enter Britain. They are Chinese by ancestry but chose to be second-class British subjects in exchange for servitude to their colonial masters."

He was somewhat mystified.

"What's the word you used? Compra . . . something. Well, forget it! I will stamp the entry permit on your Hong Kong identification paper. You can go to the customs officer over there now."

Thus, I officially entered the United States, as I walked from the immigration building back to the TWA plane on the tarmac on September 7, 1961, shivering in a freezing summer day of Anchorage, Alaska. I was twenty-one years old, six feet tall, appearing more like a skinny boy than a young man who had already legally come of age.

SEATTLE, WASHINGTON

UPON ARRIVAL IN SEATTLE, THE STEWARDESS INSTRUCTED ME to disembark and board a different plane to Boston in two hours. Having never traveled by plane before and unsure of the transfer, I was somewhat apprehensive as I walked into the Seattle airport terminal until arriving at the gate for the Boston-bound plane. Regaining my bearings, I started wandering around the terminal. It offered nothing beyond numerous boarding and disembarking gates, each of which was surrounded by rows of chairs bolted to the floor. There were cigarette machines. The stench of cigarette smoke in the terminal was worse than that in the cabin of my TWA flight from Hong Kong. I didn't want to wait for my Boston-bound plane by sitting and inhaling cigarette smoke at the designated gate. Besides, sitting, even without cigarette smoke, never appealed to me. After having suffered many long hours of confinement on the flight from Hong Kong, each seat in the Seattle airport looked like a miniature prison. The last thing I wanted was to sit for two additional hours even though I was well aware that I needed to control my peripatetic propensity. It caused my parents and their peers to conclude that I was a problem child, cursed with the lack of social grace for the inability to sit still. In China, the ability of a child to sit still for a long time was an indicator of his/her good character. I was an obvious disaster.

One of the teacher's evaluations at the end of my first year in secondary school shortly after I joined my parents in Hong Kong in 1950 stated, "Incessant movement and vulgar speech characterized Li Na's behavior." That evaluation brought on a bout of lashing by my father.

My second-grade teacher in Shanghai, annoyed by my fidgeting and incessant need for activities in an assigned seat, where I was supposed to sit rigidly and quietly all day long like every school kid did in China at the time, publicly reprimanded me by announcing to my class that I was born with thorns in my ass. That public humiliation succeeded in inducing me to sit still for ten minutes. As I started to fidget again, the teacher looked in my direction, shook his head and gave up. He could tell that I would be a problem child, destined for trouble and social estrangement.

At the Seattle airport, I thought two hours was too long a period of time to loiter in a dull, smoke-filled terminal building, in an era before airport terminals acquired restaurants, shopping centers and other consumer attractions. Then an idea popped in my head: Visit the city of Seattle!

I had never heard of Seattle before this journey. When the TWA plane took off from Hong Kong, I only knew that I was supposed to end up in Boston. No one explained to me that the plane had to stop at numerous points, and I had to change planes along the way. What led me to the idea of visiting Seattle was pure curiosity. I wanted to know how an American city differed from Shanghai, Hong Kong or Nanking (Nanjing), the three cities I had lived in. The plane had already stopped in Anchorage, my port of entry to the United States. Anchorage was gray and tiny from the air. The snow-capped mountains at a distance looked alluring. But Anchorage itself appeared like a village from the airplane. One could hardly call it a city. When I disembarked in Anchorage, the air temperature was near freezing, cold enough to shock someone from the hot and humid climate of tropical Hong Kong.

When my plane flew over Seattle, the city looked like a metropolis spread over a vast area. Tall skyscrapers dotted the landscape, and the narrow passages of blue-green water between some islands and the mainland looked enticing. But how could I pull off a quick tour of Seattle from the airport?

Then, I remembered what James Dean did in the movie *Giant* before he hit a jackpot of black gold and became a "giant": He hitchhiked when he didn't have a car. "Hitchhike" was a memorable English word I learned from that movie. In the Chinese subtitles, it was given an ad hoc translation which didn't make much sense. But the English word stuck with me. It had an appealing ring to my ears. It also gave me the idea that Americans were generous, because in Hong Kong, if you tried to hitchhike, you were liable to be run over on the narrow road. Besides, a person driving a car in Hong Kong, who had to be rich, would never stop for a stranger standing along a road.

I surmised that if the movie *Giant* showed James Dean hitchhiking, it was a common practice in America. Gathering my courage, I walked out of the terminal, stood by the side of a highway, raised my arm and stuck out my thumb.

In no time, I got a ride in a gigantic car, which didn't look like any of those 1950s British-made automobiles in Hong Kong, such as Morris Minors, Triumphs and Austins, typically smaller than a Volkswagen bug. This American car looked like a boat, somewhere between a sampan and a junk, the common water taxi or floating home that plied the water of the Hong Kong harbor. It would have been impossible for such an enormous contraption to negotiate some of the narrow streets in Hong Kong.

As I settled into what looked like a luxurious leather sofa in the front part of the cabin and thanked the driver for picking me up, he asked gently, "Where do you want to go?"

"Oh, I don't really have a destination. Just want to see the city of Seattle."

"Alright, let me think of a good location to drop you off," he said as his "boat" sped down the freeway. The speedometer indicated that the car was going 70 miles per hour, an inconceivable and exciting speed for me. Yet, I didn't feel that we were moving fast in that wide, open space along the freeway outside of the Seattle airport. In addition to the excitement brought on by the car's high speed, the cornucopia of new and fresh sensory input was overwhelming: the smell of pristine air—the air in Hong Kong and Kowloon was always foul, reeking of pungent automobile exhaust mixed with the putrid smell of perspiration along crowded sidewalks; the wide open space as far as I could see through the car windows; the snow-capped mountains at a distance shaped like volcanoes with the top already blown off—years later I learned that they were indeed volcanoes, called the Cascade Mountains; and the dark green conifer forest blanketing the mountain slopes below the snow line. It was expansive and primordial, invoking images of the rich flora and fauna associated with forests in my reading of *Tarzan* stories. The corrugated stretches of clouds resting on top of the tree line looked like perfect lairs for the hidden dragons of Chinese folklore. According to Chinese mythology, dragons always conceal themselves in clouds, which is why humans can only imagine them. Finally, there were the fast-moving automobiles, speeding by on both sides of me, sounding as if they were tearing up the asphalt of the road. All of those new, mesmerizing scenes. They nearly put me in a trance.

But the driver jolted me out of my private world of thoughts when he spoke again, "Perhaps I will drop you off somewhere downtown. Does that sound good to you?"

"Sure! That sounds perfect!" I responded, even though I didn't understand "downtown"—I never heard of such a word in British English.

"Where did you come from?" he asked with a smile.

"Hong Kong."

"What? You just came from Hong Kong?" He sounded startled. "Where is your luggage?"

"I think it's being loaded onto a plane bound for Boston." I didn't understand what startled him.

"Are you going to Boston?"

"Yes, yes. I am going there to attend a college not far from Boston."

"Which college?"

"Bowdoin college. It's in the state of Maine."

"Bowdoin! That's an excellent liberal arts college. Congratulations!" I didn't know what "liberal arts" meant. But I thanked him anyway.

"When are you leaving for Boston?"

"Oh, in about one hour and thirty minutes."

"What?! " He sounded really alarmed. "You can't go to Seattle. We are more than twenty minutes away from downtown. You need to get back to the airport!"

He slammed on the brake and pulled onto the shoulder of the highway.

I was completely baffled.

In old Hong Kong, the runway of the airport, known as the Kai-De, was less than 500 feet from one of the most densely populated residential and commercial neighborhoods, called the "Kowloon Citadel" because, until the 19th century, the area was enclosed by a tall stone wall. The runway almost abutted the rows of apartment houses, separated from the airport by a four-lane paved road, which was exceptionally wide by Hong Kong standards. Buses, lorries, cars, rickshaws and pedestrians always filled the road. The citadel sat at the bottom of a thousand-foot rocky mountain, called the Lion Mountain because the ragged, rocky ridge at one end of the top looked like the silhouette of a lion's head. As planes approached the Kai-De airport, they headed straight toward the mountain as if they were on a suicide dive. While descending rapidly over the citadel, they flew like warplanes strafing the markets, apartment buildings, and a multitude of people before banking sharply toward the runway. The noise generated by the planes was deafening, but the people living there were inured to it. Nobody in the crowd even bothered to look at the planes flying less than a couple of hundred feet over them. Just part of the daily ruckus of life. Among the pilots of international commercial airlines in those days, Kai-De airport was infamous as the most difficult and dangerous airport for them to land.

In Seattle, when I walked out of the airport terminal and saw an enormous expanse of open field, I inferred that the city of Seattle wasn't 500 feet away like Kai-De airport was from the Kowloon citadel. Nonetheless, I reckoned that it couldn't be more than one or two miles away. When the driver told me that the city was fifteen miles away, I was flabbergasted and began to panic.

Fifteen miles was an incredibly long distance in Hong Kong!

In fact, hardly any point on the Hong Kong island was fifteen miles from another point. Obviously, I was heading into a disaster on the very day of my arrival in the United States.

At the next exit, the driver got off the highway, turned 180 degrees around on a country road, and kindly drove me back to the air terminal.

By the time I arrived at the gate of departure, the plane had already started boarding its passengers. In the plane, there were only about twenty passengers scattered among rows and rows of seats. Relieved that disaster had been averted, I began to chuckle at my little misadventure to Seattle.

"Wow, America is a big country," I thought to myself.

So was China. But in the China I knew, people rarely ventured more than a couple of miles away from where they lived. In rural areas, most residents spent their entire life without ever leaving their village, except women who departed permanently for their husbands' homes through arranged marriages. Even in a city, people tended to stay within its confines. When a person moved to a different city, as I did in my childhood, it was tantamount to bidding farewell indefinitely to friends, relatives and a familiar world, as if one were moving to a different country. After all, the inhabitants of a different Chinese city would most likely have a different diet, observe some unfamiliar social conventions, and speak a language or dialect that was unintelligible to a newly arrived resident.

Compared with China, Hong Kong was just a small speck along the southern coast of Guangdong (Canton) province. It had two urban centers during the 1950s and 1960s: the waterfront separated from the mainland by the narrow Victoria Strait, and the larger region of Kowloon adjacent to the rural and undeveloped New Territory located on a peninsula of the Pearl River Delta of the mainland. The combined urban area of Hong Kong was so small that my friends and I often eschewed the readily available buses crisscrossing the colony in order to save the 25-cent bus fare (equivalent to 4 cents in U.S. currency, which should be measured against the fact that a rice bowl, our regular dinner, cost two Hong Kong dollars—which was equivalent to 33 U.S. cents). When we headed to some destination on foot, we wouldn't say that we were walking. Instead, we said "taking #11 bus," because the number "11" symbolized two legs. But the distance we covered on foot rarely exceeded one or two miles, which, at the time, approximated the diameter of an imaginary circle enclosing all of the densely inhabited urban districts.

BOSTON, MASSACHUSETTS

I HAD A MISSION IN BOSTON: FIND MY AUNT, HELEN, WHO TOOK care of me in Shanghai after the Second World War until 1950 when she brought me, age ten, to my parents in Hong Kong. During those years in Shanghai, Aunt Helen and I survived the civil war with all of its terrifying chaos, violence, mayhem and anarchy prior to the triumph of the Chinese Communist Party and the establishment of the People's Republic of China. After Aunt Helen returned me to my parents, I did not interact with her throughout my teens in Hong Kong because of my father. Without ever offering a reason, he forbade his family members from contacting Aunt Helen—an edict based on his absolute authority dictated by Confucian ethics. My older siblings, who often heard information about my parents' lives from relatives, claimed that bad blood existed between him and Aunt Helen. In the early 1920s, my father, mother and Aunt Helen met in Beijing, a political and cultural center of China. They traveled from their native province, Shandong, a large peninsula immediately south of Beijing, jutting into the Yellow Sea toward Japan, in search of opportunities for education and social advancement. Nobody knew the details of the "bad blood" between father and Aunt Helen. It was a taboo subject. In Beijing, father had won admission to Peking (Beijing) University, the preeminent institution of higher learning in China at the time. I never knew why mother and Aunt Helen ended up in the same city, which for more than two centuries served as the capital of the Qing (Manchu) Dynasty. During the late 19th and early 20th century, Beijing was the epicenter of revolutionary activities before and after the collapse of the Qing Dynasty in 1911.

Before Aunt Helen brought me to my parents in Hong Kong in 1950, I attended a grade school in Shanghai. Upon the establishment of the People's Republic of China on October 1, 1949, all citizens were instructed that the Communist government had established a new "class system." At the bottom of the system were "counterrevolutionaries," which included anyone formerly associated with the Nationalist government, no matter how tenuous or contentious the association, and their family members. They became China's "untouchables." That untouchable caste also included all landlords in rural areas, regardless of their standing among their tenant farmers. During the first few years of communist rule, most counterrevolutionaries were executed or killed by mobs at the instigation of communist cadres. In Shanghai, I soon came to understand why mother and father escaped to Hong Kong before the Communist takeover and left me under the care of Aunt Helen. Following Aunt Helen's instruction, I never brought up Father's name in school or to any stranger to ensure no one would know that I was the son of a very important counterrevolutionary. Fortunately, we lived under the Communist rule for only one year before departing to Hong Kong. If we had stayed longer, government agents would surely have caught up with me, labeled me the son of a counterrevolutionary, and probably banished me into a labor camp.

Upon my graduation from a Chinese high school in 1957, I, like a fool, returned to China from Hong Kong to seek a tertiary education. Political naivete, paternal prodding, and resentment of the British colonialists drove my imprudent decision. Underlying those reasons was the stark reality that I had neither the financial resources nor the opportunity to seek a university education anywhere else. In China, the authority told me that as the son of a counterrevolutionary, I needed to attend a thought-reform school to undergo indoctrination before I could be considered a candidate for admission to a university. They didn't tell me outright that I had no chance of becoming a normal citizen. On the contrary, they implied that there was a slim hope for me if I reformed myself and cleansed my poisoned mind.

In thought-reform school, I received daily political indoctrination, endured harsh physical labor, and studied for the university entrance examination, only to be told at the end of the year that I would never gain admission to a university on account of my family background. Despondent and emaciated, I returned to Hong Kong, the colony from which I so desperately wished to escape.

Yet I was by no means the only young overseas Chinese who tried to seek a new life in China. During the 1950s, many young people of Chinese ancestry from Southeast Asia, beguiled and blinded by their enthusiasm for the communist-led emancipation of their mother country from the yokes of Western domination, chose to return to China. Unfortunately, most of them belonged to well-to-do merchant families in Hong Kong, Macau, Thailand, Vietnam, Malaysia, the Philippines and Indonesia. The economic status of their family relegated them into the undesirable class of bourgeoisie in the Chinese communist caste system. Many of them landed in the same thought-reform school where I was, and most of them ended up as outcasts, condemned as manual laborers for life on collective farms. Like a ship of fools, we merrily flocked toward our ruination.

When I returned from China to Hong Kong in 1958, Aunt Helen had already immigrated to the United States. Mother, who was Aunt Helen's sister, told me that Helen worked for the Rescue Mission in Boston. She gave me a Boston address as I said goodbye to her at her Christian theological seminary in Hong Kong.

At Boston's Logan Airport, mindful of my misadventure in Seattle, I sought assistance by showing Aunt Helen's address to a man at the information booth and asked for the cheapest way to get there. Following his instruction, I boarded a bus to downtown and hailed a taxi from there. At $10, the combined cost of the airport bus and the taxi ride struck fear in me. It amounted to one-tenth of all the money in my possession for the coming academic year. To put that expenditure in perspective, ten U.S. dollars was equivalent to sixty Hong Kong dollars at that time, which would buy thirty "rice bowls" from the street vendors, roughly the cost of feeding myself for two weeks in Hong Kong in 1961. In addition, I had not yet purchased a bus ticket from Boston to Brunswick, Maine, the location of Bowdoin College, and didn't know what other expenses lurked ahead for the next nine months, at the end of which I hoped to get a summer job to earn some money.

Upon arriving at Aunt Helen's address, I tried my best to conceal my anxiety as she opened the door of her apartment at the Rescue Mission.

At the sight of me, she broke into a happy grin, showing hardly any wear and tear from sixty-some years of a rough-and-tumble life. She remained tall, lanky and upright. Sporting a long beige dress printed with polka dots and small plum flowers, as if made from some old wallpaper, she wore her black hair tightly combed back into a chignon just as I remembered when I was a child living with her in Shanghai.

"My prodigal son has returned!" she said happily.

"Here she goes again with her non sequiturs," I thought to myself as her comment triggered a flood of memories.

As a child, I liked Aunt Helen, who was kind and loving to me. Together we survived several harrowing years of civil war between the insurgent communists and Chiang Kai-shek's Nationalists in the late 1940s. In Shanghai, where Aunt Helen and I lived, the civilians did not suffer from the battle between the Communist army and the Nationalist army. There wasn't any firefight, artillery duel or house-to-house combat. The Nationalists simply melted away before any Communist soldier came into sight. It was the anarchy and lawlessness in the vast metropolis of Shanghai that inflicted unspeakable trauma and suffering to the millions of frightened residents. Days before the Communist soldiers arrived in the city, employees of the police department, the fire department, the civil service bureaus, the utility companies and the mayor's office abrogated their duties, looted their workplaces and simply vanished. Subsequently, Shanghai became an open city, where gangsters, hooligans, thieves and riffraff robbed, raped and killed with impunity.

Overcome with fear, people sought refuge in their homes, hoping that the locked doors and blocked windows would deter brigands and intruders. For three days the tenants in our building huddled together on the ground floor, piling heavy furniture against the front door. Everyone trembled and some sobbed at any unusual sound that reached us. Aunt Helen and I often clung to each other at those moments of great tension. Yet, in spite of our bond that strengthened during the final days of the civil war, Aunt Helen often put me ill at ease with her unsolicited, unprovoked and sometimes oxymoronic pronouncements such as:

"Jesus loves you!"

"He will kill the infidels!"

During the days of the open city, she prayed on her knees repeatedly, dragging me onto the floor, crying out loud for Lord Jesus to show mercy on us. My reaction to her pronouncements bordered on a mixture of bewilderment, guilt and shame, mostly because I harbored the thought that she was a little strange. In the traditional Chinese culture, it would be extremely disrespectful and shameful for a child to think of an elder as a little strange, especially when the elder was a guardian.

Now, after eleven years of separation, the first thing she did upon seeing me in Boston was call me her prodigal son. She knew that I wasn't her son, and she understood that in traditional Chinese culture, claiming someone as a son had serious consequences. If one young man called another young man his son, that would be the cause of a fistfight, because doing so would usurp the paternal authority, superiority and control over the victim. In defense of his honor, the victim would lash out physically.

In a Confucian society, every child learned that parents were irreplaceable, no matter how they treated you. They were your gods, because they gave life to you and therefore, you owed them everything. It was their prerogative to treat you in whatever manner they saw fit. If they neglected or abused you, it would be your karma. If they treated you well, it would be your good fortune. Parents could give a child away without ever feeling an iota of guilt or remorse, and the child would not be allowed to harbor any resentment. Filial loyalty was the cornerstone of the Confucian ethic, which, in turn, underpinned the East Asian civilization. During the late 19th century, Empress Dowager Ci-Xi ruled China for decades, presiding over the decline of the Qing (Manchu) Dynasty, as she took advantage of the canon of filial loyalty to cow the Emperor, her adult son, and forbade him to initiate political and economic reform, which could have rescued China from the brink of political and economic collapse. From the perspective of an offspring, the unbridled authority and revered role of parents could never be usurped. In the history of feudal Europe, patricide during the struggle for power within royal families was not uncommon. During China's era of imperial dynasties, which endured for more than two thousand years, power struggles in imperial families were just as common and murderous as they were in the families of European monarchs—but patricide was unheard of in China, whereas filicide occurred not infrequently.

In addition to not being Aunt Helen's son, I was by no means "prodigal." I had never squandered any money, nor did I have any money to squander. No one, no elders, had ever given me a penny. No pocket money, no spare change. In secondary school, when I needed money to buy supplies like a pencil, ruler and eraser, I had to ask Father for the precise amount. Making the request always felt like pleading for leniency in front of a stern judge, frightening, painful and humiliating. Before I earned any money at the age of nineteen, my pocket was always empty.

I knew the expression "prodigal son" came from a biblical story, and Aunt Helen was a pious Christian. So, when she called me a prodigal son, I smiled, bowed, and told her that I was happy to see her, which wasn't a lie.

She lived in a very humble one-bedroom apartment behind the office of Boston's Rescue Mission, down from Beacon Hill, in the direction of Chinatown.

Leading me to her living/dining room cum kitchen where she had set up a cot in one corner for me, she served me a bowl of soup noodles, which were delicious.

The two days I spent with Aunt Helen were not easy. We spent the whole time in her cramped apartment, never exploring Boston or

Cambridge, both of which had loomed large in my mind because of Boston's revolutionary history and Cambridge's two great institutions of higher education: MIT and Harvard. She badgered me with all kinds of questions about my parents and siblings. Most of those questions I couldn't answer, not out of reluctance to proffer any information, but because I was clueless. She was unaware of the estrangement between my parents and me, which was extremely rare, to say the least, in a Chinese family. It soon became apparent from our conversation that she knew more about the lives of my parents and siblings than I did, because Mother and she, both devout Christians, kept in touch with each other by mail regularly. She knew that my mother had left my father many years ago. Since then, Mother had earned a degree from a theological seminary and became an ordained minister of a fundamentalist protestant church. Aunt Helen told me that she was in the process of sponsoring my mother to immigrate to the United States. That piece of information was a million times more newsworthy than anything I could tell her about anyone in my family.

Typical of a traditional Chinese elder, she never asked me directly what I did during the decade of our separation, although it was perfectly acceptable to enquire about my parents and siblings. I suspected that she had learned from my mother that I had gone to China after high school, only to return to Hong Kong one year later, rejected, emaciated and despondent.

She also wanted to know what I would study at Bowdoin. When I said mathematics or physics, she chuckled and commented, "Those are not my favorite subjects. But they set you up for good careers."

I had no idea if mathematics or physics would lead to a good career, but it was comforting to hear the message.

In Hong Kong and China, high schools had two tracks for those lucky enough to pass a school's entrance examination. The children who earned high scores were placed into the science track. The placement did not take into account the youngster's interests or preference, even though it would shape his/her life and profoundly impact the child's eventual career. For many children and their families, being in the science track in high school was also a matter of pride, a badge of honor, even if the youngsters happen to love the arts, social sciences or literature. That frame of mind remained steadfast in me after my arrival in the United States.

Early in the morning on the third day after my arrival in Boston, I left for Bowdoin. To save money, I walked to the Greyhound bus station, which happened to be not far from the Rescue Mission. At the ticket booth, I was relieved that a one-way fare to Brunswick, Maine cost $5. I still had $85 to see me through the academic year.

BOWDOIN COLLEGE

THE CAMPUS OF BOWDOIN WAS IDYLLIC AND BEAUTIFUL. BUILT around a large quadrangle with lush lawns crisscrossed by paved walkways and shaded by magnificent oak, maple and poplar trees, the campus looked like an upscale resort. Surrounding the quadrangle stood several Victorian-style buildings adorned with patterned masonry framing and

leaded glass windowpanes. There were also many ivy-covered redbrick buildings displaying rows of windows with white trim.

A church with an exceptionally tall spire stood behind the administration building directly across the campus. It was the First Congregational Church. Snow white, the tall spire of the church looked imposing against the azure sky on the day of my arrival, as if James Bowdoin III, the founder of the college, whose father collaborated with Benjamin Franklin in his pioneering research on electricity, had intended for it to watch over Bowdoin's welfare. The college was established in the town of Brunswick, Massachusetts, before the American Revolution. That portion of Massachusetts plus a region adjacent to Quebec became the state of Maine.

I had never heard of the state of Maine or Bowdoin College until a Commission of the World University Service selected me, after a series of written exams and interviews, as a recipient of a World Refugee Year Fellowship to attend Bowdoin. In 1961, when I arrived on the campus, Bowdoin College was the town of Brunswick, Maine.

From the Greyhound bus station bordering the campus, I followed the signs and headed straight to a small, rectangular administration building, lugging my suitcase in one hand and a brand new manual typewriter in the other. The suitcase contained all of my worldly belongings, and the typewriter, in a metal box, was the major piece of equipment I purchased in Hong Kong in preparation for a college education in America. It cost me the remainder of my savings, after converting the lion's share of it into one hundred U.S. dollars, the amount of money I had for incidental expenses during my first year at Bowdoin.

At the entrance of the administration building, a plump, bespectacled man with pink cheeks, wearing a checkered sports jacket and a bowtie, came out to meet me. With a wide grin, he introduced himself as a staff member of the Admissions Office of Bowdoin College.

Calling me by my English name, he greeted me cheerfully as we shook hands, before I had uttered a single word. "Welcome to Bowdoin, Charles!"

36

I was surprised. I didn't wear a nametag. Of course, in Hong Kong, I was known only by my Chinese name, Li Na. How did he identify me and augur my English name? Weeks later, the answer came: I was the only person of Asian origin of the 1961 class, and the college knew of my arrival on that day because the World University Service in Hong Kong had sent the relevant information ahead of me.

After informing me that I had been assigned to live in the Kappa Sigma fraternity house, he commenced to lead me there.

As we ambled across the campus, he asked if I had a pleasant trip from Hong Kong and what my first impression of America was. I told him that everything in America was unusual to me, and I felt a little overwhelmed. He tried to comfort me by saying that I would love Bowdoin, which, in his opinion, was a hallowed institution of learning that graduated renowned literary figures like Nathaniel Hawthorne and Henry Wadsworth Longfellow. I responded with what weighed heavily on my mind:

"Yes, I have a lot to learn!"

Jumping at an opportunity to ask questions, I went on,

"Speaking of learning, could you please explain what a fraternity house is?"

"It's a kind of a club, where students share room and board with like-minded students," he explained. "The term 'fraternity' is related to the word, 'fraternal,' which means 'brotherly.'"

"Oh, I know the word 'fraternal.' Learned it in biology: fraternal twins vis-à-vis identical twins," I responded.

"Very good," he said, smiling. "Your English is excellent!"

"Thank you." I was a little embarrassed by the compliment. "I would say that my English is barely functional. So, what is the Kappa Sigma fraternity then?"

"At Bowdoin, we have many fraternities. Kappa Sig is known as the athletes' fraternity," he said with pride. "Almost all of the members of the football, baseball, basketball and track teams belong to it. And we're looking forward to seeing you on our track team. Aren't you the 100-meter champion of Hong Kong?"

"Well, I was," I said haltingly, "but that's another story. I am no longer interested in track. My mission here is to study."

He looked at me quizzically. "You can do both. Our athletes have to study too!"

I didn't wish to volunteer the information that sprinting on a track never captivated me, even though winning was always exhilarating, as if each victory were a small payback to a fate that had doomed me to fail. The training amounted to pure torture: running around the track, sprinting in spurts, gasping for air, nursing muscle aches. In Hong Kong, I ran track to escape depression and gain enough recognition to attract students to tutor. It was another survival strategy. There was nothing appealing about being a sprinter. I had also learned from track coaches that with my lanky physique, I had no chance of elevating myself into a world-class sprinter, no matter how much fast-twitching muscle I had. Experts told me that I had amazing acceleration and lightning reflexes but lacked stamina. In every race, I attained maximal speed long ahead of my competitors. Then I began to fade twenty to thirty meters before the finish line. I needed to bulk up, they told me, especially my upper body, by consuming more protein. The advice meant that I should eat more meat, fish and eggs. I would have loved to do so. But my budget didn't allow for such extravagance. My meals in Hong Kong consisted of mostly rice with a tiny amount of meat or fish as a condiment, a flavorful enticement to fill the stomach with empty carbs. In short, sprinting did not appear to be an option for a career, even though it helped me gain some visibility and increase my chances of being sought out by wealthy families as a tutor for their children.

Now, granted the rare opportunity to pursue a college education, I didn't want to waste any time on sprinting. But I kept the thought to myself. It would be impolite to contradict my host from the Admissions Office.

The walk ended quickly. Located diagonally across the campus from the administrative building, Kappa Sigma house was a two-story white wooden building that sat at the corner of an intersection bordering the campus. Behind the fraternity house was a grove of conifer trees.

At the door of the fraternity, an affable young man who didn't look athletic at all received us.

"This is Pete Webster, the president of Kappa Sig." The staff person gestured at the young man and then, pointing at me, said, "This is Charles Li from Hong Kong."

As he turned back toward the administration building, he added, "Well, Charles, I'm leaving you in good hands. Thanks, Pete."

Pete led me through the living room: a spacious place with dark wood-paneled walls, furnished with well-worn leather sofas, brass standing lamps, and a couple of nondescript coffee tables. The furniture pieces seemed randomly placed, as if they had been moved around constantly. That turned out to be the case, I soon found out. When two Kappa Sig brothers played cribbage in the living room, they would pull two sofa chairs facing each other and insert a coffee table between them. If a group of people came into the living room to shoot the breeze or drink beer, they would assemble a couple of sofas near each other.

On the left of the living room, a glass-paneled double French door led to the dining room, which connected to the kitchen. On the right of the living room was a stairwell with stairs going up and stairs going down. Upon my arrival, Pete was the only one in the house.

He told me that I arrived on campus early. In two days, which would be Sunday, the day before instruction began, everyone would be arriving and the house would be full, he reassured me.

When we reached upstairs, I realized that there was a small third floor, hidden from the outside because of the gable roof. It held two small bedrooms for seniors. Pete showed me my bed on the second floor, a single steel-framed bed diagonally placed among eight or nine similar beds in a large room without a closet, bureau, desk, chair or any other furniture. It was the largest and the most austere room in the house, designated for new members of the fraternity. Rectangular in shape, with a linoleum floor and white walls absent of any decoration, the room could have been a hospital ward of a bygone era if one imagined the presence of a nurse wearing a white cap and apron. The fraternity house did have bedrooms furnished with carpet, desks, chairs and even sofas. Each of those rooms housed two or three residents who were upperclassmen. Occupying them represented a privilege of seniority.

After I placed my suitcase and typewriter under the bed assigned to me, Pete led the way downstairs. In the kitchen, he introduced me to the cook of the fraternity house, Mack, a large, congenial middle-aged fellow with blue eyes and thin, reddish-blonde hair meticulously combed back and parted on the right. He looked very much like an Englishman stripped of his colonial entitlement in Hong Kong. When Pete and I showed up, he was busily stocking up provisions in the kitchen: enormous cans of meat, tomatoes, corn, green beans; buckets of oil; sacks of potatoes; bags of pasta and rice. The stockpile of cans surprised me. In China and Hong Kong, spam and ham were the only meat sold in tin cans, typically imported from the United States. People rarely ate them because they were neither tasty nor inexpensive. For daily meals, meat and vegetables were always eaten fresh, no matter how meager the quantity. Even the poorest people ate fresh vegetables, especially green vegetables, in great variety. Rich people who could afford to eat chicken always purchased live chickens. In public markets, the stall that sold chicken had a couple of large bamboo cages filled with cackling chickens trying to escape their pending demise. The stockpile of cans of food in the kitchen of the fraternity induced me to assume that Americans liked canned food. I thought it was a strange practice for an affluent nation.

Pete and the cook, Mack, made clear that any time I wanted to eat, Mack was the person to go to as long as he happened to be in the kitchen.

"I hope you like being here," Pete said. "There is one thing I must make clear to you. You cannot go downstairs to the basement. That's where the brothers hold meetings and conduct fraternity business. Kappa Sig does not admit colored people, although we, at Bowdoin, do not discriminate against anyone. It's the national organization of Kappa Sigma that does not allow colored people to become brothers.

I don't like the policy of the national fraternity, but I have no power to change it. You are a guest at this house, and you cannot participate in our meetings. Okay?"

I nodded, not fully grasping his words while understanding that I was not allowed to enter the basement. As for being a "guest," meaning someone who didn't belong, I knew it well.

At age four, when my memory began to form, I lived with my wet nurse in our own quarter in my father's mansion. My siblings were all in their teens. I rarely interacted with them. Rarer still was the company of my parents. All of them seemed to belong to a different world. I felt like a "guest" in my parents' mansion.

When my father went to prison and Chiang Kai-shek's government confiscated all of his properties, I was liberated from his mansion and moved with what was left of my family to the slum of Nanjing. Slum dwellers were expendable riffraff. It would be a flattering understatement to call them "guests" in their homes. They were necessarily transient, and they didn't belong anywhere, not even their slums, because the authority could forcefully remove them any time without warning.

In high school, after my mother had walked out on my father, I lived as a guest in my father's office flat, where he served as the Editor-in-Chief of China Press, the Hong Kong vestige of a major publishing house in China. Setting up an army cot in the dining room every evening, I slept fitfully most nights, waking up whenever an editorial assistant or a janitor entered the room looking for an umbrella, a journal, a book or a misplaced personal item. It was definitely not a home to me. I was a "guest" imposed on the editorial staff by my father, their ill-tempered authoritarian boss. Understandably they didn't tolerate my presence with grace. None of them ever talked to me.

After high school, I returned to China for one full year, trying in vain to attain a college education. It took a year in a thought-reform school to convince me that I didn't belong to China, even though I thought of myself as a Chinese. Returning to Hong Kong, a full-fledged, old-fashioned primitive colony, where nobody belonged, I joined a horde of "guests."

The Brits in Hong Kong didn't belong there. Transient overlords, they tried to make a fortune by hook or crook in as short a period of time as possible so that they could retire comfortably to England. The Chinese people of Hong Kong in the 1950s were either refugees from the communist mainland or local-born. As stateless colonial subjects, they had minimal human rights. The British government excelled at imbuing its colonial subjects with the sentiment that the colony was not their homeland, even if they and their ancestors were born there. The colonial rulers wanted to make sure that the natives understood they existed to serve the economic interest of the British Crown. On the first of January during the 1950s, the governor of Hong Kong celebrated New Year's Day by performing the public ritual of announcing through the media how many million British pounds the colony had contributed to the British treasury the past year.

The colonial government did not even spend money to educate Chinese children. When the Chinese people created their own tuition-driven primary and secondary schools, the Hong Kong government decreed that those schools were not educational institutions, regardless of their academic rigor and the quality of their students. They were forced to register with the colonial government as business enterprises similar to retail stores. The diplomas earned by the graduates of those Chinese schools had no value in the colony or the British Commonwealth. They did not qualify the graduates to compete for a civil service job in the Hong Kong government, and they did not qualify the graduates to apply to any officially recognized university in the British Commonwealth, which in the 1950s included Singapore, Malaysia, Australia, Canada, New Zealand, South Africa, Jamaica, most of East Africa, etc. In the eyes of the colonial officers, the diplomas issued to the graduates by the Chinese schools in Hong Kong meant nothing more than the receipts given to customers of a retail store.

When Pete Webster told me that I was a guest in the Kappa Sigma fraternity house, I was neither startled nor offended. It was life as usual.

What did appear murky and puzzling to me was his statement, "not allowing colored people to become brothers" in Kappa Sigma. It was the first time I heard the term "colored people." I had thought every person was colored and human skin color changed in response to age, health and an array of environmental factors. In my Hong Kong Chinese high school, a teacher taught us the old European classification of human beings according to four skin colors: white, black, yellow and red. If white is a category of color, it follows that every human being is colored. The term "colored people" sounds like "feline cats," redundant and senseless.

Being reserved, I did not respond to Pete's statement about the national Kappa Sigma fraternity's segregation policy. It didn't mean anything to me. But his term "colored people" did elicit a smile from me and drew me into a reverie about my high school class of wisecracking smart alecks, who prided themselves on being analytical and sarcastic. They responded to the European classificatory scheme of humans on the basis of skin color with derisive snickers when our teacher presented it to us in class and called for a discussion.

"Can you believe that we, Asians, are yellow?" one student mused.

He then asked the class, "Anyone here have the skin color of a banana peel? If you do, you are probably suffering from jaundice. You'd better rush to an emergency hospital."

Laughter began to break out, which prompted the teacher to admonish the class, "Let's adhere to a discussion based on empirical data!"

Heeding the teacher's admonition, a student noted, "Asian people's skin color changes seasonally, depending on the level of exposure to the sun. During the summer, swimming in the sea darkens our skin. During the winter, an ivory tone prevails because of the monsoon rain and indoor living. This is an empirical fact. I wish to add that the Italians and Portuguese in Hong Kong and Macau seem to darken in the tropical sun, just like us Asians. But they are classified as 'whites,' I suppose, because they are Europeans. This classificatory scheme looks like a fraudulent sham!"

Another student chimed in, "Native Americans are red according to this European classificatory scheme. Are there actually red people in this world? They must be 'sweating blood' like the hippos, no? Well, if they sweat blood, what about the Native Americans living in the Arctic? The Arctic is not warm enough to cause anyone to sweat. The people who proposed this bogus classification of human beings must be retarded."

The laughter in the classroom began to get louder and more boisterous. Then that same student who suggested that Native Americans sweated blood quickly added, "It is an empirical fact that the Native Americans look just like Asians in the dark phase of their skin, at least according to the images in cowboy movies I have seen. I assume none of us has met an American Indian. But in those Hollywood movies, the American Indians are always portrayed as ruthless bandits, murdering the putative 'white' people crossing the great plains of North America."

Yet another student observed, "The only people who have 'red' skin are the Brits in Hong Kong. They are incapable of acclimatizing to the tropical heat of Hong Kong. Their cheeks and noses are covered with red capillaries. Drinking beer and alcoholic beverages makes them even redder."

This final observation caused the class to explode into a cacophony of noises, ranging from chattering and howling to roaring and hooting. Any insult of the British colonial overlords would win the heart of those wise guys, who were painfully aware and bitterly resentful that the British government considered their school a mercantile enterprise.

I was lost in the memory of my high school classmates' mischief until Pete Webster jolted me back to reality with his reassurance that he and his Kappa Sigma brothers did not discriminate against colored people.

"Kappa Sig's exclusion of colored people is unfortunate." He found it necessary to reiterate what he had already said. "It is a policy of the national headquarters. At Bowdoin we are not prejudiced against colored people. Having you as a guest for an entire academic year attests to the liberal attitude at Bowdoin."

In Hong Kong, even though the Brits didn't refer to the Chinese as "colored people," racial discrimination against the natives was an integral part of the British colonial policy. The life of a Chinese in Hong Kong was never rosy, regardless of financial status and conventional success, especially if one was intelligent, sensitive and desirous of a dignified and upright way of life. He or she was constantly reminded that his or her social standing was close to that of a dog. Even a wealthy comprador with a British passport could not escape that fate. No, the British overlords never literally made their colonial subjects bend down like a four-legged animal, as some French colonial officers did to the natives of French Indo-Chine. My father told me that he couldn't believe his eyes during a 1938 visit to Hanoi, Vietnam, when he witnessed a Vietnamese attendant bend down on his knees and hands, like a four-legged animal, to serve as a stool, so that a French officer could step on his back to mount a horse. When my outraged father inquired about what he saw, he learned, much to his horror, that the incident was by no means odd or exceptional, but a customary colonial practice in all of Indo-Chine.

The colonial practice my father witnessed provided a telltale clue to the outcome of Vietnam's independence war in the 1950s. At the time, the victory of the Viet-Minh surprised the world, especially the Western nations. By any conventional standards, the French military constituted a far more superior fighting force than the Viet-Minh, who sought the independence of Vietnam. The French had bombers, fighter jets, naval ships and cutting-edge armaments, in addition to the well-trained, highly disciplined and heavily armed Foreign Legions, while their adversary, the Viet-Minh led by Ho Chi-Minh, didn't have a single airplane or warship. They often fought with World War II weapons and equipment captured from the Japanese at the end of World War II.

What turned out to be more potent than arms and technology was the Viet-Minh's indomitable will to rid their country of the French overlords and the wholehearted support of the general populace. The Vietnamese never hesitated to sacrifice their lives in order to assist or join the Viet Minh in their war against the better-trained, better-armed French Foreign Legions and other well-equipped military units. After all, who would choose to live like an animal, i.e., getting down on your knees to become a stool for the French national, when the alternative promised a future in which your children could live with dignity as human beings, even if fighting for that alternative entailed a high probability of sacrificing your life?

The British, though not as brutal and barbaric as some of the other European colonialists (the Belgian King Leopold whose rapacious plundering and murderous exploitation of Congo in the 19th century comes to mind as an egregious example), were no less ferocious in exploiting and oppressing the people of their colonies. The Brits made it abundantly clear in every way that the lives of their colonial subjects were worthless and expendable. Signs declaring "NO DOGS OR CHINESE" guarded the entrances to many parks and prestigious neighborhoods in Hong Kong until 1947.

British colonial disdain for human rights even left its mark on the English language. The word "coolie" was borrowed from a Chinese word that literally means "bitter labor." The Romanized first syllable *coo* means "bitter," and the second syllable *lie* mimics the pronunciation of the Chinese logograph that means "labor." This Chinese word sprang into existence shortly after the Opium War in the nineteenth century when Britain annexed several territories along the eastern seaboard of China. Those territories included Hong Kong, parts of Shanghai, Canton city (Guangzhou) and parts of Tianjin, a seaport near Beijing. In those newly acquired territories, the British employed a vast number of manual laborers who served as beasts of burden on the waterfront in factories and at train stations. The coolies' compensation was opium, not money. The British agency and officers that conceived this unusual scheme of compensation—opium for backbreaking hard labor—were as pernicious and ruthless as they were clever and calculating. Opium is a palliative drug. An addict becomes docile and inured to pain. He has no appetite and only craves the next fix. In the British colonies and concessions, the colonizers, by paying opium to the laborers for their long hours of inhumane, harsh labor, created a situation in which the Chinese laborers toiled obediently and never complained about the excessive workload or the physical devastation. Most important of all, the practice cost the employers next to nothing to feed and house the laborers, since opium suppressed the appetite of the addicts and made them oblivious to pain and discomfort.

What could be better or more expedient for the British colonialists whose goal was to make a quick fortune?

They had invented the most efficient and effective way to accumulate capital at a negligible cost in a colony. The only consequence was the loss of lives among the colonial subjects—an irrelevant issue to the colonialists. In addition to the advantages of this colonial practice, the British paid a pittance for the opium. In those days, opium was mostly produced in another British colony, Burma, not far from China. The exploitation of farmhands in one colony lubricated the wheels of commerce in another colony.

On average, a coolie survived only a few months of the grim regime of harsh labor and opium addiction. Towards the end, as his body began to break down from malnutrition and overexertion, he was prone to cardiac arrest and sudden death. If, before his death, a coolie stumbled and hurt his back or broke a limb, he became unemployed. The employer simply recruited a replacement. The death of coolies in Canton, Hong Kong, Shanghai and other coastal cities where the British had established their extraterritorial jurisdiction during the late 19th century was so common that the Chinese accepted the phenomenon as a routine matter of semi-colonial life. Neither injury nor death of a coolie triggered any compensation to his family.

The impoverished Chinese accepted injury and sudden death as part of the occupational hazard of a coolie, the "bitter labor." "Bitter" because the labor and the opium sucked the life out of a laborer in a short span of time.

Once, a 19th century British colonial officer, commenting on the sudden death syndrome among the coolies, remarked casually in his Queen's English, "Yes, it is unfortunate, but the coolies are Chinese, and by God, there are so many of them."

Today, the word "coolie" remains in the English language, designating an over-exploited or abused unskilled laborer.

With those memories and thoughts churning in my mind during the guided tour of the Kappa Sigma fraternity house, I hardly spoke other than responding with, "yes," "okay," "thank you." My reticence stemmed, in part, from my Chinese upbringing, which instructed a young person to be reserved and hold his tongue in a new environment, and in part from my limited proficiency in English and almost total ignorance of American culture. I simply didn't know what would constitute a proper response, as Pete Webster explained everything to me politely. When he finished showing me the fraternity house, I wanted to retreat to the bed that had been assigned to me on the second floor. Since he had told me that was my bed, I felt confident that it was not improper or discourteous for me to seek refuge there.

By the time I sat down on my bed, extreme fatigue had overcome me. Yet I didn't want to sleep. Pulling out a pad of paper from my suitcase, I began writing in Chinese, one character after another, to Kim, my Hong Kong girlfriend, and the two roommates with whom I spent my last evening before coming to the United States, telling them what I had seen and how I had felt. I had been traveling for several days and seemed to have completely lost track of time. The plane ride from Hong Kong, the encounter with the immigration officer in frigid Anchorage, the misadventure in Seattle, the déjà vu reunion with Aunt Helen in Boston, and finally, the arrival at Bowdoin. Every place and each experience left an indelible mark in my memory.

Before embarking on the trip to the United States, I could not have anticipated any of the events and experiences that unfolded along my journey. I might just as well have been plucked up by a tornado and dropped into a fairyland, a land that was neither rosy nor despicable, but strange and unusual. Now, sitting at the edge of my bed, I felt an overwhelming need to be grounded and connected. Writing to my girlfriend and roommates in Hong Kong and writing to myself in my journal to record, in detail, my experiences along the trip and my interactions with my hosts satisfied that need.

KAPPA SIGMA FRATERNITY

BY SUNDAY AFTERNOON, ALL OF THE KAPPA SIGMA BROTHERS had arrived—some in their own automobiles, some brought by their parents.

In 1961, Hong Kong remained a relatively unknown, backward British colony, long before the Chinese entrepreneurs from Shanghai, Guangdong and other coastal cities, who escaped from the communist mainland, reinvented the colony as Asia's financial center and a glamorous tourist destination in the 1980s. China, at that time, known as Communist China, was demonized in Western nations. It was not only behind the "iron curtain," but also populated by the "Yellow Horde." (In the late 1950s, the longest-serving prime minister of Australia, Robert Menzies, warned against the potential invasion of white Australia by Asia's Yellow Horde.) In addition, memories of the savage Korean War, during which China's Liberation Army became the main combat force on the side of North Korea and fought the U.S. to a stalemate, remained fresh among many Americans at the time. I reckoned that there wouldn't be any questions about Communist China from the Kappa Sigma brothers. Besides, they might not have known that I once lived in Communist China. Hong Kong, however, could be a topic of interest. They should have known that I came to Bowdoin from there.

A British colony, I thought, might pique their curiosity. Based on my conjecture, I was prepared to answer questions about life in Hong Kong, the history of British colonization, the relation between the Brits and the Chinese, the standard of living as well as other topics before and during my first dinner at Kappa Sigma. But my conjecture was wrong. Very few members of Kappa Sigma asked me any questions about Hong Kong. Everyone talked incessantly, reminiscing and recounting their summer adventures. I tried to listen and learn. But the language and cultural barriers were insurmountable.

On the language side, I had the illusion that my English was relatively fluent, partly because I displayed a negligible amount of non-native accent and partly because I functioned smoothly as a private tutor in mathematics and sciences to the high school children of the American Consul General in Hong Kong for one year before I left for the United States. During my long trip to Bowdoin, I also seemed to communicate without a hitch at the Immigration Control in Anchorage, interact with the gentleman who picked me up as a hitchhiker outside of the Seattle airport, and make inquiries at the information booth in Boston's Logan Airport. But English remained a formal language to me, learned in a classroom at a time without a language laboratory equipped with audio-visual equipment. In those days, students never acquired fluency in a foreign language in a classroom. At best, they learned a stilted, formal speech that allowed them to function in very limited social contexts. My deficiency in spoken English struck shortly after all of the fraternity brothers showed up. The speed of their conversation rendered it incomprehensible to me. Then, there were slangs and a myriad of ways to say things in English that I had never encountered before.

One evening, Asa, an unassuming and congenial underclassman from Tennessee occupying the bed a few feet from mine, asked me about my feelings when I left Hong Kong. I said, "When I ascended the TWA airplane, I felt very conflicted."

Before I could continue, Asa interrupted me, "You mean, when you boarded the TWA plane."

Surprised, I asked, "Was my sentence ungrammatical?"

"Well," Asa responded, "Your sentence is grammatical. But we just don't say 'ascend an airplane' in English. We say, 'board an airplane.'"

I thanked him for his instruction. Upon some reflection, I realized that my mistake was caused by the Chinese way of saying to board an airplane, which literally translates into "ascend an airplane."

Many years later, I came to understand that every language has its own ways of saying things, numbering tens of thousands that constitute a dimension of a language distinct from its grammar and vocabulary. These ways are determined by the culture and tradition of its speakers, forged over generations. Contrary to popular belief, which exaggerates the role of grammar and diction in the acquisition of a new language, fluency in a language depends fundamentally on the command of how things are said in that language.

As my roommate Asa had pointed out to me, the sentence, "I ascended the TWA airplane," is perfectly grammatical. It is just NOT the English way of stating that activity.

After I attained fluency in English and had acquired some basic knowledge of French, I understood why a French friend of mine said one time, "I have hunger," which caused his American friends to burst into laughter. He was speaking French English. Again, "I have hunger" is perfectly grammatical and easily understood, but it is just not the way of expressing the sensation of hunger. Because of the tens of thousands of idiosyncratic ways of speaking in each language, one must spend a significant period of time immersed in a community of native speakers before achieving fluency in that language. A native speaker community can be simulated to some extent in a sophisticated language laboratory or instruction program nowadays, but not in the 1950s, and definitely not in colonial Hong Kong.

Before arriving at Bowdoin College, I had never functioned in an English-speaking community, real or simulated. The first few weeks at Bowdoin were nerve-wracking. I was constantly embarrassed. My deficiency in both comprehension and production of the English language was so glaring that it inhibited my social interaction and created an anxiety in me that was incapacitating. Worse still, I tried to cover up my language deficiency by enrolling in as many courses as I was allowed to. The Kappa Sigma brothers assumed, on the basis of my enrollment, good accent and reasonable diction, that I was a fluent speaker of English.

Even many months after my arrival, when my command of the English language was nearly up to par, I was astonished by the unpredictability of the meaning of "houseboat," especially in contrast with the meaning of "boathouse." Someone from California in one of my classes mentioned that his family owned a houseboat. I inferred the meaning of the word from the context. What astonished me was that a learner of English could not possibly predict the semantic relationship between the nouns in a nominal compound. Why should "houseboat" mean "boat which happens to be a house" or "a house which happens to be a boat," while "boathouse" designates a covered structure for mooring a boat?

Many years later, I learned that not only is the semantic relation between the nouns of an English nominal compound unpredictable, but native speakers can improvise and create hitherto unknown nominal compounds. For instance, if you see a van parked at a street corner in your neighborhood every afternoon, you may end up calling that van a "corner van," which would be perfectly comprehensible to your neighbors, even if no one had heard of such a compound in the past. I remember once on a camping trip in California long after I had achieved fluency in English, the jagged, black branches of a dead live oak tree appeared macabre to me.

Pointing at it, I said to my companion, "Look at that ghost tree!"

"Ghost tree, a nice description!" she responded.

I surmised that I had made up a nominal compound that was novel.

The language barrier, not in terms of grammar or vocabulary, but in terms of adapting to the English ways of saying things, was merely one of the many handicaps I had to overcome after my arrival at Bowdoin.

The cultural barrier constituted a much more perplexing hurdle.

Conversations between members of the fraternity tended to revolve around sex, sports, booze, automobiles and summer travel. Some of those topics rarely occurred in the economically backward China and

Hong Kong. Some were forbidden because they violated Chinese social conventions.

Students in China and Hong Kong during the 1950s never consumed alcoholic beverages. Booze and brands of liquor or beer, not to mention cocktails, were not in our vocabulary, Chinese or English. A young person, especially a teenage student like myself, was completely ignorant of the immense variety of alcoholic beverages in the Western world. My high school friends and I believed that people who indulged in alcoholic consumption were degenerates.

In the realm of sex, the taboo was so stark that any hint of it among young people would lead to embarrassment accompanied by giggles or laughter. Parents, teachers and social conventions reinforced the taboo. Censors in the Hong Kong government routinely cut out the sex scenes in Hollywood movies before they were shown in theaters, even though Hollywood movies of the 1950s never depicted sex acts implicitly or explicitly. The upper limit of sex-related displays in movies was kissing. The censors cut any activity or behavior beyond kissing between a male and a female in a movie to avoid corrupting public morals.

In China, the prohibition of any sex-linked activity was even more extreme than in Hong Kong. Hollywood movies were categorically banned. Kissing never occurred in public, not in movies, not anywhere. Nor was it ever mentioned in media or social contexts. There, in a nation of six hundred and sixty million people during the late 1950s, a romantic gaze set the bar of sexual insinuation permitted in the media and the public. No one ever appeared scantily clad in photos, movies or real life.

In my Hong Kong secondary school, the students learned the anatomy and physiology of mammalian sexual reproduction during a year-long biology course. We had to memorize all of the anatomical details, from ovum to fornix, from sperm to epididymis. We also learned that conception and embryological development began with the fusion of a sperm and an ovum. As for the question, "What brings on that fusion?"—the teacher avoided it, the textbook conveniently left it out, and even the mischievous smart alecks in my class didn't dare raise it.

The anatomy and physiology of mammalian sexual reproduction constituted our exposure to "sex." There was no such thing as sex education in schools. It would have been considered outrageous and detrimental to the cultivation of upright character among the youth. Sex never entered into teenagers' conversation. For sure, the boys instinctively ogled beautiful girls, but only in the sense of hoping to marry someone like that in the future. Any sexual motivation would have been subconscious. All sexual desires were sublimated.

Over my first dinner with the Kappa Sigma brothers, I heard them excitedly describing to each other their summer sexual exploits and adventures. To the extent I could understand them, I was embarrassed and felt ill at ease, as if I was staring at a yawning chasm separating the old world in which I had lived since birth and the new world I had just stepped into. I simply didn't know what to do or how to respond. Over time, my embarrassment and persistent silence on sexual topics led the brothers to suspect that I was a homosexual, a social pariah in the mind of most Americans in 1961. But I didn't even know what the term "homosexual" meant. I had never heard of it or its Chinese equivalent.

Other than talking about sex, the Kappa Sigma brothers loved boozing. It began with beer-drinking immediately after the first dinner of the academic year. A few years earlier in Hong Kong, I had tried a sip of beer out of curiosity. The beer made me grimace, and I couldn't understand why anyone could be fond of that bitter, fizzy water with a sour aftertaste. My companion, who led me to taste it, told me that beer consumption was an acquired taste.

"If you make an effort and try it several times, you will end up liking it," he assured me.

"No, thanks," I responded without hesitation but didn't wish to let go of an opportunity to disparage the Brits. "No wonder the Brits are the way they are! Their favorite drink is piss."

I also thought it would be absurd for a person to work toward acquiring a taste for such an outlandish beverage.

Now, at Kappa Sig, everyone loved beer. I was careful not to reveal my prejudice against alcoholic beverages. Nonetheless, the brothers were offended when I consistently refused a proffered Coors or Budweiser. They looked at me askance, as puzzled as they were nettled.

My cultural ignorance was by no means confined to sex and boozing. Steeped in the Confucian civilization, I knew hardly anything about American society and its history. Neither could I imagine the enormity of the disparity between Americans and East Asians in terms of attitudes, values, worldviews, protocols, social etiquette and traditions in every domain of life.

At the time I arrived at Kappa Sigma fraternity, I didn't even know what New England or the Midwest stood for. When someone told me that most of the Bowdoin students came from New England, the term drew a blank from me.

"Well, what's New England?" I wondered quietly. "Is 'England' Old England?"

Although the civil rights movement had begun to gather strength in 1961 in some parts of the United States, I knew nothing about the American South and its institutionalized racial segregation. Looking back, I wish my English teacher in high school had made me read *The Adventures of Huckleberry Finn* or *To Kill a Mockingbird* and *Uncle Tom's Cabin* instead of abridged versions of *Ivanhoe*, *David Copperfield* and *Wuthering Heights*. Alas, in a British colony, "English" meant exclusively British, and English literature referred only to literature written by British authors. In high school, I did enjoy Dickens, Walter Scott and other British writers/poets. But reading Twain and Lee or Stowe would have set me on a much better footing to understand America and start a life there.

I was also ignorant about American sports and their vital roles in American life. In addition to being one of their favorite topics of conversation, sports figured prominently as an entertainment and an activity in the world of the Kappa Sigma brothers. They argued and debated the quality and the standing of various professional teams and displayed detailed knowledge of the skills, physique, athleticism and personal information of individual players, as if they were all close friends to those star athletes. It took me a few days after my arrival to discover that football did not mean soccer, baseball had an outfield and an infield, hockey was played on ice in a rink, lacrosse was a team sport, and to my consternation, professional basketball and football players came from collegiate teams.

At the time, the concept of a university graduate becoming a professional athlete completely boggled my mind. In my view, it was ridiculous and insane that a person would abandon all the prestige and advantages conferred by a university education and choose a career using his brawn instead of his brain. Of course, I didn't know what a large percentage of American youth could access tertiary education, nor was I aware that a university degree did not command the same respect and bestow the same privilege as it did in China and Hong Kong, where a tertiary education remained accessible only by a privileged few.

In 1961, there seemed to be an endless number of new things about life in America that I didn't know or understand: from pizzas and hamburgers (which, to my astonishment, had nothing to do with ham) to drive-in movie theaters and supermarkets, from turnpikes and Howard Johnson's to laundromats and automobile junkyards, from boozing and sex to individualism and the nature of human relationships. Shocked by my inadequate command of American English and my ignorance of the American way of life, I began to panic, spurred on by the apprehension that my linguistic and cultural deficiency would lead to failure of my attempt to forge a new life in America. Under stress, I became even more withdrawn than a stereotypical reticent, reserved and proverbially "inscrutable" Chinese immigrant. I avoided social interaction, shunning everyone, including the Kappa Sigma brothers. At the fraternity house, I gulped down my lunch and dinner each day quietly in a corner of the dining room after most brothers had finished their meals. On campus, I sought refuge in the library. Every morning, I left the fraternity house while everyone remained asleep and went to a classroom to study until the library opened. It would be a rare occasion if I returned to Kappa Sig before 11 p.m.

Pete, the president of Kappa Sig, commented one evening as I was rushing out of the fraternity house after dinner, "Charles, you are always rushing away. Why don't you stay and play a game of checkers or cards?"

"Thanks for the invitation, Pete. But I have to study!"

The brothers of Kappa Sigma perceived my absence at the house and aversion to social interaction a sign of arrogance and antipathy. They were not pleased.

A few weeks into the Fall semester, I discovered that, despite the claim of the staff member of the Admissions Office who met me on my arrival, a lot of the Kappa Sigma members disdained studying. Supported by well-to-do families, most of them were confident of settling into a comfortable career after graduation either in their family business or a corporation. At Bowdoin, they intended to enjoy life and play sports. Studying hard was not cool! It contradicted their air of entitlement and privilege. With a few exceptions, the Kappa Sig brothers preferred to score a passing grade with minimal effort in their classes, and they were proud of getting a C or a D in a course without studying the assigned material.

When the issue of my joining the track team came up, I announced that I had given up sprinting. My announcement provoked fierce hostility and complaint from the fraternity brothers.

"We want to see your yellow legs accelerating on the track and crossing the finish line in record time," one of the Kappa Sig brothers opined.

"Yeah! We want to see if you can beat Milo," another chimed in. Milo was a member of Kappa Sigma fraternity. Short, thick-necked, compactly built and sporting a crew-cut, he was an excellent sprinter and the leading running back of Bowdoin's football team.

"Come on, Chuck! We took you in because we wanted a champion sprinter. You can't disappoint us," Pete spoke for the rest.

Determined that my only salvation rested in academic distinction, I ignored the pleas as well as the insults from the Kappa Sig brothers, making clear that I intended to study at all times. My unyielding resolve to dedicate myself to an activity that most of them disliked quickly eroded whatever goodwill they had toward me.

A storm was gathering on the horizon and my life would become hell. But I was totally oblivious.

STRUGGLES OF AN IMMIGRANT

APPROXIMATELY ONE WEEK AFTER MY ARRIVAL AT KAPPA SIGMA fraternity, I remained unaware of the existence of a coin-operated laundromat in a street bordering the campus, because laundry machines were unknown in Hong Kong in 1961. The standard of living in Hong Kong at the time did not warrant the luxury of household appliances like washing machines. Even a refrigerator was a rarity in those days. At Kappa Sigma fraternity house, I took my laundry to the communal bathroom and started to hand-wash it in a sink.

No sooner had I started soaping my laundry, a crowd gathered around the door of the bathroom gesturing at me and laughing hysterically. Then I heard someone saying, "Hey, can you believe it? The fucking Chinaman is opening up a laundry shop already!"

Everyone roared.

Even though I understood their words, what they said and what they did made no sense to me.

How was I opening a laundry shop? I was merely washing a few pieces of my own dirty laundry.

And what was so funny?

Without the knowledge of the historical context of Chinese immigrants in America, who, being denied the right to engage in farming or own real estate, often ended up in the laundry business, I was completely lost.

Then, Pete came up to tell me that I should do my laundry in the laundromat in town, not in the second-floor communal bathroom of the fraternity. When he found out that I didn't understand what a laundromat was, he explained it to me and told me where it was in Brunswick.

One day, passing through the fraternity living room on my way to the library, I overheard a brother telling his companions who were sipping beer that he preferred to have a screwdriver instead of the beer. After returning to Hong Kong from China in 1958, I had barely heard of the word "cocktail." It had remained in my vocabulary only because it appeared to be such a strange word—I didn't see any connection between an alcoholic beverage and the tail of a bird. No one I knew in China or Hong Kong drank cocktails. Some adults might drink Chinese hard liquor or Western whiskey and brandy during their meal, but never cocktails. Restaurants didn't sell cocktails and hotels didn't have a cocktail lounge. The few English restaurants in Hong Kong, like Jimmy's Kitchen, might serve cocktails. I wouldn't know. Their clientele was almost exclusively British. Chinese thought those English restaurants were a culinary disgrace. Even my father, who spent three years studying in England, never set foot in Jimmy's Kitchen, and he was known for being fond of gourmet food. When this Kappa Sig brother talked about drinking a screwdriver, I couldn't believe what I had heard. I knew some of the Kappa Sigma brothers engaged in bizarre activities. But drinking a tool like a metallic screwdriver? That defied common sense. My curiosity was so piqued that I couldn't refrain from posing the question,

"How do you drink a screwdriver?"

Stunned, the brothers looked at me as if I had gone mad.

"What do you mean, how do you drink a screwdriver?" one of them retorted while demonstrating with a can of beer. "You can sip it, or just pour it down your gullet."

"Well, you can't pour a metallic tool like a screwdriver into your mouth, can you?" I put up a challenge.

To my consternation, everyone howled with laughter.

"A screwdriver is also a drink. It's a cocktail, fuck'ng retard!" yelled one of the brothers, the first person to recover from laughing.

In my Hong Kong high school, teasing and mocking each other was a primary venue of games and diversion among the students in a high-strung and competitive academic environment. We gave nicknames to each other, often related to a person's physical peculiarity so that Lin, who was short in height, would be called "Short Lin." Wang, who was overweight, would become "Fat Wang." Lam, who squinted his eyes incessantly, would be named "Blinking Lam." In America, giving a nickname to someone to mock their physical peculiarity or deficiency would be considered cruel and unacceptable. In my high school, it was a normal practice as long as a strong friendship and camaraderie buttressed the relationships among the students. Everyone understood that the pranks, the nicknames and the mockeries, villainous as they might seem, were done in jest and a harmless manner. No one intended to hurt another person's feelings. The student named Lam who squinted uncontrollably, for instance, never took offense at being called "Blinking Lam." He responded to his nickname without rancor, as if it were an alternative to his real name. I was, therefore, not unaccustomed to rough treatment by my peers. But friendship never existed between the Kappa Sigma brothers and me. When they jeered at me or called me a derogatory name like "retard," they appeared mean-spirited to me. It was my perception that they aimed to denigrate and humiliate. Worse still, I couldn't understand what prompted their hostility.

The food at Kappa Sigma was typical post-war American institutional fare: dull, tasteless and unappetizing. Most of the dishes were novel to me—creamed chipped beef on toast, greasy hot dogs on soft powdery buns, dry and chewy hamburgers, baked macaroni that stuck to your gums and teeth, deep-fried fish that smelled fishy and tasted of unappetizing oil, goulash with a brown gravy that looked like a nightmare, different kinds of canned vegetables that imparted to the palate a uniform metallic flavor. There was always a large bowl of iceberg lettuce on each dining table and some kind of salad dressing that looked weird to me. At the end of dinner, the most frequently served dessert was apple pie, resembling some overdone chunks of potato doused with syrup and covered with some form of putative dough. The lettuce salad and the apple pie reminded me of an elderly Chinese in Hong Kong who, having spent some years of his youth in England and America, unleashed his chauvinistic opinion on me:

"English and American food is unrefined. We stir-fry our vegetables, they either eat their vegetables raw or boil them to a mush. We eat our apples and peaches fresh in order to savor their sweet fragrance and constituency, they bake their apples and peaches with sugar and dough. We flavor our chicken with a variety of spices, they boil their chicken in water. I wouldn't dignify English or American food with the term cuisine!"

After arriving in Bowdoin, I yearned for Chinese food day and night: the cornucopia of flavors of Chinese dishes, the crispy and tasteful green vegetables, the delicately seasoned meat and fish . . . They appeared in my dreams frequently.

At the fraternity, I began to feel that even the cheap rice bowl prepared by the street vendors in Hong Kong had become irresistibly appealing, as if the meager quantity of meat and vegetable on top of the rice originated from some Michelin-starred gourmet kitchen. After one month of living in the fraternity house, eating had become a chore, an activity that I was obliged to carry out two or three times a day in deference to my physical needs.

One morning, longing for some tasty food, I got creative and asked the cook, Sam, to give me a bowl of hot oatmeal and two sunny-side-up fried eggs. Oatmeal looked like rice gruel, a porridge that Chinese people eat at breakfast with salty pickles, pan-fried peanuts flavored with various condiments, deep-fried twists made of salty dough, and occasionally a fried egg or some meat dishes. In a teahouse, known as a dim-sum restaurant in American cities nowadays, the rice-porridge is often cooked with minced beef, chopped "thousand-year-old" eggs, shaved scallions, and seasoned with freshly smashed garlic, ginger, sea salt and finely ground white pepper. It is served piping hot, a heart-warming, delicious but inexpensive dish to kick-start your day.

That morning at the dining room of the Kappa Sigma fraternity, dreaming of the mouth-watering Chinese breakfast and pretending that the oatmeal was a thick version of the Chinese rice gruel, I transferred the fried eggs from a dish to the bowl of oatmeal, poked the yoke out, sprinkled some salt and a heavy dosage of ground pepper into the bowl. As I was stirring that concoction with my spoon and getting ready to eat, an ugly scene unfolded.

One of the Kappa Sigma brothers who happened to walk by while I was constructing my rendition of rice gruel with, admittedly, improper ingredients, saw what I did. He froze in his tracks, and with a contorted face, screamed, "Jesus!"

The scream instantly drew a number of brothers to the dining room. Standing in front of me as if I were a failed street vaudeville performer, they looked solemnly aghast.

One of them said, "Oh, my God, the Chinaman is eating crap here."

Another one commented, "How can you mix oatmeal with egg yolk and black pepper?"

As usual, I was befuddled. But this time, anger welled up in me in addition to perplexity. I was just trying to eat my breakfast and didn't deserve such insult and commotion. I wanted to say to them, echoing Oscar Wilde's caustic quip on Britain's foxhunt:

"You are the unspeakable living on the inedible. What do you know about food?"

Of course, I didn't say anything of the kind. Holding back my anger, I got up, abandoned my breakfast, grabbed my book bag and stormed out. As I exited the fraternity, I heard a voice trailing behind me.

"For Christ's sake, that fuck'ng Chinaman is crazy."

It didn't take long for me to become the laughing butt and the bête noir of the fraternity.

One day, I heard a brother muttering to another, "Oh, that Chinaman, he is really inscrutable!"

"Yeah, an odd bird. Probably retarded. What do you expect from a Chink?"

Shortly after the mid-term exams during the fall semester, the Kappa Sig brothers wanted to know how I performed in my courses. They were curious. Perhaps they wanted to find out if I were also academically retarded, since they had ample evidence of my social and linguistic incompetence. One day, they cornered me in the living room after dinner and demanded I tell them my grades. When I told them that I scored in the 90 to 100 percent range in all of my courses, a few nodded approvingly, but the majority booed. They, especially the ones who exuded an air of privilege and entitlement, told me that they prided themselves on passing their courses at the lowest threshold with minimal studying.

"It is the tradition and practice of Kappa Sig. Pass a course without doing any homework. That's what being smart is all about!" one of them said as if he were teaching me a lesson.

That was the one occasion when I stood my ground and expressed my disagreement, "Well, Pete told me that I am not a member of Kappa Sigma and I should not poke my nose into the affairs of the fraternity. I am afraid that your tradition is not mine, and you should refrain from imposing it on me."

Even though I spoke without rancor, my forthright response caught them by surprise. They chose not to retort and became silent. After that occasion, no one denigrated me about my bookworm existence.

But they had a trick up their sleeves.

A couple of weeks after discovering my grades, the brothers told me that as a reward for my outstanding academic performance, they would fix me up with a blind date. They said they were concerned about my well-being. For nearly two months, I had buried myself in my studies. I never played cards, attended sporting events or participated in social activities at the fraternity.

"It is not healthy for anyone to study so much," one of them explained their shared sentiment. "You've got to have some entertainment. We've decided to find you a blind date."

I figured, "Here they go again, trying to set me up with a girl who is blind so that they can make fun of me for the entire weekend."

I declined their offer, making it clear that I didn't want a date, blind or not blind. But they refused to take no as an answer and re-affirmed that by Saturday afternoon, my blind date would show up in the fraternity.

That Saturday afternoon, I went to the main library, wearing my pea coat for winter even though it was a balmy autumn day. As 4 p.m. approached, the bell rang, alerting everyone in the library that it would be closed in a few minutes. Instead of leaving the library like everyone else, I sneaked into the basement stacks. Shortly afterward, a muffled bang signaled to me that the main library door had been closed, which meant that the library was locked up until Sunday afternoon.

I was happily relieved.

No one had detected my presence in the basement, and I had managed to escape the dreadful prospect of dealing with a date, not to mention the Kappa Sig brothers' taunts, jeers, and harassment that I could vividly imagine, if I were to escort around the campus a blind girl whom I had never met, knew nothing about, and wouldn't know what to do with.

In the basement of the library, I settled on the floor between the tall bookshelves and buried myself in books of geographical explorations. I had always dreamed of exploring remote places like the Amazon, the Taklamakan desert, equatorial Africa, Papua New Guinea, seeing exotic animals and perhaps cavorting with them. Reading other people's description of the fauna and flora of those places was as close as I could get to my dreams.

As hours went by, books became tiresome. I switched to the volumes of old *LIFE Magazines* whose photo essays kept me entertained. It was particularly interesting to see the issues printed during the Second World War. Their contents, extolling patriotism, glorifying the heroic exploits and sacrifices of American soldiers on the battlefields, celebrating the production of armaments—General Motors rolling out columns of tanks and armored vehicles from its assembly lines, Bell Aircraft churning out squadrons of P-39 fighter planes in the Midwest, and the Consolidated Aircraft Company assembling B-24 bombers in its hangers in San Diego, reminded me of the sort of propaganda material that the Chinese government produced during the 1950s for the Chinese population. I wondered if the American government at the time maintained a Ministry of Propaganda as the Chinese government did.

Several issues of *LIFE Magazine* also featured the role of American women in the war effort, showing them in factory jobs that had been reserved for men before the war. It was interesting to find out that American society did not approve of women working in the manufacturing sector before the Second World War. With a long tradition of oppressing women, Chinese men never betrayed a hint of compunction for making manual, agricultural or industrial workers out of women throughout the history of China. Indeed, Chairman Mao referred to women as important as "half of the sky," implying that women, on the one hand, constituted half of the nation and, on the other hand, should work to support the national economy like men did. In practice, Communist China remained as male chauvinistic as the old China. Mao's policy only made Chinese women's lives twice as burdensome as it was in the old era. Under Mao, a Chinese woman had to shoulder two full-time jobs, one working for the country as men did, another taking care of their children and doing all the household chores.

The *LIFE Magazines* offered grand entertainment that night when I felt tired, bleary-eyed and a little famished. Some of their photos also kindled my childhood memories of World War II. I used to be mesmerized by the B-24 bombing raids in the city of Nanking (Nanjing), which was under Japanese occupation. I watched from a distance dozens of bombs float out of the belly of each plane, like salmon squirting eggs out of their abdomen in spawning grounds during their reproductive frenzy, and then hearing, after a little delay, a series of rolling explosions. There, in the library basement, I saw photos of proud American pilots in their flight gear climbing into the cockpit of their bombers and wondered if they were the ones who flew over my head in Nanking in 1945.

Late that night, exhaustion overtook me. Settling into a wooden chair placed in front of a wall, I popped my feet on a warm radiator and dozed off.

The next afternoon, I emerged from the library, hungry but in good spirits. My first order of business was to get some food from the kitchen in Kappa Sigma fraternity. There, a hostile crowd confronted me.

"The fucking Chinaman is back," someone hollered. A crowd began to gather around me.

Pete Webster came downstairs and asked, "Where have you been?"

I told him I was in the library reading books and magazines.

"You did that for twenty-four hours?! Jesus . . . !" Pete said in exasperation, "We had a date for you yesterday afternoon."

"Yeah, I know. But I had made it clear that I didn't wish to have a date."

Someone in the crowd yelled, "The Chinaman is a fucking queer."

At first, I didn't say anything and headed for bread and butter in the kitchen refrigerator. Then, I thought it was perceptive of them to consider me "strange and quaint," the only meaning of the word "queer" I knew at the time. It appeared to me that I surely fit that description at Kappa Sigma, because I differed so drastically from the brothers in every way. I was a non-conforming and ignorant alien, quaint and strange. Before stepping into the kitchen, I turned around and said to them:

"Yeah, I am queer."

To my utter bewilderment, my response brought down the house.

It mattered not that I didn't say, "I am a queer." In my vocabulary, the word "queer" existed only as an adjective, and I used it as an adjective when I said, "Yes, I am queer." But they heard only what they wanted to hear.

They were howling, roaring and pan-hooting in the midst of cussing, swearing and other undecipherable chattering emanating from the crowd gathered around me. Through the revolving kitchen door, I heard Pete's stentorian voice:

"Leave him alone."

The episode settled one issue: No one tried to fix me up with a date again during the remainder of my two years at Bowdoin.

<hr />

The thought of complaining to the college authority about the abuse I suffered at Kappa Sigma had occurred to me. But I did not think it would be appropriate for a guest to complain. From a Chinese perspective, filing a complaint would be similar to a guest informing his or her host that his home stank. It would be extremely impolite at best and provocative at worst. Being ignorant of how an American college functioned, I also feared that the authority might frown upon my complaint. For all they knew, I could have brought on myself all of the pranks and insults. So I told myself to endure the abuse and harassment and consider the torment dished out by the fraternity members part of my training for survival.

Another reason that made me hesitate about complaining was that a good part of the Kappa Sigma members' habits and behavior appeared strange and incomprehensible to me, and my opinion would be negative and disparaging if I were to reveal it.

Was my opinion valid? I wasn't confident at all.

The Kappa Sig brothers differed from me in every way. I was an alien, and an alien's perspective was likely to be biased on account of his or her own cultural background. After all, I judged them according to my values, which they obviously didn't share. Perhaps I was just as prejudiced in my opinion of them as they were judgmental of me. Yet, independent of that awareness, I couldn't help harboring some resentment at their hostility or avoid negative sentiments about the behavior of the Kappa Sig members.

One of my negative feelings concerned their penchant for inebriation. It was strange enough to see them loving and consuming alcoholic beverages. But it seemed incomprehensible and degrading that some of them occasionally guzzled beer and liquor for the explicit purpose of getting plastered. When that happened, they were definitely not enjoying the alcoholic beverage. Pleasure had nothing to do with the activity. They aimed to be drunk. The faster they became disoriented, started moaning and began vomiting, the more successful they would be. On weekends, some of the Kappa Sig brothers who didn't have a date for some reason often put on such gruesome performances, as if they hadn't, they would no longer be able to face the world.

Having struggled all my life to survive, and survival meant doing your utmost to avoid physical and psychological harm lurking in your environment, I couldn't help wondering, "Why do they inflict harm on themselves purposely? To what end was vomiting, losing your balance and being incoherent recreational?"

It was utterly bizarre and incomprehensible to me.

Another negative opinion of mine arose from seeing them petting and making out with their dates collectively in the fraternity living room on weekends: kissing, necking, groping, hands on breasts, hands up skirts . . . I understood the yearning for beautiful young women. But why did they engage in sexual activities in public? Instinct told me that among all human behavior, sex represented the ultimate intimacy and demanded the ultimate privacy. Of course, I was totally inexperienced in that arena, having grown up in an environment where holding hands between a young man and a young woman marked the limit of physical contact during courtship. This restraint on the part of unmarried Chinese youth in the 1950s did not stem from either moral concerns or religious admonitions. It was a voluntary effort to ensure self-preservation. Contraception was unknown to us. Young Chinese in Hong Kong suspected that kissing and petting would lead to sex, sex would lead to pregnancy, and pregnancy, for young lovers who couldn't count on their next meal, meant being sentenced to hell for the rest of their lives. In that world, it was practical and sensible to draw the line at holding hands until the young lovers' financial condition permitted marriage.

At Kappa Sigma, pre-marital sex seemed common, at least on the basis of what I had overheard. That alone bewildered me, although I didn't feel judgmental about it. I reckoned that they didn't have the same concerns that the young Chinese had. What appeared strange and reprehensible to me was that they not only exhibited their sexual pursuits by necking and petting in the fraternity's living room, albeit in the dim light of the evening, but also loved to brag about their exploits in graphic detail the next day, especially if they had spent a weekend with their dates. Sexual relations should be private in my worldview. What was the point of displaying sexual activities and bragging about it?

But I never uttered a word to reveal my judgmental thoughts or negative opinions.

Even though I refrained from complaining to the college authority about the jeers and insults inflicted by the Kappa Sigma brothers, the abuse was hurtful. But the hurt was a feeling that I nursed only when I was alone in the book stacks of the library or on a solitary walk. My status as a guest always weighed heavily on me. I did think it was strange for them to treat a guest in such a hostile way. At the same time, I didn't know if I had the right to complain. Instead, I vented all my anger and feelings in my diary, late every evening, after I had finished my study, usually at a hidden desk in the bookstacks of the library where I felt safe and private. There I wrote down everything that happened during the day in the hard-covered notebooks my Hong Kong friends gave me as a farewell present. When I opened those notebooks, I felt the companionship of my Chinese friends, and when I finished, I felt a sense of relief, as if I had succeeded in pleading my case in a courtroom.

In hindsight, I realize that the fraternity brothers had not planned to mock and discriminate against me from the beginning. Coming from New England upper middle-class families, most of them had little or no experience interacting with anyone or understanding anything from a culture and background that differed dramatically from theirs. Their milieu was primarily affluent, suburban and Yankee. Their behavior and manners conformed to the prevalent norm among the youth of the upper echelon of the American society in the early 1960s, the end run of a mentality and attitude that tended to be insular and intolerant. They relegated anyone or anything from a different culture to the absurd and outlandish, even if their prejudice and contempt did not stem from malicious intent. Indeed, the Kappa Sigma brothers never thought of themselves as prejudicial or racist. Had one accused them of being racist, they would've probably defended themselves by claiming that they were perfectly capable of befriending an African, a Mexican, an American Indian or an Asian. I wouldn't doubt the veracity of their claim, as long as that African, Mexican, American Indian or Asian shared their values, traditions and background. But if they had to live with an immigrant who did not know or understand their values, traditions and background, they would have difficulties interacting with the person. Like little children incapable of introspection and unconscious of their own value system and mental framework being not better or worse than that of other people, they were unaware of their assumption that their world was the only righteous and acceptable one. They couldn't help jeering and poking fun at a person with a different appearance, dissimilar values, and non-conforming behavioral patterns. In their world, everything other than what was familiar to them was deviant and condemnable. I am sure that when I was in high school in Hong Kong, my classmates and I were not different from the Kappa Sigma brothers in our tunnel vision of the world.

In 1961, I lacked the knowledge of American history and the understanding of American society to put the behavior of the Kappa Sigma brothers in its proper sociological context. I could only debunk the surface manifestation of what I saw, what I heard and what I experienced, and my conclusion at the time was that they were hostile.

That was a conundrum.

I couldn't fathom the root of their hostility. Having never behaved rudely or truculently, never questioned their values or activities, and never expressed any disapproval of their behavior, I couldn't figure out why they were angry with me. Confronted by this hostile and puzzling situation, I resorted to the quintessential East Asian defensive mechanism: shutting down and turning off, retreating into a world of saying nothing, seeing nothing and hearing nothing, like a clam hiding in its shell. My silence and retreat from the Kappa Sig brothers' antics probably irked them more than my ignorance and naivete did, and I could very well have been responsible for goading them into becoming increasingly aggressive in order to elicit some response from me.

After the blind date incident, a magnificent spectacle unfolded: the autumn foliage of Maine. I could hardly believe the blazing color in the distant hills visible from the Bowdoin campus. They looked more beautiful than a Paul Klee canvas. Nature's expansive design was not framed and did not appear in squares. It blended shades of red, yellow, maroon, amber, scarlet, burgundy into an enormous montage accentuated by slivers of birch white and patches of conifer green. The spectacle blanketed the hills and dales, an inimitable display of colors without borders, more brilliant and more dazzling than any painting of the Impressionists and the Pointillists. Indeed, the colors of *A Sunday Afternoon on the Island of La Grande Jatte, The Pine Tree at St. Tropez* or the gorgeous paintings of Van Gogh and Gauguin seemed almost dull in comparison.

I was awestruck.

But the colorful foliage exceeded beauty. It also signaled drama in the tradition of a Greek tragedy. The autumn breeze, sending jet streams of chill air to herald the approach of winter, rustled the trees, causing their colorful leaves to break away from the boughs and branches, fluttering and swirling in the air, before settling on the ground. They served as notice that beauty and splendor, no matter how exquisite and alluring, were irrevocably fragile and ephemeral.

During the two weeks when Maine blazed with autumn foliage, I walked away from the Bowdoin campus into the countryside at every opportunity to immerse in the flaming landscape, sometimes skipping dinner to gain a little more time to enjoy the spectacle. On those long walks, the hell in Kappa Sigma fraternity receded from my mind. More significantly, nature and its captivating beauty enabled me to view all of my woes and troubles in a larger scheme of things in life, rendering my troublesome existence insignificant. The wonder of nature reminded me that I was no more than a speck in the wide world, trivial and negligible. It also laid bare the absurdity of my worldly ambition and the mad pursuit of conventional success that was so prevalent and obsessive in the world of my youth. The broader perspective brought on by the amazing grace of the autumn foliage was relaxing, and it rendered my difficulty at Kappa Sigma fraternity insignificant. In spite of infinite loneliness, which haunted me frequently after I boarded the TWA plane to come to the States, I even began to think that the life of a hermit living in the woods could be appealing.

The fall foliage of Maine solidified my life-long love of nature, a love that began when I first wandered into the mountains of the New Territories of Hong Kong to escape my father's wrath, long before hiking and exploring the wilderness became popular. It grew as I lived in America. After graduate school, I have taken advantage of every opportunity and vacation to visit the magnificent National Parks in Utah, Arizona, California, Wyoming and Idaho. They were an inexhaustible source of comfort and strength. Before I married and established a family in my early forties, I escaped to a national park with my sleeping bag and tent whenever I felt overwhelmed by nightmares or approaching the end of my rope. There, in the midst of majestic mountains, glacial lakes, idyllic trails, towering trees, gurgling streams and imposing cliffs, I found not only beauty but also serenity and relief.

The brief splendor of the autumn foliage quickly gave way to Maine's bitter cold winter. Trees, with the exception of conifers, became barren. Grass turned brown. Grey clouds cloaked the sky, shielding the sun at most hours, and the air became frigid.

In tropical Hong Kong, the weather consisted of a rainy season and a dry season, even though the people there clung to the tradition of dividing a year into four seasons. The dry season wasn't really dry because occasional showers occurred, albeit not as heavy and persistent as the endless precipitation of the rainy season. Bitter cold winter with ice, snow and cutting wind didn't exist.

Before leaving Hong Kong, I knew that I would have to cope with the cold winter in America. Yet neither I, nor my friends who always had my welfare on their mind, could imagine the severity of the winter in Maine. None of us had been to the United States, so we had no experience with the sub-zero climate that occasionally laid siege to Maine. Even on a mild winter day in Brunswick, the temperature could be below freezing.

My two soul brothers in Hong Kong, anticipating the cold winter I would have to endure in America, pooled together whatever little money they had and presented me a gift package before my departure. The package consisted of a secondhand navy peacoat, probably robbed from a drunken American sailor by a Hong Kong street urchin who would have immediately sold it to a secondhand clothing store; a new pair of grey flannel pants; a Schaffer fountain pen with a silver cap; and two beautiful notebooks for me to jot down my thoughts and daily experience, a practice I had cherished since my childhood. Next to the hand-knit sweater from Kim, my girlfriend, that gift package from my friends was the most generous and luxurious one I had ever received. I counted on the peacoat and the flannel pants to keep me warm in Maine's winter, and I treasured the Schaffer fountain pen, using it to write my journal for years until its gold tip broke away.

Armed with the gifts of warm clothing from the people with whom I identified, I thought I was ready to take on the winter at Bowdoin. But as the month of November advanced, the cold intensified with howling wind and the occasional blizzard. My peacoat, sweater and flannel pants turned out to be woefully inadequate to ward off the frigid, icy wind of Maine. When I walked from one building to another on campus, my ears burned, my nose dripped, my teeth chattered, my hands turned red and numb, my feet stiffened as if rigor mortis were creeping up my legs from the frozen ground. Each time I left a classroom or the library, I had to overcome my reluctance to step outdoors to battle the inclement weather. Worst of all, I had to give up my only entertainment: walking into the hills outside of Brunswick to escape the Kappa Sigma fraternity house.

How to combat the frigid weather of Maine became an urgent issue in my life.

During the Thanksgiving weekend, which I spent at Aunt Helen's apartment, I went from store to store in Boston to seek employment, any kind of employment, for the five weeks of Christmas and New Year's vacation, so that I could earn money to buy some warm clothing. Three days of trudging in the dirty, salt-laden snow of Boston, which almost ruined my only pair of leather shoes and precious flannel pants I had never taken off since the cold weather began, landed me a clerkship at a bookstore. The job paid the minimum wage of $1.15 per hour. I didn't mind at all. In fact, earning Yankee dollars was exciting. I could hardly wait for the three weeks between Thanksgiving and Christmas vacation to pass so that I could start.

The first day on my job, the store manager told me that I could take an hour of lunch break. I politely declined, figuring that skipping lunch would mean, first, an additional $1.15 in my pocket, and secondly, a physical reminder of the long and difficult path ahead of me so that I would not weaken my resolve to work hard.

"A little hunger, like a gnawing irritant," I thought to myself, "will always keep you on your toes in the struggle for survival."

Skipping lunch became a routine for me during my one-and-half month stint at the bookstore in Boston. The manager of the bookstore nicknamed me "No-lunch Li."

The job suited me well. I loved the setting.

Books lining the walls, books on freestanding shelves, books displayed on tables, books in nooks and crannies, books everywhere. They seemed to impart a kind of coziness all by themselves, as if they constituted a large cocoon, offering a warm haven to those who sought to learn and know.

I also liked the unique scent of books in the bookstore. Unlike books in a library, which always had a tinge of mustiness mingled with the odor of mites and other microscopic parasites, new books emanated an aroma of woodsy cleanliness. After all, paper was just a few steps removed from natural wood.

In addition, opening up a new book brought forth the faint smell of ink from the printing press, reminding me of the painstaking labor in the production of a book, not just by the author, but also by the workers toiling in the printing factory.

Finally, there was the pleasure of simply holding a book in hand, anticipating the surprise of what its content might offer, while I dreamed that one day I would become an author.

Before taking on the job at the bookstore, I had spent a lot of time immersed in books in the Bowdoin library, a grand Victorian building in the neoclassical style, with a large, cavernous reading room consisting of many rows of long, heavy mahogany tables resting on polished oak floor. At the center of each rectangular table were two parallel rows of table lamps, each adorned with a soothing green glass shade. Oriental runner rugs, ornate and florid, covered the floor, muffling the sound of steps as people walked by.

In the library, one sat in an armchair at the table in front of a lamp to read and write. The atmosphere was somber and formal, almost like a temple. It offered a completely different ambiance from the little bookstore I worked in. The campus library was imposing, a stately dome that inspired ambitious endeavors and grandiose dreams. The little bookstore where I worked was warm and homey, a familiar niche that offered comfort and intimacy.

Sitting behind a counter near the entrance of the bookstore most of the time, six and a half days a week except Christmas Day and New Year's Day, I felt like a privileged creature curled up in a cozy nest, only to be interrupted by a modest workload of answering customers' questions, gift-wrapping, and showing customers where to find a particular book.

In the early evening, I stocked the shelves with newly arrived books and tidied up the place before the manager closed the door. When customers were sparse, there was even time for me to read. I could also buy books from the store at a 50% discount. It was a tempting bargain. There were many books I would love to own so that I could browse leisurely to gain some acquaintance with American fiction, poetry and history, all of which I had just begun to learn. But I couldn't afford to spend any of my $1.15 hourly wages.

I liked my job so much that when the bookstore closed in the evening, I secretly wished I could stay and spend the night there. Going back to Aunt Helen's place did not appeal to me at all, even though it wasn't hell, like the Kappa Sigma fraternity. The only attraction of her place was the Chinese food that she cooked up, which consisted of richly marinated and well-seasoned meat and vegetables, stir-fried on a high-heat burner to retain the ingredients' freshness, juice and texture. Since restaurants were off-limits to me for financial reasons, Aunt Helen's cooking represented both a luxurious treat and a reminder of my Chinese roots. For her, the pleasure stemmed from watching me devour the food she prepared. When food was tasty, I ate with great enthusiasm, like a sea otter lying on its back amid floating seaweed, chomping on an abalone with gusto. When I ate, Aunt Helen would sit across the table looking at me, transfixed and delighted, as if I were the living vindication of her culinary skill that would qualify her to be a good mother. She was, in fact, an excellent cook, as Chinese women often were in those days. Expertise in the kitchen was a part of their survival tool kit in a male chauvinistic culture because good food appeased their men. But tragically, fate had denied her the opportunity to be a mother.

By the end of the vacation, I had saved enough money to augment what was left of the one hundred dollars I brought from Hong Kong to buy myself a hooded winter coat lined with artificial fleece, a pair of rubber winter boots, two pairs of thick socks and long johns, and one pair of woolen gloves. With this extensive purchase, I was ready to battle the inclement weather of the remaining cold months. Indeed, when I returned to Bowdoin in January, protected by my new armaments, I could walk from one building to another on campus feeling like a normal person. My ears, protected by the hood of the new coat, did not burn; my legs, wrapped in long johns under my pants, did not feel the cutting wind; my hands, snug in woolen gloves, no longer turned red and raw; and my feet, protected by the thick socks and the rubber boots, no longer stiffened.

The Christmas/New Year vacation also clarified in my mind why I found Aunt Helen strange and sometimes incoherent when I was a child in her custody during the late 1940s. Aside from spouting non-sequiturs now and then, she had nothing to say beyond proselytizing and asking per-functory questions. An evening with her was, at best, dull and tedious, and at worst, irritating and exasperating.

Her perfunctory questions typically revolved around food and eating:

"Does the dish taste good?"

"Have you had enough to eat?"

"Why don't you eat more?"

Even though she knew the answers—I loved her cooking and always ate her food until my stomach could hold no more—she repeated those questions every evening anyway.

Interspersed between those questions would be a related but repeated refrain: "You are too skinny and need to eat more in order to grow." Yes, at 130 pounds and six feet in height, I was thin. But my body seemed to refuse to put on any weight, as if being thin was in my genes.

Aunt Helen's questions were perfunctory because she did not seek answers, and if I did proffer an answer, she never paid attention to it.

On exceptional occasions, she did ask genuine questions that were information-seeking. The first time I went from Bowdoin to her apart-ment on a weekend, she asked if Bowdoin fed me well, probably because she remembered the dorm food at a women's college in Pittsburgh, Pennsylvania, during the late 1930s when she studied Home Econom-ics. I could imagine her curling her lips and wrinkling her nose at the American dorm cuisine of that era.

I told her that Bowdoin gave me plenty of food, even though it did not always appeal to my palate.

"What's the worst?" She wanted to know more.

"Chipped beef," I answered without hesitation. There was no need to think or choose. "It tastes like thin slices of pounded rubber immersed in a putative sauce laced with fat and salt."

Aunt Helen laughed. "I had the same dish once a week thirty-some years ago in Pittsburgh. It was pretty darn awful!"

I also complained about another frequently served lunch dish: a long hotdog in a bun with a powdery and spongy taste. Worse than its taste, the bun stuck to my gums and teeth, and the hot dog itself was nothing but fat, salt and purported meat. At this point of our conversation, Aunt Helen was surprised by the similarity between her experience thirty years ago and my experience at Bowdoin.

"Hotdogs were also regularly served in my dorm in Pittsburgh during the 1930s. It's unbelievable that American dorm food hasn't changed much in thirty years."

"I should have probably done what the other boys did," I confessed. "They smothered the hotdog in the bun with ketchup, mustard and relish before wolfing down the whole thing. But mustard looked like some kind of yellow bird guano, and ketchup, I don't know what it is. The Bowdoin boys told me that it was a Chinese invention. News to me! I had never seen it anywhere until I came to Bowdoin."

It felt good to vent some of my grievances to a person outside of my diary. But I shied away from bringing up the shenanigans at Kappa Sig in my conversation with Aunt Helen, fearing that it might provoke her to interfere on my behalf. I just didn't want her to get involved in my Bowdoin life, no matter how unpleasant and abusive it might be. Also, I couldn't predict the outcome if she complained to Bowdoin about the way I was treated. But I came to the conclusion that talking about the poor quality of the food at Kappa Sigma fraternity wouldn't stir up any controversy.

"Well," I ventured on, "once a month, the fraternity cook serves steak. It isn't bad, but neither is it some haute cuisine like the Bowdoin guys made it out to be. Just a slab of grilled beef without any spices to modulate and enhance its flavor. In my opinion, it represents a rather primitive way of cooking meat, as if we were early hominids living in an era not long after the discovery of the hearth many hundred-thousand years ago. I could hardly eat a single piece of the steak. But some of the guys could eat several at one sitting."

She shared my sentiment about American steak and commented, "To a Chinese, American cuisine, if you can call it that, is pretty backward. When I first arrived in this country, it really caught me by surprise. The steak is an example of a good ingredient transformed into a bad dish. They also boil their vegetables into a mush, obliterating all of their savory flavors. It is horrendous! We, Chinese, stir-fried our vegetables. In addition, America doesn't even have a fraction of the green vegetables we have in China. Just talking about it makes me miss all the wonderful greens like A-tsai, Chinese chives, green scallions, cilantro, kong-xin tsai, baby bai-tsai, Napa cabbage, not to mention a great variety of tofu, freshly harvested bamboo shoots, soybean sprouts, and oh, my favorite: Chinese eggplant, which is long, thin and tasty, unlike the bland, gourd-like American eggplant. Just thinking about those vegetables makes me want to return to China."

Her comment about dorm food in America reminded me to bring up another meal at Kappa Sigma.

"Oh, there was a lobster dinner, late in October. A major culinary occasion. Every student talked about it for several days beforehand. Unfortunately, I didn't participate."

"Why not?" Aunt Helen knew from my childhood that I adored delectable food and would eat up a storm, given the opportunity.

"Well," I said, "many days before the dinner, the Kappa Sigma brothers were eagerly anticipating it. They talked about how many lobsters they would eat, and how they would dip the lobster meat in melted butter. In my opinion, eating lobster with dripping butter seemed as absurd as dressing filet mignon with pork fat. The butter would smother the flavor of the lobster like the pork fat overwhelming the delicacy of the filet. When the time for lobster dinner arrived, some Kappa Sig brothers were so excited that they stood at the kitchen door and lobbed bright-red, boiled lobsters, fresh out of the steamer pot, like heated missiles, to their fellow diners. I went into the dining room, took one look at the scene of flying lobsters, and decided to skip dinner. I just didn't wish to take the risk of being pierced by a red, hot lobster with sharp armored tips on its head."

She laughed and shook her head.

I went on to say, "Of course, none of the food at Bowdoin comes close to the quality of your creation," as I pointed at the five-spice beef stew she made that evening, a versatile dish that would go well with either rice or Chinese noodles. The beef was lean sirloin cut into cubes. Aunt Helen seared the cubes in vegetable oil before covering them in a homemade clear chicken broth. Then she added several kinds of ground peppercorn, fresh ginger root, nutmeg powder, some cinnamon stick, several star anise, red pepper flakes, fennel seeds, chunks of carrots, a pinch of sugar, some rice wine, a good amount of scallions and soy sauce. The pot was placed on the stove, brought to a boil and slow-cooked for an hour. At the end of an hour, Aunt Helen stirred into the pot some rice vinegar to accentuate the taste of the meat. When she opened the pot, a tantalizing aroma floated toward me that instantly made my mouth water.

Earlier in the day, Aunt Helen had made fresh Chinese noodles from flour and water. They were al dente and tasty. Boiled separately and placed in a bowl, the noodles were covered with the tender and flavorful five-spice beef stew and its sauce.

"It is heavenly!" I exclaimed as I savored the meal.

Aunt Helen smiled with the utmost delight. It was a rare occasion of successful interaction between us.

While food served as a pleasant medium for Aunt Helen and me to interact harmoniously, her goal to convert me into a Christian had the opposite impact on our relationship. She had always wanted me to become a Christian. Converting heathens was probably her mission in life. But converting a nephew close to her heart commanded special urgency. She would launch her missionary effort with me as a target at any moment of a day, in any context. To her, a particularly propitious moment would be the time when I sat quietly reading. All of a sudden, she would begin with the incantation:

"Jesus is our savior. He loves you."

Following that would be warnings, demands or questions such as, "The day of reckoning will come sooner or later!" or "I pray for you every day. When will you submit to Jesus?"

Throughout each barrage of Aunt Helen's attempts to convert me, I refused to engage. Most of her formulaic exhortations, warnings and threats were already deeply etched in my memory from the four years I spent in her custody in Shanghai during the 1940s. In Boston, I didn't know the nature of her job at the Rescue Mission, because she never told me anything about it. But I suspected that a good part of it involved preaching individually to the homeless people who sought help from the Mission. Perhaps preaching to me was just an extension of her job.

At Bowdoin, I had to endure the harassment of the Kappa Sigma brothers, who could be crude and hurtful. In Aunt Helen's apartment, I also faced harassment, albeit a relatively gentle kind. But Aunt Helen's version of harassment, repeated ad nauseam, could be just as devastating because there was no escape. At Bowdoin, I typically walked away from the fraternity house and disappeared into the library as soon as the brothers mounted an assault. In Boston, I didn't know where to go or what to do outside of her apartment.

Aunt Helen's evangelical pronouncements made me think of one of Father's musings, which resonated with me even when I was a young teenager:

"Religion does not differ from politics," he said. "Both involve the business of persuading, corralling, manipulating and controlling people. So, my son, if you ever become a politician, you must harness organized religion to advance your political goals."

Father probably learned this tactic from the Communists during the 1920s when they collaborated with Chinese politicians of different ideological convictions.

Of course, Father intended to shape me into pursuing a political career in China at all costs. For him, life's only worthwhile goal was climbing the political ladder in one's country of birth. But he failed to forge me into a politician, just as Aunt Helen failed to convert me to Christianity. On the contrary, by the time I was in senior high school, I thought professional politicians were primarily self-serving egotists hiding behind the pretense of "helping the masses" and other altruistic-sounding slogans. It made sense that "manipulation and control" was an important principle of operation for politicians. But many politicians went beyond manipulating and controlling the people. Under pressure, their manipulation, especially in China, would quickly devolve into mendacity, a conspiratorial deceit to mislead the masses for personal gain. In the early 1950s, Chiang Kai-Shek announced on New Year's Day of each year that he would launch a military invasion from Taiwan to retake Mainland China from the communists. One New Year's Day, upon hearing Chiang's harangue on the radio, I asked Father if the generalissimo could indeed retake Mainland China.

"No, he doesn't stand a chance," Father answered matter-of-factly.

"Then why did he claim he would in his speech?" I queried.

"He was lying," Father responded without any hesitation.

I was stunned. In my school, a pupil got slapped on the cheek as a routine punishment for lying. How could an adult, especially a leader of the Nationalist government in Taiwan, lie so blatantly to the public? So, I continued my query,

"Why did he lie?"

"He is a politician," Father answered casually.

I didn't have the heart or courage to ask him, "Do you also lie?" But he volunteered some clarification.

"All politicians lie," he sighed. "Some lie when they have to. Some, like Chiang Kai-shek, unfortunately, are habitual liars. They lie even when there is no reason to lie. As if lying is embedded in their brains, pounded into their souls, and ingrained in their personalities."

Many years later, Hannah Arendt reiterated Father's observation, "all politicians lie," more eloquently in an essay: "Lying in Politics: Reflections on the Pentagon Papers" in *The New York Review of Books*, November 18, 1971. She wrote,

> Truthfulness has never been counted among the political virtues and lies have always been regarded as justifiable tools in political dealings. Whoever reflects on these matters can only be surprised **HOW LITTLE ATTENTION HAS BEEN PAID**, in our tradition of philosophical and political thought, to their significance . . .

I wish there was a movement to rectify people's passive acceptance of lying politicians all over the world. After all, children are routinely punished for lying, and in the adult world, perjury is a criminal offense. Instituting an ethical standard to disallow a lying politician from holding office seems a good way to elevate the moral standard of politics and ameliorate societal ills.

Mother never approved of Father's desire to pursue a career in the political arena of China. I agreed with her when she blamed politics for his ruination. It had given him an unsavory character, not to mention that it also landed him in jail.

Nevertheless, I thought he struck gold in his observations about religion, even though he wasn't as eloquent and succinct as Dashiell Hammett. In the words of the enduring detective Sam Spade in *The Maltese Falcon*:

"The crusades were largely a matter of looting."

Partly out of my respect for Aunt Helen as an elder and my erstwhile guardian, partly out of my suspicion that the core of the antagonism between Father and Aunt Helen might very well have been their colliding views of religion, I refrained from reacting to Aunt Helen's effort to convert me.

When she preached incessantly, I either read or daydreamed endlessly.

I also understood that Aunt Helen, Mother, my sisters, and countless men and women needed religion as an anchor in life. Religious faith enabled them to survive, to cope with the absurdity of life, the hardship and the tragic events which could happen not infrequently to anyone, at any time in the China I knew. Personal religious conviction never offended me. Unbridled proselytization did!

Mother, in contrast to Aunt Helen, never tried to convert me. She prayed and read the Bible, sometimes in my presence, but never asked me to share or participate in her faith or her religious activities. In return, I respected her relationship with her God.

At her funeral in the San Francisco Bay area in 1996, my siblings, whom I had rarely ever interacted with, asked me to speak on behalf of our family. Thinking about Mother and the importance of religion to her, I chose to recite Psalm 23 instead of giving a speech.

"The Lord is my shepherd. I shall not want. He maketh me to lie down in green pastures . . . "

To the surprise of everyone, including me, I choked with tears halfway through the recitation and was forced to stop. I had to regroup and compose myself before finishing the poem.

There was no apparent reason for me to shed tears at Mother's funeral. I never spent much time with her. She and I never established a close relationship. At the funeral, even my siblings didn't shed tears, in spite of the fact that they had spent many good years of their lives with her. Mother died in peace, with absolute confidence that she was going to heaven. Her pastor and all members of her Chinese evangelical church in Hayward, California, shared and reinforced her confidence. At age 94 and in failing health, she decided that she had had enough of life on planet earth and reckoned it was time for her to meet her Lord. At that point, she had stopped eating and, within a few days, passed away in her sleep.

During the last fifteen years of her life, Mother and I saw each other periodically. Through one of my sisters, I found out that by the mid-1970s, Mother had retired to the Bay area from a career as a social worker for the Commonwealth of Massachusetts, counseling and helping Chinese immigrants in Boston who lacked English language proficiency. She emigrated to Boston from Hong Kong with the help of Aunty Helen shortly after I graduated from Bowdoin College in 1963. Since she retired to the San Francisco Bay area, I visited her several times every year, sometimes accompanied by my wife and children, and took her to her favorite Chinese restaurants to eat dumplings and dishes that she could not easily cook in her kitchen. Our relationship was distant but respectful. I admired her for her incomparable courage and strength. Coming from a culture in which women belonged to men almost like a piece of property, she was never cowed by Father or anyone else. In her late 40s, when she could no longer tolerate Father's temper tantrums and violent outbursts, she left him, without a penny to her name and without any work experience, attended a Christian seminary, got a tertiary degree, and became an ordained minister of a fundamentalist Christian church in Hong Kong. In 1963, she immigrated to the United States at an age when most people would look forward to retirement.

It was a mystery that I choked up at her funeral. I had no explanation. Even my ever-vigilant self-monitor in the frontal lobe of my brain was at a loss.

During that Christmas vacation in Boston in 1961, I came to the conclusion that I could no longer tolerate staying under the same roof with Aunt Helen, even though I spent every day happily working at the bookstore at the time. Being harangued by her multiple one-liner sermons every evening was not unlike being subjected to psychological torture, similar to what Comrade Liu did to me at the Thought Reform School in China during 1957-58.

By the second semester at Bowdoin College, it was clear to me that I would major in mathematics. Actually, it had been a foregone decision long before my arrival at Bowdoin that I would choose a major in science or engineering if and when I was lucky enough to get a college education. After the Second World War, just about every Chinese boy who had done well in secondary school chose to study science or engineering. It never occurred to me to buck that prevailing trend, no matter how appealing literature and social sciences might be. Since Bowdoin didn't have a school of engineering, I became a math major because of my aptitude for abstract mathematics and my disdain for laboratory work, which drove me away from physics, biology and chemistry. On the one hand, the process of conducting an experiment in order to arrive at a predetermined result appeared pointless to me. I felt that I didn't learn anything new from the effort. Taking meticulous measurements, dissecting a frog or an earthworm, mixing chemicals in a test tube to confirm what I had already learned bored me. On the other hand, the logic and reasoning in abstract mathematics were appealing because they led to new knowledge. Working through the proof of a theorem yielded a pleasure similar to that of coming to grips with a piece of intricate classical music. You acquired some new insight. In addition, the awesome power of mathematical logic was tantalizing. It allows the development of new mathematical knowledge on the basis of a few well-defined concepts.

Toward the end of my first year at Bowdoin, my professors, especially those in the Mathematics Department, were so pleased with my academic performance that they secured another year of full financial support for me at Bowdoin. The U.S. State Department fellowship that brought me to Bowdoin was limited to one year. Now, Bowdoin was granting me another year of full fellowship covering tuition, fees, room and board. More significantly, the professors told me that if I kept up the pace of my academic progress, I might be able to graduate by the end of my second year.

My professors' encouragement and support gave me such a boost that I felt, notwithstanding the situation at Kappa Sigma fraternity, attending Bowdoin College was an incredible stroke of luck in my life. For the first time, I was no longer staring into the abyss of abject poverty or the possibility of the life of a street urchin. I was on the cusp of moving beyond the preoccupation of seeking food and shelter, and most importantly, I had a future to look forward to. Indeed, hope and new prospects beckoned, even though it wasn't at all clear what the new prospects entailed beyond a college degree and a job.

The endorsement from the faculty of the math department also emboldened me to seek advice from some of them on a non-academic issue that had been on my mind throughout the academic year:

Where could I find a job during the summer vacation?

A young, newly minted professor asked if I had any preference for a summer job. I responded, "Any job that pays me well. I need money for room and board during the summer in addition to saving some pocket money for the following academic year."

He suggested that I check out the employment opportunity section of *The Boston Globe* before the summer. I did and found an ad stating that an upscale lobster restaurant on the waterfront in Cape Cod would hire additional waiters during the summer months.

When the school year ended, I took a bus to Boston, transferred to Cohasset, and headed straight to the lobster restaurant, lugging my suitcase and typewriter. The owner, Mr. Zakarios, a poor immigrant from Greece who had worked day and night for decades to become a prosperous restaurateur in America, was impressed that a foreign student who had finished only one year at Bowdoin College had the courage to come directly to him at Cape Cod on the first day of his summer vacation to seek employment. He hired me on the spot at $1.25 per hour, starting the next day, reminding me that I would earn a lot more income from tips. I asked him where I could rent an inexpensive room for the summer. He directed me to a private home about half a mile away, and there, a very nice elderly couple told me that I could rent a room in the back of their modest house for $35 per month. The room was spartan but comfortable. Ensconced in my new nest, I felt I had accomplished quite a lot in one day.

That evening, I wrote to Aunt Helen from Cohasset to inform her that I had obtained a summer job and found a place to stay near Cape Cod. She wrote back to say that she was glad I found a job but sad she wouldn't have me around for the summer. Her response elicited a mixture of relief and guilt from me. While I was glad to escape from her orbit, I also felt terrible for abandoning her. There was nothing that pleased her more than playing the role of a mother to me. She never complained about not having a husband. Her face, pockmarked from a bout of smallpox at age four, doomed her to spinsterhood. But her maternal instinct was irrepressible.

In a pre-modern Chinese village, a child infected with smallpox was usually abandoned in the wilderness far from the village to die, because the virus was so virulent that a village community would not tolerate the presence of anyone infected with such a contagion. The bereaved parents would have no choice but to take the sick child, semi-comatose from high fever, up to a mountain and leave it in a cave with a big bucket of drinking water, knowing that a fever-raked child would be thirsty during those brief bouts of consciousness before death.

Three or four days later, the parents would return to collect the body and bury it.

In Aunt Helen's case, when her parents came to bury her, she was, miraculously, alive. The poxes on her body and face were already covered with scabs. But their joy at the miracle of regaining their child was overshadowed by their awareness that Helen would be scarred for life. No man would want her as a wife because of her pockmarked face. In the male-dominated rural society of China, a woman without a husband was a non-entity, as good as a stray canid without a territory. Being devout Christians, Aunt Helen's parents brought her up as an independent woman. Her ill-fated destiny made her strong and feisty in a world dominated by male chauvinism. But being left on a mountain to die in the depth of her illness must have been a devastating experience. I often wondered if her oddness resulted from the shock and trauma of being abandoned at the direst moment of her need, when she was fighting for her life against the smallpox virus at the tender age of four.

For decades, Aunt Helen had survived, by hook or crook, as a single, professional woman in China—a laudable achievement and not an easy one. She was self-sufficient, except she could hardly contain her desire to mother me ever since I lived with her in Shanghai while Father was in prison. She often claimed that those years in the late 1940s, when she took care of me in Shanghai, were the best years of her life, and I, in turn, always felt grateful to her for her love and kindness.

Wary of hurting Aunt Helen's feelings, I reassured her in my letters from Cohasset that I would visit whenever I had a day off from the restaurant. Cohasset was separated from Boston only by a bus ride of approximately one hour.

Much to Aunt Helen's delight, I visited her several times during the summer. My visit, usually brief, always cheered her up, while I had a handy excuse at any moment to leave on account of my job.

After retiring from Boston's Rescue Mission, Aunt Helen settled into a Chinese Christian retirement home in southern California and survived until her mid-nineties.

Working at Zakarios was brutal. I had known hard physical work at the thought reform school in China where intense labor was extolled as the cure-all for bourgeois deviation. But the work at Zakarios was, in addition to being incessant and physically demanding, also frantic and psychologically stressful.

A waiter ran constantly between his station consisting of four or five tables of clients, the bar, the lobster holding tank and the kitchen throughout the evening without a moment of respite from 5 p.m. to 11 p.m. Customers always began their meals with at least one round of cocktails, before their salad, clam or lobster chowder, followed by whole lobster and ended with desserts. The first few days were particularly nerve-wracking. I encountered the names of all kinds of cocktails that I had never heard of. They seemed so outlandish, like Singapore Sling, Daiquiri, Pink Lady, Martini, Manhattan . . . Even though I had learned my lesson about Screwdrivers at Kappa Sigma fraternity, each name as I heard it for the first time at Zakarios astonished me. In addition, there was a vocabulary associated with alcoholic beverages that I had no knowledge of. Within that vocabulary, the term "dry," which my customers frequently used in their order, seemed the strangest when I first heard it.

How could a beverage be dry? I shook my head in disbelief.

Further complicating my job was the peculiar specification of the cocktails many customers desired: a particular brand of gin or vodka, a special type of whiskey or scotch or bourbon, the different brands of vermouth, the exotic names of sherry or champagne like Don Fino, Oloroso, Clicquot, Mumm, Don Pérignon, etc. When a party of customers gave me their cocktail orders, I had to write them down. But I didn't know what to write down during my first few days on the job, because I had never heard of those names and brands of liquor. Just about every word the customers used in the domain of alcoholic beverage was new to me. As common etiquette prevented me from asking customers to spell the names or brands of alcoholic beverages they ordered, I was overcome with anxiety when I took their cocktail orders. Concealing my panic with a faux smile, I scribbled down the orders in my own spelling. But my effort was not always successful. Sometimes, the bartender became royally irritated because my scribbling made no sense. Sometimes, he would crack up in laughter as he read out loud my scribblings such as "Black Johnny Worker," "Don Perry Nun," "Die-curry." Unbeknownst to me, the job of a waiter, in addition to physically taxing, was mentally demanding as well.

By the time the restaurant closed at 11 p.m., I typically collapsed on the floor in the waiters' changing room to give my legs a brief respite before walking to my lodging place. Even after I had acquired most of the vocabulary concerning alcoholic beverages by the second week, I found the work exhausting. The job was no longer nerve-wracking by then, but the workload kept growing as the summer moved on. I realized that Zakarios was a popular eatery for the well-to-do denizens of Cape Cod and the Boston area.

I was lucky that Zakarios was an upper-end restaurant for the rich. At the time I applied to be a waiter there, I had no inkling of what I was getting into. It turned out that the income from my job, mostly in tips, far exceeded my expectations. I was earning up to a hundred dollars or more every evening. Surprisingly, the most generous tipper wasn't any of the celebrities like Teddy Kennedy, Zsa Zsa Gabor or Howard Johnson that came in, but a priest in his clerical attire, who dined at the restaurant alone at the beginning of each month, consuming a two-pound lobster and one full bottle of Moët Chandon from France. The lucky waiter who served him always received a twenty-dollar tip.

On Saturdays, work began at 9:30 a.m. because the restaurant was a popular venue for weddings, which typically drew a large and heavy-drinking crowd. Each Saturday would be the most exhausting day of the week. Other than a thirty-minute dinner break at 5 p.m., I was on my feet for fourteen hours, rushing from one place to another. But the wedding party would add forty or fifty dollars in tips to each waiter.

By the end of July, after more than two months of waiting tables, I estimated that I had saved a good sum of money, although I never counted it. Every evening, I emptied the cash I earned from my pockets into a metal box, which I purchased in a variety shop.

Ever since my experience in Shanghai during the Chinese civil war, witnessing the collapse of banks and the anguish of the victims who trusted the banks for holding their money, I had always equated banks with robbery, or more precisely, institutionalized looting. All I knew was that, under normal circumstances, a bank would pay a depositor a certain amount of interest every fortnight, but on any day, a bank could shut its doors without warning, and a depositor's money would've vanished. By the summer of 1962, I had learned in a course on economics at Bowdoin to understand that banks were a necessary part of the financial system of a modern nation, and furthermore, unlike pre-Communist China, developed nations had enacted laws and regulations to protect depositors and insure their money in case of the sudden collapse of a bank. But that was all textbook knowledge acquired in a classroom. My real-life experience came from witnessing the practice of fraudulent banks during the Chinese civil war in the late 1940s. The trauma of the victims being robbed of their hard-earned savings by the bank left such an indelible impression on me that my fear of banks continued to haunt me during the summer of 1962. I wasn't going to take a chance by keeping my money in a bank, not even in America.

In Cohasset, every late evening, when I arrived in my little room, exhausted from the back-breaking work, I didn't turn on the light. After locking my door, I would reach under my bed in the darkness and fish out my winter rubber boots from my suitcase. Inside one of them was my metal box. Then I would transfer that day's earnings from my pocket into the box before returning the box to the boot, and the boot to the suitcase. Only upon completing my money-transferring would I turn on the light, take a shower, brush my teeth and go to sleep.

In early August, having been granted an off-duty day by my boss, Mr. Zakarios, I decided not to visit Aunt Helen in Boston and gave myself a holiday. It was a balmy day with a pleasant breeze. The blue sky was adorned with puffs of white clouds. In my landlord's small but pictur-esque garden, songbirds squabbled and fluttered, dragonflies flitted here and there, honeybees buzzed among the flowers, feeding and dancing. Lounging in an Adirondack chair by an ancient oak tree, I lost myself in *The Portrait of a Lady* by Henry James. It was one of the few books I bought at the Boston bookstore where I worked during the Christmas vacation. The owner highly recommended it. He had good reasons for his recommendation. What a riveting novel! It captivated me so com-pletely that more than seven hours elapsed before the glare of the setting sun jolted me back to reality as if I had been gone in another world.

That evening, I decided to count the money in my strongbox, some-thing I had not done before. I suspected that money got my attention because it loomed large in the life of Isabel Archer, the lady in *The Por-trait of a Lady*.

Much to my surprise, I had nearly three thousand dollars. It was a fortune, a windfall I had never seen before.

There was no way I could spend that much money during the coming academic year, even if I allowed myself to indulge in buying some books and treating myself to a pizza now and then, a common practice of the Kappa Sigma fraternity brothers on weekends. I put twenty dollars in my pocket and went out to dinner in a modest seafood restaurant. Sitting at a table by myself, I thought about my little "fortune" and wanted to do something unusual, ambitious, pleasurable and edifying. I came upon the idea of mounting an automobile tour of the United States before the start of the school year in early September.

The next day, I went to see Mr. Zakarios and announced that I would like to quit my job immediately. He glowered at me and demanded an explanation since the summer had not yet ended. I responded with the excuse that I was burned out by the hard work at the restaurant and needed some time to prepare academically for the coming school year. My response satisfied him. Without further questioning, he accepted my excuses and paid me cash for the wages he owed me.

As I went around Cohasset hunting for a suitable secondhand car to launch my tour, it didn't escape me that I had lied like a politician when I fabricated excuses to mollify Mr. Zakarios. Even worse, my excuse came up spontaneously without any premeditation.

At that point, I wished that I didn't monitor myself so relentlessly. There was a part of my brain that never ceased to monitor and scrutinize all of my words and behavior. Even worse, this monitor system, this invisible "person" hovering above and controlling my brain at all time, remembered everything, especially my substandard or unethical utterances and deeds, so that sometimes, out of the blue, it would bring up a particularly embarrassing incident just to make me cringe and put me on edge. Like a curse, this omnipresent monitor probably took form during the weekly session of self-criticism in my thought-reform class in China during 1957-58. That class was conducted by Comrade Liu, a merciless former political commissar of the People's Liberation Army from the Korean War, who had absolute power over the students in her class. She decided each student's fate, with a stroke of her pen signaling whether or not the student should receive a university education, regardless of his/her academic merit. Attendance at the weekly self-criticism session was absolutely compulsory. Comrade Liu didn't accept any excuse. Students would have to show up and confess their wayward behavior and counter-revolutionary thoughts even if they suffered from a high fever.

At the beginning of the year, every student took the self-criticism sessions seriously, because everyone wanted to demonstrate to Comrade Liu that they embraced the process of thought reform wholeheartedly and strove to become proper and acceptable socialist citizens of China. Each of us diligently prepared for every session through daily self-examination, writing down our offenses in our journals, ranging from capitalistic daydreams of yearning for a protein-rich meal or the bourgeois transgression of lacking enthusiasm in long hours of back-breaking manual labor, to questioning the validity of the past directives of the Communist Party, like the indiscriminate killing of the "landlords," real as well as alleged, during the Land Reform Movement in the early 1950s and the murderous "struggle" against anyone whom the Party had designated a Rightist during 1956-57. However, several months into the weekly self-criticism sessions, our enthusiasm waned, because so many new Party directives were irrational, unwarranted and unjustifiable, like mobilizing the entire nation to kill flies and birds while halting all industrial and agricultural production. A rational and sensible person couldn't honestly criticize himself for harboring misgivings about the merit of some of those Party edicts. In addition, we all knew that voicing misgivings about current Party policies, even in the context of self-criticism, might be detrimental to our future. The misgiving went on your record, and one day in the future it could be the cause of your banishment. Gradually the weekly self-criticism session degenerated into a farce. The students would criticize themselves and each other on anything and any behavior, mostly trivial and irrelevant, such as going to the bathroom too frequently or taking too long a shower. Sometimes the criticism could be a masked sarcasm, a parody of the Communist Party's ruthless control of the body and soul of every Chinese at a time when an adult could not even marry or divorce without the prior approval of the Party.

By that time, the habit of monitoring oneself for having done or said anything improper or untoward was already irrevocably established in every student's life. The brain-washing process, under the supervision of the ever-vigilant Comrade Liu, our ideological supervisor, created a different mental framework in each student, permanently altering a student's neuronal wiring system.

When I arrived at Bowdoin, I certainly did not feel obliged to monitor or examine myself constantly. But my brain seemed to do it regardless of my wish and circumstance, as if the genie of self-criticism and perpetual self-monitoring were out of the magic lamp.

In an attempt to overcome my guilt for having lied to Mr. Zakarios, I plunged headlong into the mission of finding an affordable automobile, walking briskly ten to twenty miles each day around Cohasset, Situate and other nearby towns. But the cars in secondhand car lots were either too expensive or too big. As I began to lose hope of finding an affordable car, on the third day of my search I found, in a local newspaper advertisement section, a suitable candidate: a Morris Minor, put up for sale by a private owner. I bought it immediately for $300.

The Morris Minor was a midget British car that looked like a shrunken Volkswagen beetle. In the 1950s, when the British automobile industry remained robust and flourishing mostly because it had a captive market in British colonies all over Asia and Africa, the Morris Minor competed with the smallest and cheapest Fiat from Italy and the tiny, cockroach-like Citroën from France in the European and third-world automobile markets. Barely capable of reaching 60 miles per hour even if one floored the gas pedal, the Morris Minor was not intended for the U.S. It was popular in Hong Kong because, aside from being a British colony, big cars would have difficulty maneuvering the narrow, crowded streets. Additionally, gasoline was expensive by the local standard of living.

In Cape Cod, I was lucky to find a secondhand Morris Minor. It suited me well because it was inexpensive to own and operate. At the time, most Americans would consider my car a joke, undeserving of being included in the category of automobiles. When I cruised the streets in it, people who drove by often cast a disdainful glance in my direction, as if to say, "You shouldn't be allowed on the road with that contraption."

Keenly aware of the un-American nature of my little car in an era when gasoline price hovered around 20-25 cents per gallon and American automobile design emulated spaceships with fins, I drove cautiously in the right-most lane, whether on a turnpike or a street. When a semi-truck sped past me on a turnpike, my Morris Minor shook violently from the air turbulence, as if it could disintegrate at any moment. Nevertheless, it accommodated me, my suitcase and my typewriter, and would carry me all over the United States on my tour.

THE BEAUTIFUL COUNTRY

DURING THE 1950S, EVERY YOUNG PERSON IN HONG KONG, fascinated by America's reputation of affluence and opportunities for professional advancement, dreamed of moving to America. American products in every domain of life, from apparel (Arrow shirt), luxury household goods (Frigidaire), heavy machinery (Caterpillar), to airplanes (Boeing), motorcycles (Harley Davidson), and machine tools (Black and Decker), were celebrated for their design and reliability. All American products carried a high price tag, partly because of the high value of the American dollar, but they stood for quality, and Hong Kong people reasoned that the sterling quality of American merchandise deserved higher prices. To the people who lived in an unforgiving colony of the fading British Empire, America was paradise, the land of dreams.

Once every fortnight, a large ocean-crossing passenger ship of the American President Line docked on the Kowloon side of the Hong Kong harbor and took on hundreds of passengers to sail to the United States. The departure of the liner always attracted a throng of pedestrians on the street. Longing to be the lucky passengers on board, they stopped in their tracks to watch the large ship slowly backing away from the pier into the deep water of the harbor while blasting its foghorn to warn the sampans, junks and Walla-Wallas (a small water taxi) to stay clear of its path. One could read the yearning on the face of the onlookers:

"Why am I not one of those lucky passengers?"

After all, the name of America meant "beautiful country" in Chinese. No other country had so laudatory a name in the Chinese language. Not France, not New Zealand, not Italy. Who wouldn't want to live in a beautiful country!?

One year of living in the Kappa Sigma fraternity had sown some doubt in me about living permanently in America, but the concept of America as the beautiful country, reinforced by the autumn foliage of Maine, remained steadfast in my mind. I had seen photos of Yosemite, Yellowstone and other National Parks in magazines before leaving Hong Kong. Now that I had some money, a car and three weeks before the start of another year at Bowdoin, I wanted to see the great national parks of the beautiful country. With the help of maps, I planned a W-shaped route: starting from Cape Cod, southward to Florida's Everglades, and then turning northwest toward Niagara Falls; from Niagara Falls, drive west via Mount Rushmore and the Badlands before heading southwest toward the Rocky Mountains and New Mexico; the last leg of the trip would cover the Grand Canyon before going north to the Grand Tetons, Yellowstone and ending in Seattle, Washington. There I planned to sell the car and fly back to Boston.

First stop, the Rodin Museum, Philadelphia.

I learned about Auguste Rodin and Philadelphia's Rodin Museum in the late 1950s from a magazine in a public reading room of the United States Information Service (USIS) in Hong Kong.

The USIS air-conditioned reading room frequently served as my refuge from the oppressive heat of Hong Kong's long hot and humid months. I went there to improve my English by reading journals like *Time, Newsweek* and *Reader's Digest* with the aid of an English-Chinese dictionary, or flipping through photographic magazines like *LOOK, LIFE* and *The Saturday Evening Post* while sitting comfortably in an armchair. There were other magazines and journals like *The New Yorker, Harper's,* and *National Review,* but their contents frequently posed too much of a barrier for me. Occasionally, I would gather up enough courage to tackle a grade school level book, often a *Tarzan* story. One day, as I was scanning the shelves, the book title *The Naked and the Dead* caught my attention. It captured two themes that loomed large in my past. I pulled it from the shelf and started to read it.

A difficult undertaking! Nearly every page contained some words that were new to me. As I tried to read the book, I was looking up my English-Chinese dictionary so frequently that an onlooker could have thought that I was reading two books simultaneously. But Norman Mailer's narrative grew more and more captivating and dazzling as I labored from one page to the next. I refused to give up reading the book, arduous as it might be. In the end, it took me more than three weeks of spending several hours each day to plow through the book at the USIS reading room. Many years later, when I met Norman Mailer in Berkeley at an antiwar protest, even though I had already grown into a different person, I was thrilled.

The work of Rodin that caught my attention in the USIS reading room was *The Thinker (Le Penseur)*. I didn't know at the time that *The Thinker* was so popular in America and Europe that mentioning it among the au courant might give the impression of a novice speaking in clichés. But there couldn't be a better introduction to sculpture appreciation than *The Thinker*, with the possible exception of some of the works of Henry Moore and Isamu Noguchi. *The Thinker* was not as abstract as Alberto Giacometti's attenuated human figures or Constantin Brancusi's symbolic *Bird*. At the same time, it conveyed much more than a commemorative bust or statue of a real person in life, like many of the Classical Greek and Roman sculptures. With its posture, intense concentration, and Herculean anatomy, *The Thinker* captured one of the most important activities in human life. All human beings, young and old, strong and weak, rich and poor, THINK from time to time, without necessarily exploring any grandiose topic or erudite theme. Thinking is random, constant and universal. It is the unavoidable activity of the human brain and even the animal brain to some extent. Yet, if someone were to ask what thinking was, the answer might not be easy or transparent. But Rodin seemed to have encapsulated the answer in one powerful sculpture.

Viewing the photo of *The Thinker* in the USIS reading room, I decided, then and there, if I ever went to France or America, I would make a special effort to see Rodin's sculptures.

Now in the courtyard of the Philadelphia Rodin Museum, *The Thinker*, larger than life, perched on a marble plinth, appeared in front of me. I walked around it, examined the broad back and muscular limbs of a powerful male figure sitting on a rock, his chin resting on one hand, deeply engaged in thought, its palpable pensive face and heroic struggle conveying the travail of deep thinking. I walked around it again, draped in curiosity about art and creativity. It was easy to admire *The Thinker*, but not some modern art such as the works of Jackson Pollock, which seemed remote and obscure to me.

The architecture of the museum, however, was much less appealing than the contents it housed—an injustice to Rodin's œuvre. Dull and graceless, the building looked more like a fortress or an oversized mausoleum than a place housing precious art.

Inside the museum, a large number of Rodin's sculptures, his drawings, plaster studies, prints and letters were on display. Especially memorable among the sculptures was the *Burghers of Calais*, a larger-than-life bronze work depicting six leading citizens of the coastal city of Calais surrendering to the victorious Edward III, the King of England, in the 14th century during the Hundred Years' War between France and England. Instead of presenting the burghers in fake heroic glory, the sculpture was faithful to the reality. It depicted the pain and anguish of the six civic leaders as they volunteered to sacrifice their lives in order to save the citizens of Calais from massacre, even though ultimately the Queen of England persuaded her husband to spare the six burghers from execution.

After spending most of the day at the Rodin Museum, I went to see the Liberty Bell to pay homage to American independence before spending a night in a suburb of Philadelphia "sleeping" in my Morris Minor without ever straightening up. Lodging in a motel room was a luxury. I would allow myself such a luxury only if I felt the necessity for a shower.

While in Philadelphia, I decided to skip major metropoles along the tour. My experience in Boston and Philadelphia informed me that big cities were expensive, complicated and somewhat intimidating. Cities tended to breed tension. In an urban environment, there seemed to be many more aggressive and hostile inhabitants than in small towns and rural areas. I admitted to myself that a reason for my perception might be my ignorance of American culture. So, I decided that cities should be savored during future tours when I became better educated and more knowledgeable.

Next destination: Southern United States.

It took me two long days of driving to reach Durham, North Carolina, my first stop in the South. In Hong Kong, I had heard about Duke University as an outstanding institution of higher learning. That was why Durham was my first stop. It turned out that was as far south as I reached.

Having secured a free parking spot on the edge of Durham, I boarded a bus and sat in the back, noticing that all the passengers who appeared to be of European descent sat in the front end of the bus, and all the passengers of African descent sat in the rear. I did not think of the distribution of passengers as anything significant. Just a coincidence, I thought.

Arriving downtown, I was surprised that it didn't look like a city center in any fashion. There were no bustling markets, no high-rise buildings, no throngs of pedestrians. Some retail stores and restaurants dotted the landscape. The ubiquitous sight was the small signs declaring "white only" and "black only," or "White" and "Black."

I was mystified.

The only way these signs could make sense was that they referred to the skin color of people.

Immediately, the notion of "colored people," which I first encountered at the Kappa Sigma fraternity, jumped to mind.

If my interpretation of the signs was correct, I reasoned, the people of Durham must have never seen Asians, whose skin color ranges from pitch black (some of the Dravidian people, for example) to ivory white (which include, for example, some of the forest dwellers like certain subgroups of the Dayak people, in Borneo). I looked at my uncovered arms under the oppressive summer sun. Their color appeared midway in the range. Dark, definitely not ivory white, yet not black. Unclear to which category I belonged, I nearly had a panic attack. In the end, I braced myself and decided to ignore the signs.

Walking around Durham that sultry afternoon trying to find something worth looking at or some landmark worth visiting, I failed. After an hour or so wandering in the nondescript city center, I ducked into a store and asked the clerk for directions to Duke University.

"You don't want to go there," he said with a menacing grin. "There is a bunch of no good rabble-rousers on that campus helping the Negros organize a Freedom Rally to tear apart our town."

Other than his hostility and anger, which registered on me instantly, the content of his warning completely went over my head. I walked out and stepped into a barbershop. The barbers thought I wanted a haircut. I explained that, as a tourist, I just wanted some information.

One of them said, "Well, there isn't much tourist attraction in this town. Durham is the heart of the cigarette industry. Go visit the American Tobacco Company owned by the Duke family, if you are interested. It was, not so long ago, the largest cigarette-producing company in the world."

While the barber went on talking about the history of the cigarette industry in Durham, he offered me a Lucky Strike, which I politely declined, saying that I didn't smoke. When I was about to leave, he offered a friendly recommendation:

"If you're not interested in the history of the cigarette industry, I would advise you to leave town. In a couple of days there will be a major demonstration by them Negros trying to desegregate our Howard Johnson's restaurant. Troublemakers are coming in town from out of state. All hell will break loose here!!"

As I walked away, I was totally lost, like a Martian who had just arrived on planet Earth. Nothing made sense: the so-called city of

Durham, the absence of a city center. It would not even qualify as a suburb. The people there seemed strangely angry. Even worse, what they said, or what was on their mind, was completely incomprehensible to me. Everything hinted at an unsettling and untenable situation. I decided to heed the barber's advice to leave town and headed back to my car.

Along the way to my car, I drank from several public fountains and munched on the raisins and peanuts I brought for dinner, paying no attention to the signs for white or black.

No one upbraided me for my behavior. My innocence and ignorance were genuine. But some people watched me with astonishment and some degree of amusement as if I were either a prankster trying to attract attention or someone who had lost his marbles.

Of course, I wasn't cognizant of the reaction I drew from the few people on the streets. After all, I was a Chinese who had just spent an entire year immersed in mathematics and physics in a liberal arts college in Maine, with a cursory understanding of American people and history acquired in classrooms and the library. The reception, if the Carolinians' reaction to me could be construed as a "reception," didn't frighten me. It puzzled me, because back in Maine, people did not react to me in the same way, even though the Kappa Sigma boys could be mean and hostile.

Abuse and insult, I recognized and understood. But there, in Durham, nobody called me nasty names, made derogatory comments about me, tried to turn me into a laughing butt, or attempted to goad me into a fistfight, as the Kappa Sigma boys did from time to time. The North Carolinians seemed to be as much startled by my drinking from random water fountains as I was befuddled by their reaction. I did not think that I posed a threat to them. But I also wondered what I had done to provoke the local people's amused and startled ways of looking at me. For the life of me, I could not understand the situation.

Years later, when I became an activist in the antiwar and civil rights movements, I uncovered what was on the mind of some Durham residents on that day in early August, 1962: The African Americans, with the support of some residents of Durham and some students of Duke University, were in the midst of a protracted, nonviolent struggle to desegregate the town. Specifically, on August 12, 1962, just a few days after my brief visit to Durham, a Freedom Rally aiming to desegregate the local Howard Johnson's restaurant took place. NAACP's Roy Wilkins and CORE's James Farmer led a march of several hundred protesters from the St. Joseph's AME church toward the restaurant. This protest march occurred less than a year after the success of a series of sit-ins led by a group of local high school students supported by a good number of students from Duke University and the North Carolina State University to desegregate the movie theaters of Durham in 1961.

In Hong Kong, I had learned that America differed significantly from the European nations in ways that meant a lot to me. America began as a colony and successfully fought for its independence from the British in the 18th century to become the United States of America. Living in a colony and resentful of being a colonial subject, considered inferior and uncouth, I always thought America, having been a former colony, would be a model nation characterized by freedom, equality and meritocracy and serve as a melting pot of immigrants from all over the world, where anyone could achieve conventional success by hard work and intelligence.

I knew that America had had a slavery system. But I mistakenly thought the Civil War in the mid-19th century had put an end to it, and since then, America had been putting into practice that noble statement in the Declaration of Independence:

"We hold these truths to be self-evident, that all men are created equal ... "

No one had told me that "all men" meant "all men of European descent" to the founding fathers of America. Neither had I encountered in the USIS reading room in Hong Kong any magazines or journals that described apartheid in the southern states where segregation on the basis of skin color was enforced by law. My experience in Durham in early August of 1962, brief as it might be, was a conundrum.

Mercifully, enlightenment came early next morning after a night of dozing on and off in a fetal position in my Morris Minor. At a breakfast joint not far from where I parked, a waitress kindly explained to me the laws of segregation in her thick southern dialect, which I could barely understand. She reaffirmed that some Negros were trying to upend the local social order and instructed me to sit in the section marked for Negroes.

After wolfing down the scrambled eggs and toast, I got into my car, started the engine, and headed north toward Niagara Falls, aborting my original plan to visit the American South: the bayou country, the Everglades, the land of Mark Twain and William Faulkner.

As someone who had experienced racial discrimination, I noticed that prejudice in the United States differed from the British colonial brand. The Brits never saw their colonies as their home. They went to the colonies to earn money, much more money than they could dream of earning in Britain. The prejudice they enforced and the abuse they inflicted on the natives was aimed at keeping the multitude of colonial subjects docile, compliant and aware of their subordinate status. The Brits didn't belong to the colony and didn't want to belong to the colony. They were transients, i.e., "guests," or parasites if one wished to be merciless. The only permanent residents were Chinese colonial subjects. One could call them the reluctant "hosts" of the parasite metaphor. The last thing the Brits wanted was to be identified with their "hosts." In addition, an Englishman, whether from East London or the provinces, would immediately morph into a member of the ruling elite upon arrival in a colony as if he had become an aristocrat in a re-enacted social order of the Victorian era. Even if he were penniless and barely educated in England, he had an infinitely superior status in a colony, never to be confused with the colonial subjects. As rulers, the Brits could be contemptuous of the natives, and sometimes institutionalized their contempt. But most of them maintained some decorum in their daily interaction with their unfortunate hosts for the sake of expediency. Civility was a worthy price to pay as long as it facilitated the execution of duties of the colonial overlords so that, at the end of their tour of colonial service, they could return to their homeland with their coffers filled.

In the United States, racial prejudice was imposed by one group of citizens against another. Like it or not, the Native Americans, the immigrants and their descendants from Africa, Asia, Europe, Central and South America were all living permanently in their homeland. All of them were Americans. Nobody was an expat waiting to return from America to an ancestral land after a tour of duty. In such a situation, when one group harbored prejudice against another, no one could escape from the consequences of discrimination and hostility. Even segregation mandated by Jim Crow laws in the South could not alter the fact that all ethnic groups there belonged to the same society and lived in the same country. Everyone spent their lives interacting with everyone else. Thus, prejudice and intolerance of one group by another bred rancor, stoked anger and promoted hostility from all sides.

When I left Hong Kong for America, I thought I had left racial discrimination behind. Now, in North Carolina, a new kind of prejudice based on skin color, which appeared even more insidious than colonial prejudice in some respects, confronted me. It shocked me to the core because it shattered my naïve and glowing image of the United States as a land of equality and freedom. I wanted to understand this American prejudice and delve into its history. How could a nation create an apartheid system using a defunct and bogus 17th century anthropological classification on the trumped-up basis of skin colors? I assumed that everyone knew that skin color varied, dependent on the amount of exposure to ultraviolet radiation in combination with genetic factors. Even teenagers like my high school classmates could see that classifying human beings on the basis of skin color was unscientific and hocus-pocus. Yet to this day, the American public and institutions continue to describe people as black, white and brown, even though there are plenty of "black" Americans whose skin color is lighter than many "white" Americans.

In Durham, I was relieved that the general public had, by and large, shied away from using "yellow" to refer to Asian Americans or "red" to describe Native Americans.

The persistence of categorizing humans in terms of their skin color is particularly galling in view of contemporary paleogenetics and paleoanthropology. It is by now firmly established on the basis of indisputable evidence that all modern humans are descendants of dark-skinned people of Africa. Our African ancestors were dark-skinned because Africa's abundant sunshine favored the selection of dark skin during human evolution. Dark skin offers better protection against melanoma from ultraviolet light than light skin. Even in Africa, where Homo sapiens originated, the human gene pool (as in, the genes of all human beings) has always included the genotypes for all shades of human skin color.

About 40,000-50,000 years ago, some dark-skinned Africans settled in Europe. New paleogenetic data indicate that as recently as 8500 years ago, the hunter-gatherers of the region covering present-day Hungary, Spain and Luxembourg had dark skin, dark hair and dark eyes, whereas the 7000-year-old skeletal remains of the inhabitants of Northern Europe yielded genetic data for light skin, blue eyes and blonde hair. What happened in the interim between 40,000-50,000 years ago and 7,000 years ago in Northern Europe?

Even though the people who arrived in Europe from Africa 40,000-50,000 years ago had dark skin (i.e., they all had the genotype for dark pigmentation), scattered within the gene pool of our African ancestors were genetic components that, combined by chance through reproduction, could result in offspring with the genotype for light pigmentation.

Ten thousand years ago, the glacial climate of Northern Europe, with its lack of sunshine and heavy overcast, favored the selection of those with the genotype for light pigmentation, because light pigmentation facilitates the absorption of scarce ultraviolet sunlight in that glacial climate, and ultraviolet light is needed by the human body to synthesize vitamin D, a critical compound in many essential physiological pathways. In other words, those Northern Europeans born with the genotype for light pigmentation through genetic recombination had a higher probability of survival and reproduction than those who were born with the genotype for dark pigmentation. Over thousands of years of natural selection in the environment of reduced sunlight, dark-skinned northern Europeans gradually disappeared. This is how "white" people evolved in Northern Europe.

Contrary to the propaganda of some religious cults and political organizations that traffic in hatred, there is no mythology in the origin of light skin, and light skin definitely does not imply any genetic superiority.

After aborting my tour of America's South, I wanted to learn the nature and the history of segregation in America. That did not happen until I went to graduate school at Stanford and became involved in the civil rights movement. At Bowdoin, I had heard some students talking about Martin Luther King Jr. To me, Martin Luther King Jr. was just another American name that went over my head during that period of my hermetic life.

When I steered my Morris Minor north, in the midst of confusion and bewilderment, the only thing that mattered to me was that I did not wish to spoil my first automobile tour of America. As compensation for not visiting the South, I decided to add coastal California to my itinerary. It was a serendipitous decision that led me to a region that would eventually become my permanent home.

After Durham, my next stop was Niagara Falls.

The thunderous waterfall at Niagara was magnificent. The tumbling rapids and the swift eddies reminded me of a poem entitled *The Vermillion Cliff* by the great Su Shi, a Song Dynasty poet/artist/scholar of the 11th century who pioneered the Chinese literati tradition of integrating poetry with brush painting and calligraphy. The poem commemorated an epic battle between three rival kingdoms at a spot called "The Vermillion Cliff" in the part of the gorges of the Yangtze River that was as majestic as some sections of the Colorado River in the Grand Canyon. The battle was fought in 208-209 AD, described in detail in the celebrated 14th century Chinese novel, *The Romance of the Three Kingdoms*. When Su Shi visited the Vermillion Cliff, he was moved by the river's raging current, the awesome cliffs and the history of the epic battle fought there 900 years ago. What struck him was that the kings, the generals, the soldiers in the battle were gone, as if they had been swept away by the current. Only the mighty river and the awesome cliffs remained steadfast. His reflection called into attention the brevity of human life, and he began his poem with the lines:

"The great river flows eastward.
  Since antiquity, its waves washed away everyone
  regardless of fame and achievement."

The poem rekindled my memory of devoted friends and close-knit human relationships in the Chinese culture, which I had forgotten during the all-consuming struggle for psychological survival at Bowdoin. That memory brought on a sad feeling. It also made me question the validity of the pursuit of conventional success, plunging me into an existential crisis.

"Why is worldly success the necessary goal of life?" I asked myself.

Depression, a feeling of being lost, began to overwhelm me. The ominous ailment of infinite loneliness lurked on the horizon. I wanted to abandon my automobile tour of America, give up my pursuit of education and return to the comfort of companionship and loyalty among devoted and mutually dependent friends in Hong Kong.

In the struggle against surging emotions, I called up my old therapy of running. But I couldn't run in a city whose streets and geography were unknown to me. So, I hopped into my Morris Minor, drove away from the thundering Niagara Falls, focused on the road, stayed clear of trucks and other automobiles, and fought against the spiraling depression until it receded after two days and two nights behind the wheel, interrupted only by brief naps and minimal eating.

Heading west, I found the scenery through the Midwest underwhelming, which suited me well, because the boring landscape kept me driving until I reached the Rocky Mountains in Colorado. Nestled in the Rockies were glaciers, pristine alpine lakes, conifer forests, magnificent scenery and diverse wildlife.

Meeting wildlife on their turf was scintillating. Their graceful agility and sprightliness exuded a vitality far exceeding that of big-brained humans, as if evolution had exacted a steep price for developing human cognition. Wild animals also served as the perfect antidote to loneliness. I felt comforted and reassured by their lust for life. They never posed a threat to me, even in close proximity. Not a moose, not an elk, not a bear, not a buffalo. Many years later, I learned that animals are capable of reading human facial expressions like fear and aggression. A hard stare, for example, is a universal signal among mammals communicating hostility and aggression. In my encounters with wildlife on my trip, they typically raised their head, looked in my direction, presumably checking my facial expression and body posture, and immediately resumed the activity in which they were engaged. In return, I felt deeply grateful to them for gracing my visit with their presence, even if it was brief. During my ignorant and unhappy childhood, I often escaped from my father into the wilderness of the mountains in Hong Kong's pristine New Territories, hoping foolishly to encounter a tiger in my wild belief that it would become my kindred spirit.

From Colorado, I headed toward the West Coast on Route 66. Along the way, a chain of spectacular landscapes unfolded: the vermillion southwest with its enticing mesas, canyons and rock formations; the orange and yellow sandstone cliffs of Zion rising thousands of feet from the banks of the Virgin River; the mighty Colorado River tumbling through canyons it had carved out among endless chaparral-covered plateaus until it finally reached the awesome Grand Canyon, displaying ever-changing colors among myriad geological formations; the towering granite sentinels and cathedrals of Yosemite; the eerie silence and grandeur of Death Valley; the breathtaking and dreamlike coastline of California; the azure Crater Lake of Oregon that glittered like an enormous sapphire encrusted in the mountain. All of them were beautiful, spectacular and splendid beyond words.

When my tour ended in Seattle, Washington, I sold my Morris Minor for a pittance to a secondhand car establishment and flew back to Boston.

LEAVING BOWDOIN

MY SECOND YEAR AT BOWDOIN WAS RELATIVELY CALM AND
uneventful. No longer a novelty to the brothers of Kappa Sigma fraternity, I encountered less harassment. The fraternity remained my place
for food and lodging. But I lived a hermetic life. Shunning social contact,
I studied at all times. My presence in the fraternity became irrelevant
to everyone, including me. Showing up only at mealtime, I ate quietly
and speedily in a corner by myself. In the evening, I rarely went back
to Kappa Sigma to sleep before midnight, preferring to spend my time
in a small library in the Mathematics Department. The department
had granted a key for me to use the library after office hours, a unique
privilege bestowed on the best student. The one-room library was where
I holed up, studying mathematics or reading books I took out from
the main library. By late afternoon, the professors would all leave their
offices, and I'd have the library to myself. It was a perfect hideout, peaceful and quiet, cozy with books lining the walls.

In the meantime, academic honors began to come my way. At the
beginning of the school year, the college designated me a James Bowdoin
Scholar. Before the end of the Fall semester, I was elected to Phi Beta
Kappa and nominated by Bowdoin to compete nationally for a Danforth
Fellowship, which awarded funds for tuition and fees plus a monthly

stipend to pursue a Ph.D. at any university. By March, the Danforth Foundation notified me that I had won a fellowship, and I decided to attend Stanford University on the West Coast after graduating. That decision was undoubtedly influenced by my automobile trip during the summer of the previous year. The West Coast, especially California, was physically more attractive than any place I had seen. Californians seemed laid back. During my tour, nobody looked askance at my Morris Minor, and I didn't perceive any tension between different ethnic groups. The clincher was the coastal climate of California. It was temperate and beautiful throughout my trip.

Before graduation at Bowdoin, the Danforth Fellowship and my admission to the Ph.D. program in mathematics at Stanford clearly set me on a path for an academic career.

I had never planned for an academic career. In fact, I had not planned for any career. Since childhood, my preoccupation had been survival. To me, any career path would have been welcome. But a scholarly career meant so much more. To a traditional Chinese mind, scholars enjoyed the highest social prestige. For thousands of years, scholars in China perched on top of the social hierarchy, so much so that the scholar who scored the highest mark at the ultimate national scholarship examination during the dynastic era always became a son-in-law of the reigning emperor. That tradition of holding scholars in high regard lingered into the 20th century. In my youth, a professorship commanded respect and deference. Throughout Chinese history, wealthy merchants felt obliged to support scholars financially. For someone who had difficulty accessing a university education a few years ago, I was excited by the prospect of attending graduate school, even though anxiety and fear continued to gnaw at me.

Years later, in 1976, when I was a professor and went to Taiwan to conduct a research project on how children acquired tones in their first language, some of the Chinese academics were concerned that I remained unmarried in my thirties. I told them that marriage didn't interest me. They interpreted my statement as an oblique reference to my failure to acquire a wife because of overwork. In their attempt to help, they told me that if they placed an ad in the local newspaper announcing that a young professor of Chinese ethnicity in America had come to Taiwan to seek a wife, dozens of wealthy merchant families would respond with offers of their daughter plus a significant fortune. I thanked them for their offer of help and told them that I was too eccentric to be a good husband.

By April, 1963, as I was looking forward to graduate study in mathematics, Bowdoin College informed me that I had been chosen to be one of two valedictorians at the commencement. It was a weighty assignment. For weeks, I carried on an internal debate on what the focus of my speech should be. On the one hand, I wanted to express my deeply felt gratitude to Bowdoin for my education, which had changed my life forever and opened up new avenues for me to pursue; on the other hand, I felt compelled to speak out against American racial discrimination and social injustice, which I had been learning about through books and journals since my short-lived venture into North Carolina the previous summer. In the end, my reserved and conservative Chinese mindset won the internal debate, and I crafted a speech full of exhortations for the pursuit of knowledge and the glowing promises of a liberal arts education. It pleased the college authority and the homecoming alumni. I was awarded the $200 prize for the best commencement speech, even though I thought the speech by the other valedictorian, who expounded the future of a political union of western European nations, the European Union, offered a lot more thought-provoking substance than my superficial but well-composed platitudes.

After commencement, I stayed on at Bowdoin as a National Science Foundation Fellow for the summer, studying mathematics independently.

It was heavenly!

Quiet and temperate, the campus exuded charm and beauty. Without throngs of students, the buildings, instead of looking intrusive, seemed to belong to their idyllic surroundings. Among verdant trees, lush lawns and blooming flowers, they stood like silent monuments, colorful with their red brick walls on which ivies spread like a river branching out in its sedimentary delta as it entered an ocean. In the quietude, these man-made edifices gave the impression that they had become integrated into the natural environment. Walking around the large quadrangle in the middle of the campus, I felt as if I were in the woodland of Henry Thoreau's *Walden*. Hummingbirds flitted here and there; butterflies floated among flowers and trees; squirrels calmly buried acorns; songbirds chirped and sang; the dappled sunlight soothed; the summer breeze caressed. I felt serene and blessed as I engaged in mental yoga, thinking about mathematical problems.

A remarkable summer of peace, tranquility and learning.

No harassment, no insult, no menacing encounter, no obligations and no one exercised any authority over me. I learned field theory and algebraic topology, read novels and American history (a requirement at Bowdoin from which I was excused), and studied Greek and Roman civilizations. For entertainment, I read Greek mythology. There was so much I didn't know and wanted to know. My impatience for knowledge made me feel, at times, that I had never received any education. But life was enchanting, and I brimmed with hope and optimism. Every night, by the time I went to bed, I felt that I had taken a small step forward in the quest of knowledge.

STANFORD UNIVERSITY

BEFORE LEAVING MAINE FOR CALIFORNIA IN SEPTEMBER 1963, I had, with the assistance of the Stanford Housing Service, rented a room in a private home on Waverley Street. It was three blocks from Embarcadero Avenue, a main east-west thoroughfare that connects the Stanford campus with the town of Palo Alto. After arriving at my new home, I found out that unlike Bowdoin, Stanford had an enormous campus. The mathematics department, located in the northeast corner of the quad, was almost two miles from my residence at Waverley Street, too time-consuming for a daily commute on foot. I reckoned that once instruction began, I would need some means of transportation. In the meantime, I resumed my summer routine: reading, studying and walking.

One evening around 10 p.m., after working on problems in complex variables for several hours, I decided to take a walk. The temperature had fallen significantly after sunset. The cool, dry air outdoor was refreshing. The poorly lit streets didn't impede my promenade because I stayed on the sidewalk. The town was quiet, except for the sound of an occasional automobile passing by. I was enjoying my stroll when a police car stopped next to me, flashing a row of red lights on its roof. A policeman rolled down his window, blinding me with a flashlight.

"What are you doing?" he asked menacingly.

"I am taking a walk."

"We don't walk in this town," he responded.

I was dumbstruck!

I had never heard of such a pronouncement, least of all from a law-enforcement officer. But a moment of reflection seemed to support his claim. I had been in Palo Alto for three days and rarely saw pedestrians. On University Avenue, there were a few people on the sidewalk darting in and out of shops and restaurants or traversing the short distance between their automobiles and offices. Around Embarcadero, Waverley and El Camino Real, although not short of automobile traffic during daytime, pedestrians were rare. By the evening, pedestrians were non-existent in the entire city. It was true that I had not seen any person walking in my neighborhood that evening. The scarcity of pedestrians in Palo Alto simply hadn't registered on my mind. But the policeman had thrust it into my face.

"Well, I am new in this town. Have I violated any municipal law?" I asked.

"No, you haven't," the policeman said as he got out of his car to face me while keeping his blinding flashlight on my face. "Do you live here?"

"Yes, I live right around the corner," I said calmly.

"Can you show me your ID?"

"I don't have my ID with me, but if you go to my residence with me, I can show you my graduate student ID card from Stanford."

He frisked me to make sure that I wasn't carrying any weapons, ordered me to sit in the back of his patrol car, and drove the few blocks to my residence.

After showing my ID to the police and returning to my room, I thought to myself, "So, people don't walk in Palo Alto. What a strange city!"

The incident with the police lit a fire under me to acquire wheels. The next day, I decided to purchase a Vespa motor scooter for a variety of reasons. First, compared with a car, a Vespa was inexpensive; second, it was easy and less costly to operate and park; third, Vespa had made a deep impression on me when I saw the movie *Roman Holiday* in Hong Kong. I felt the scooter had a lot of charm and panache, without grasping that much of my fondness for the scooter was probably induced by the charms of Audrey Hepburn, Gregory Peck and the city of Rome.

DISASTER

PROUD OF MY NEWLY ACQUIRED WHEELS, I WAS CAUTIOUSLY cruising along the curb of El Camino Real after picking up the Vespa from the dealer, when suddenly a powerful thrust coming from nowhere propelled me into the air, and then, without any time for reaction, I dived headlong onto the road and skidded with my face along the asphalt surface.

Everything happened in a flash, out of my control. All I knew was that my head exploded when it hit the road. My immediate response was to get up and check if I still had all my body parts. When I did stand up, the world was spinning and blood was cascading down my face, partially blocking my vision.

Then I heard a voice, a female voice, behind me. "Are you alright?"

I turned around. The question came from a very blurry woman standing in front of an equally blurry automobile. Before I could say anything, she fainted and crumpled like jelly on the road. The ghastly sight of my mangled face and the blood gushing from my left temple was probably too gruesome for her to behold. As I sat down on the asphalt to avoid collapsing involuntarily like the young woman, I saw my new Vespa crushed and flattened under her car.

In no time, police and ambulance arrived. I was given first aid, bundled onto a stretcher with my head in a special harness and rushed to the emergency department of the Stanford Medical Center. On the way to the emergency department in the siren-wailing ambulance, I asked the medic what had happened. He told me that I had been hit by a car and sustained a serious head injury.

In the emergency room, I was attended by a group of medical professionals, stripping my clothes, cleaning my wounds, stemming the blood flow, connecting me to intravenous fluids and medicine, wheeling me to the X-ray room. By the time a physician saw fit to talk to me, my head was wrapped in gauze and bandages, with only part of my mouth, nose and right eye exposed. He wanted to know if I felt any pain. I shook my head.

"Good! The painkiller is working," he said with a smile.

I wanted to know the extent of my injury but had difficulty articulating. My mouth and tongue wouldn't cooperate. The physician sensed my wish.

"You are very lucky. Your skull is intact. No broken bones. Your orbital bone on your left eyebrow sustained some permanent damage. You also suffered a serious concussion. You lost the skin and some flesh on your left cheek, left chin, part of your lips and the tip of your nose. We may have to do some plastic surgery eventually. We will see. In the meantime, you need to remain in the intensive care unit for the next twenty-four hours. After that, if your condition is stable, we will transfer you to a room."

"But . . . but instruction begins in two days," I blurted out in muffled syllables. "I must attend my classes."

"No," he responded firmly. "You won't be going to your classes for a long time."

"Oh . . . no . . . " I moaned.

His instruction triggered a flood of fear and anxiety in me. Jeopardizing my future which had been so rosy and promising until just a little while ago, his pronouncement was devastating, much more so than all the physical injuries I had sustained.

Since the commencement at Bowdoin, I had been flying high, happily looking forward to graduate school and optimistically thinking that I had finally become the master of my own fate, heading into a positive life and a rewarding career. All of a sudden, my entire world had crashed, literally and figuratively, fallen from the sky. Now I was rendered dysfunctional.

Questions and dark thoughts flooded my brain,

"Is this the end of my academic pursuits? What is going to happen to me? No, no, no! I cannot fail again like I did in China. I would rather die than return to Hong Kong without at least earning a Ph.D. degree in America. Why did that woman drive her car into me? What have I done to deserve such a cursed fate?"

I began to sob.

It must have been my heaving chest and the gushing tears from my right eye that startled the doctor. Tense and concerned, he looked up at the various monitors to which I was connected. No sooner had he looked up that he relaxed.

In a gentle voice, he tried to comfort me, "Don't worry, you will go back to school in Winter quarter. This Fall quarter you will recuperate from your injury. It's only a three-month delay. Everything will be fine."

Then, he asked, "Do you have a family that can take care of you?"

I shook my head.

"Fine. You will be fine! We will take care of you." He patted me on my left arm as he left.

On the third day in the hospital, a plastic surgeon came to talk with me. He suggested grafting skin from my buttock to the left side of my face. I shook my head.

"Well, it's your choice. But you may become severely scarred. I am offering you an option."

"My face is not handsome to begin with," I responded. "Blending my face with my ass will only make things worse."

He laughed and left with the comment, "You're a tough guy!"

It wasn't my intention to sound like a tough guy at all. My response was an instinctive reaction to the life-long baggage I carried since I was ten when my parents told me that among their six children, I was the only ugly one. But when I refused plastic surgery at the Stanford Hospital, I had neither the opportunity nor the desire to explain my unintended macho response to the physician.

After my interview with the plastic surgeon, there was nothing for me to do in the hospital other than having my wounds dressed in antibiotic ointment and re-bandaged by a nurse every morning. I was no longer connected to instruments monitoring my vital signs. The nurses had stopped the intravenous provisioning of fluid and nutrients to me. I couldn't eat solid food yet because of the injury inside my mouth. But my appetite was good. Every two or three hours, I asked for a milkshake which I sucked down from a straw. As I regained energy, boredom in the hospital room began to drive me insane. I desperately needed to move, read a book or engage in some form of physical activity. By the fifth day, I had had enough of the hospital confinement. Straightening myself up, I walked to the nurse station and asked them to call a taxi to bring me to my rented room on Waverley Avenue. Shocked, the head nurse shook her head and told me that I needed permission to leave.

"I am a twenty-three-year-old adult," I shot back, "and I don't need anyone's permission to leave a hospital."

She panicked. "Let me call the doctor. Just wait a minute."

In no time, a doctor showed up.

After a few questions, he recognized my steely and unyielding determination to leave. He said, "Okay. You can leave on the condition that you return here every morning to have your wounds dressed and bandage changed, and if you feel dizziness or a severe headache coming on, come back to the hospital immediately. Finally, please do not engage in any serious mental work, like solving mathematical problems. Your brain has been injured. It needs rest."

"I will do as you say," I said agreeably. "I am not suicidal."

Back at the house on Waverley Avenue, the landlady caught sight of me and reeled in shock. Putting her right hand on her forehead, her mouth agape, her face white as a sheet of paper, she almost fainted.

When she regained her composure, she exclaimed, "My God, your head is wrapped up like a mummy!"

"Yes, the consequence of being hit by a car." I didn't want to elaborate, revisit the accident, or give an "organ" recital of my injury.

"Oh, I am so sorry! Let me know if I can help," she said kindly.

I thanked her and went to my room. Exhausted by my escape from the hospital, I fell asleep almost immediately.

Upon waking up the next day, I knew that my first priority was to acquire another set of wheels. This time, I went to a secondhand car dealer and bought a ten-year-old Buick. It was huge and heavy, with a pale green exterior, a turquoise steering wheel and dark green interior. It looked and felt like a garish armored vehicle, powerful, gigantic and hideous looking, fit for a gangster from the Caribbean islands because it was brazen and ostentatious.

As I drove that monstrosity back to Waverley Avenue, I figured if a Ford Falcon hit me from behind again, the Falcon, not my Buick, would crumple like a tinfoil toy.

The accident, though devastating, had a silver lining, but I didn't know it at the time.

After arriving in the United States and being cast into the Kappa Sigma fraternity house at Bowdoin College, I had built an impenetrable shell around me, isolating myself completely from social interaction. I shunned all human contact as if people on campus were inanimate. When some kind-hearted individuals reached out to me and solicited my friendship, I was non-responsive. During the two years at Bowdoin, my only social activities involved the acceptance of several invitations from a wealthy local businessman, a major booster of Bowdoin College, to spend weekends at his ocean-front retreat. I thought his cottage, perched on the rocky coast, was charming, the ocean, enthralling and the scenery, picturesque. He had a housekeeper who cooked meals for us and kept the cottage spick and span. When I went there, I always brought books and homework with me. Even so, I felt guilty for accepting the invitation and not using the weekends to study full time on campus. The Kappa Sigma boys asked me if I was having a homosexual relationship with the businessman. At that time, I didn't even know what a homosexual relationship meant, even after the "queer" incident when I escaped from a "blind" date. But I chose not to respond.

The accident and the forced medical leave from my studies at Stanford completely shattered the shell in which I sought protection after arriving at Bowdoin. To say I was out of sorts at the time would have been a gross understatement. Frightened like a wild fawn caught in the headlight of an approaching truck and overcome by infinite loneliness, I began to doubt my ability to survive.

I had been frightened before, in China, on the streets of Hong Kong, but never had I questioned my survival instinct, because there were always pressing issues like hunger, cold or threat that monopolized my attention, whether the fright was self-inflicted or foisted on me by a mean-spirited person. On those occasions, my instinct was to fight. Now, with the head injury, I was not allowed to work or exercise, and there was no target, real or imagined, with which I could do combat. I thought I would lose my mind.

In desperation, I reached out for social contact and human connections, which serendipitously opened up a new world to me. My focus was no longer physical survival, but mental stability and diversion. This new focus thrust me into a world hitherto unimaginable to my sequestered mind that pursued success relentlessly.

PART TWO

YUHA

WEAK, ISOLATED AND AIMLESS AFTER DISCHARGING MYSELF from the Stanford hospital, I faced a conundrum: What could I do with myself or how could I meet people?

Hardly any option seemed available.

In desperation, I hung around the Stanford Center for International Students and Scholars every day after going to the hospital in the morning for a nurse to dress my wounds and change the gauze wrapping around most of my head and face. I spent each day sitting in the lounge of the Center, reading newspapers and magazines between naps.

One day, as I woke up from a nap, a golden-haired, blue-eyed man with a goatee and a charming smile sitting next to me asked solicitously if I was alright. He was Yuha Partennen, a Fulbright Fellow from Helsinki, Finland, newly arrived at Stanford to conduct research on mathematical modeling in social science. As soon as I learned that he was constructing mathematical models, I told him that I was a graduate student in mathematics and offered my assistance when my neurologist would permit me. He thanked me and invited me to coffee at Tresidder Union, located across the parking lot from the International Center.

The next day, we ran into each other again at the International Center. He suggested that we should participate in an event organized by the

Center to see a play in San Francisco. The play was *The Wall*, based on John Hersey's 1950 novel and adapted for the stage by the San Francisco Actors Workshop. I had never attended a play in the English language before and thought Yuha's suggestion was a grand idea.

The play was so riveting that it coursed through my mind most of the night after returning from San Francisco. The next day I bought Hersey's book from Kepler's Bookstore in Menlo Park and read it immediately from beginning to the end.

The book was even more compelling than the play.

Among other things, *The Wall* put into perspective, for the first time, all the trials and tribulations that I had experienced: the absence of familial love and support, the hunger and starvation, the rejection in China, the infinite loneliness, the callous and sometimes cruel treatment by the Kappa Sigma brothers at Bowdoin, and most recently, the injury from the traffic accident at Stanford. They seemed absolutely insignificant in light of the sufferings the Nazis inflicted against the Jews in the Warsaw ghetto.

This new perspective triggered a long bout of introspection, lifted me out of my depression and doldrums, revitalized my survival instinct, and engendered in me a lifelong affinity for the Jewish people.

Before seeing the play and reading the book, I was vaguely aware of the Holocaust as an unprecedented atrocity committed by the Nazis during the Second World War, but I never understood who the Jewish people were and what being Jewish meant. Those two questions remained unanswered after I saw the play and read Hersey's book. My immediate reaction was, as usual, to seek out a book on the history of Jewish people. This time, I thought I should ask Yuha, my first friend since arriving in America two years ago, before delving into a history book that could be dull and ponderous.

When I broached those questions to Yuha, he smiled, which he always did when I asked him a question, and said there were no simple and straightforward answers, but he would try to give me a historical perspective. Then, he proceeded to tell me about the early Israelites, the Tribe of Judah, the Kingdom of David, the First Temple period, the

Second Temple period, the Roman military occupation of Judea and Galilee, the Jewish rebellion against the Roman occupation, and the subsequent diaspora of the Jewish people. Over the centuries, the diaspora created distinct regional groups of Jews because of intermarriages with local people and the influence of local cultures in Northern and Eastern Europe, Spain and Portugal, North Africa and the Middle East. These diverse groups suffered discrimination, persecution and pogroms throughout the last two millennia. When I mentioned the biblical stories of Issac, Daniel, David, Solomon and Moses, which I had learned in my Chinese high school, he told me that the Bible was based on oral traditions and all oral traditions were embellished and expanded with each narrator's creative imagination. They were valuable in their own right but should not be viewed as proper history.

Yuha's lengthy narrative fascinated me.

"As for your questions about who the Jewish people are today and what it means to be Jewish," Yuha said with a broad smile, "a Russian friend of mine, who has a typical Russian name, is not observant of the Judaic religion but proudly Jewish. He once gave an answer that is as good as any. In response to another person's query, 'Why are you Jewish?!' he said, 'If you are Jewish, you ARE Jewish!'"

That was lesson one from Yuha.

He always played the role of mentor, introducing me to a vast array of interesting information ranging from Marxism to Soviet imperialism, from Wanda Landowska's rendition of J. S. Bach's *Goldberg Variations* to Jean Sibelius' *Finlandia*, from the tragedies of Aeschylus to Henrik Ibsen's *Peer Gynt* and *A Doll's House*, from the lively depiction of biblical stories in the paintings and frescos of Giotto to the dramatic use of chiaroscuro in the work of Caravaggio and Rembrandt, from the monumental Russian novels of Dostoevsky and Tolstoy to the gripping stories of Maupassant and Stendhal.

We visited museums in San Francisco, which, according to Yuha, were provincial and second-rate. He hoped I would someday spend time visiting the great museums of London, Amsterdam, Madrid, Paris, St. Petersburg and other major European cities, which I did in the following decades. He also told me that many Italian cities such as Venice, Florence, Assisi and Pisa could be considered museums by themselves because of their architecture, sculptures, antiquity and historical significance, even though they also contained conventional museums.

We spent a lot of time in bookstores. Kepler's in Menlo Park was a nearby favorite, but we also went to the great bookstores in Berkeley, which he had heard about in Finland. I bought book after book at his recommendation. They kept me occupied, mostly during the evenings and weekends, to ward off the assault of infinite loneliness from the absence of close-knit, devoted human relationships with which I grew up. Reading the books supplemented and reinforced my conversations with Yuha, which often took the form of question-and-answer sessions with me asking the questions and him providing the answers. But those books differed significantly from the dry and dull textbooks of most courses I took in college. I read my new books with great enthusiasm. Among them, there was only one which I couldn't and didn't finish reading. That was the multi-volume *The Social History of Art* by Arnold Hauser. It was difficult reading because I was, at the time, unfamiliar with most of the artworks Hauser cited and discussed. Many decades later, even after having spent a good amount of time in the great museums of the Western world, I have not returned to that set of books.

We attended concerts whenever they were available in San Francisco, Oakland or on the Stanford campus. I saw my first opera with Yuha that year, Wagner's *Lohengrin*. It was underwhelming, and never became one of my favorites in the scores of operas that I attended over the decades after that initiation. Too many blaring trumpets, too much drumroll, and too martial for my taste.

San Francisco Symphony, at that time under the baton of the Viennese conductor Joseph Krips, was mediocre in Yuha's opinion. He advised me to attend the concerts of the New York Philharmonic, the Boston Symphony Orchestra, the Philadelphia Orchestra or any orchestra of the major European metropoles in the future.

We went to see a one-man comedy show by Dick Gregory in a small basement establishment on Broadway Street in San Francisco. I had never heard of such a form of entertainment. A new adventure for me! Dick Gregory's humor and wit on American politics and racial discrimination was not only hilarious but also revelatory. He reminded me of some of the satirical writings of the great early 20th century Chinese writer, Lu Shün. But Lu Shün, far from being a comedian, was all serious in his biting comments on Chinese behavior, Chinese character and the Chinese society during the mid-20th century, while Dick Gregory, whose monologues were just as caustic as Lu Shün's essays and novels, did not shy from burlesque or profanity as the comic elements of his performance.

One evening, Yuha invited me to dine in a high-end French restaurant in San Francisco. He did it mostly because I often complained about missing Chinese cuisine, which had an extensive variety in flavors and the choice of dishes. They became even more tantalizing in view of the ho-hum American food. In response, he wanted to show me the best of Western gastronomy, which, in his opinion, was French cuisine.

At Ernie's French restaurant, he ordered a four-course meal for both of us. Each course was paired with a glass of wine. The food was delicious. I enjoyed every bite. I had never tasted wine before that occasion and recognized only one of the alcoholic beverages he ordered. That was a glass of aged Port toward the end of the meal. My father would occasionally drink a small goblet of Port as an aperitif before the evening meal. At Ernie's, other than the Port, which was sweet and flavorful, the wines tasted strange and weird, like a slightly bitter but not so acidic vinegar. Because I wasn't about to disappoint Yuha by refusing the wine, I drank every drop of it with each course. As the dinner progressed, my face, neck and chest turned increasingly red from vasodilation, and I felt slightly dizzy, a little out of breath. As the dizziness got worse, my stomach started churning. In the end, I threw up the entire meal in Ernie's bathroom.

Throughout the academic year of 1963-64, Yuha was an inspiring friend, and he took great pride in introducing me to all facets of Western civilization. In return, I regaled him with stories and vignettes expounding Chinese history, the ethnic complexity of the Chinese people, the rise and fall of the Mongolian Empire and how the daughters, not the sons, of Genghis Khan held his vast Empire together. I went on to expound on the treasures along the Silk Road, the essence of Chinese painting, poetry and fiction, the hundreds of spoken languages, many of which are unrelated to the large Chinese language family, and the scores of written languages in China, including one invented by a group of women in central rural China, who, under the withering oppression of their male spouses, wrote to each other in their secret language to vent their anger and suffering. I told him that some of the ancient books and records kept in a secret library in an oasis called Dunhuang of the Gobi Desert were written in four or five different languages such as Uighur, Tibetan, Chinese, Tangut (Xi-Xia), Mongolian and Arabic. In the late 19th century, the contents of the entire library were carted away by an intrepid English geographer, Aurel Stein, who reached Dunhuang with a camel train. He never sought permission, never spoke to any government authority, never paid any money as he carted away invaluable treasures of antique art and books. In the manner of King Leopold of Belgium, who took Congo in Africa by a simple proclamation, Aurel Stein just packed up the contents of the library and took them to England. The books, the sculptures, the frescos, the artifacts and the steles taken by Stein now reside in the British Museum.

Dunhuang remains the repository of more than 50,000 square meters of cave paintings, primarily in the style of Buddhist art, created between the 4th century and the 14th century A.D. There are so many caves containing priceless art that the hill housing all those caves looks like a hornet nest from a distance.

I still remember Yuha's surprise and excitement when I explained that in Chinese parlance, an educated person "reads," not "views" brush painting. "A scholarly Chinese only sees/views/looks at a landscape in nature but reads assiduously a landscape painting as he or she would read *I Ching* (translated as 'Book of Changes')." A person unfamiliar with Chinese art and literature might say:

"I looked at a painting by Su Shi."

That phrase is not grammatically incorrect but could be gauche, if not uncouth. A traditional Chinese intellectual would consider "seeing or viewing" a brush painting the equivalent of:

zou   ma   kan   hua

'gallop' 'horse' 'look at' 'flower'

Which means "flower appreciation on a galloping horse."

Since the early 11th century, the Chinese literati discovered and promoted a synergy between calligraphy, poetry and brush painting, rendering those three artistic endeavors an integrated enterprise. According to them, composing a poem, conceiving a landscape painting and forging a unique style of calligraphy exuding verve and vitality involved a similar creative endeavor with a brush pen and black ink. Drawing inspiration from this synergy, the literati produced exquisite paintings, many of which were accompanied by a poem or a short narrative. These were rendered in the calligraphy of the painter-author on the same scroll of paper or silk meticulously glued onto a substrate by a skilled artisan. A viewer would not be able to grasp the meaning of such a traditional Chinese painting without deciphering the written words accompanying it. Sometimes, a connoisseur/collector, inspired by the artistry of a painter-author-calligrapher who lived centuries earlier, might add a poem or a commemorative passage onto a painting created by that artist. If such a connoisseur/collector happened to be a man of significance in his time, say, a celebrated poet, a revered calligrapher, or an Emperor, he would have enhanced the value of that painting with his added inscription.

Expressing his astonishment at this Chinese tradition in art appreciation, Yuha observed, "Can you imagine the public uproar, not to mention the travesty, if a 20th century Director of the Louvre had added a sonnet on the top right corner of Da Vinci's Mona Lisa, or if a member of the Medici family, the original owners of Raphael's self-portrait, had inscribed a couplet under the image?"

One day, over dinner with Yuha at a ho-hum Chinese restaurant serving putative Chinese food in Palo Alto, I, longing for the delectable Chinese dishes, launched into a nostalgic description of the exquisite flavors of Chinese gastronomy: the great variety of stir-fried green vegetables, crispy with subtle taste, sometimes mingled with wild mushrooms, dried shrimps or scallops, but always spiced with garlic, ginger and other condiments (which not only add culinary luster to the vegetable but also draw out the vegetable's own flavors). There were hundreds of ways to marinate and prepare meats and seafood so that the end product melted into your mouth with a cornucopia of delicate flavors; one celebrated dish was "paper-wrapped chicken"—which consisted of a whole freshly slaughtered chicken wrapped in several layers of a transparent rice paper, cooked with a medley of spices, preserving the juice and the tenderness of the meat. I described the different ways of cooking rice—some, after mixing with condiments, cured meat and shiitake mushrooms, were wrapped in bamboo or lotus leaf before being steamed, the enormous catalogue of savory soups made with seafood, assorted meats, mushrooms, different kinds of tofu products, fresh bamboo shoots, cilantro (a prosperous city, Ningpo, on the lower reaches of the Yangtze River, was so celebrated for its great variety of gourmet soups that it was known as the City of Soup); the scores of various steamed or grilled dumplings filled with marinated shrimp, scallop, crab, pork, beef, lamb, chicken, Chinese chives, chopped cabbages, scallions, or any combination of those ingredients; the different dishes of noodles made of wheat, rice or mung bean, braised or pan-fried with any number of tasty ingredients that a chef deemed appropriate.

A gourmand, Yuha was enthralled by my description of Chinese gastronomy. His eyes lit up as he made me promise that someday I would treat him to a first-rate Chinese banquet. Forty years later, when he visited me in California, I fulfilled my promise by persuading a friend and restaurateur, who immigrated to the United States on the strength of his certified culinary expertise in Taipei, to create a ten-course banquet dinner for him and my family. In spite of his poor health at the time, he savored each and every course. It was a joyful occasion. We cracked up in laughter upon recalling the comically disastrous result when he treated me to my first French "banquet" at San Francisco's Ernies.

One day, Yuha casually commented that he was deeply impressed by my ability to soak up and retain new knowledge. His comment shocked and embarrassed me.

In the Chinese tradition, family members and close friends rarely complimented each other. Compliments are perceived as flattery, and flattery is reserved only for deployment in political manipulation. This Chinese canon of social behavior is the opposite of the Western tradition, as I learned in later years. Westerners never miss an opportunity to praise each other, especially among family members and friends. If your child comes in last in a 400-meter race in America, you praise him/her for finishing the race. A typical Chinese parent would probably consider the child's performance disgraceful and would, at a minimum, admonish the child to train harder. The Chinese rationale is that compliments and praise promote complacency, and complacency impedes progress and improvement. You want your family members and close friends to improve and move ahead in the world, and therefore, if you truly care for them, you should be unrestrained and unstinting in criticizing them while holding back any praise or compliment. Ambitious parents like my father would admonish their offspring with such instructions as, "Compliment your adversaries so that they will rot; scold your loved ones so that they might flourish."

But Yuha exuded sincerity when he complimented me. It was clear that he meant well. Yet his goodwill and sincerity caused me to become even more embarrassed. I didn't know how to respond and became tongue-tied. Noticing my uncomfortable reaction, Yuha wanted to know why. When I explained the Chinese tradition to him, he laughed and said that I was no longer living in a Chinese society and should accept his compliment with pleasure. I heeded his advice, but it was impossible to ward off my feeling of embarrassment. Even today, after having lived in America for fifty-some years, I find it difficult to accept compliments graciously.

Yuha and I derived immense pleasure from the exchange of our thoughts and knowledge of cultural idiosyncrasies and diversities. To me, he was a savant on everything about the Western world, and to him, I was a source of scintillating information about the eastern Asian civilizations. Our curiosity and thirst for knowledge sustained our interaction. It was the base for a friendship that differed drastically from the loyal devotion to which I was accustomed in China and Hong Kong. Yet, the bond between Yuha and me was strong. When we got together after a two-or-three-day hiatus, he always broke into the happiest smile, which immediately lifted me into a cheerful mood. I would anticipate new knowledge to be exchanged, novel issues to be debated or teased apart, new activities to engage in, new books to be purchased and perused. Through our interaction, we both broadened our horizons, grew our intellect, and most important of all, gained insight into our own backgrounds in the light of the knowledge unveiled by the other. Beyond all those rewards from our friendship, there was an added benefit to me. Yuha, just by being himself, taught me some of the most important values and social principles in the Western world.

During the early months of our friendship, he appeared bizarre, esoteric and enigmatic to my unadulterated East Asian mind.

The first thing that struck me as utterly odd and alien was his habit of smoking cigarettes and consuming alcoholic beverages at all times. I saw him smoking and drinking in the morning, the afternoon and the evening. In my youth, I was taught that such indulgence betrayed a person's lack of self-control and degeneration. Yet Yuha was anything but degenerate. Far from being a drunkard, he was affable, unfailingly kind and courteous to everyone, always full of vitality and enthusiasm. His signature trait was his smile, which made him popular at the International Center. It appeared particularly charming in the midst of his shiny golden hair and beard, as if the gold sheen added luster to the smile. At the time, chain smokers were not uncommon in America. But I had never seen someone drinking all day long until I met Yuha. One day I asked him why he drank so much.

"I am Finnish," he smiled. "In Finland, the winter is dark, frigid and long. During those insufferable months, most Finnish people rely on alcohol to ward off the cold and cope with the darkness. Beyond the cold winter, there is the issue of masculinity. In Finland, the capacity for holding liquor is a measure of a man's masculinity. I don't want my friends to think I am a sissy. But the most important reason I drink is that drinking makes me happy!"

I understood his words. But they didn't make much sense to me. How could alcohol be connected to masculinity, I wondered, and why did alcohol make anyone happy? Masculinity, in my understanding, involved physical prowess and agility in addition to mental dexterity, whereas happiness and alcohol appeared as antidotal as fire and water. The one time I tried drinking alcoholic beverages at his behest, it made me vomit. I was definitely NOT happy. But I didn't follow up with any more questions which, even to my East Asian mind, appeared too intrusive.

Another mystery about Yuha was his relationship with his girlfriend, Susan. I didn't know how they met. Yuha introduced me to her one day over dinner. She was a schoolteacher in Palo Alto, kind and attractive. The two of them seemed to be happy together, and they were demonstrative of their affection for each other. Having seen them together on many occasions, I was puzzled that Yuha continued to spend time at the International Center, socializing and participating in evening activities without Susan. Why wouldn't he spend his free time with her, I wondered, because if I had a lover, I would spend as much time with her as I could. The situation perplexed me so much that one day, I asked Yuha, rather crudely,

"Why don't you want to spend more time with Susan?"

"Well, I care a lot about her," Yuha replied, patient as usual, "but I am here in America only a few more months. Neither she nor I wish to be too deeply involved."

Again, I understood his words, but couldn't make any sense of them. They were obviously lovers. Could they be any more involved than that? I was just dumbstruck.

One Saturday, Susan and I bumped into each other in a supermarket. Having been baffled by what I perceived as the semi-suspended nature of her relationship with Yuha for weeks, I couldn't help asking her why she wasn't spending the weekend with Yuha. My question would've been perfectly acceptable in Chinese society, but completely intrusive, if not offensive, to an American or European. Fortunately, she understood my innocence. Not only did she not take offense, she also proffered an explanation:

"I respect Yuha as a free spirit, and we see each other only when we both feel the urge to be together."

Instead of clearing up the tangle in my mind, her answer bewildered me even more than Yuha's explanation. If they were lovers, why wouldn't they want to see each other every day?

For days, I mulled over what Yuha and Susan had said before coming to the conclusion that human interaction in the Western world followed conventions that were often the opposite of the Chinese social norm. That was the first time I realized I had a lot to learn and adapt to before I could function smoothly in American society. Before the motor scooter accident, which had forced me to seek human contact, I was content to be an island by myself pursuing formal education in America. Now a new awakening had alerted me that there was a whole world of knowledge that I could not learn from reading books and attending classes. That awakening also shed light on some of my faux pas at Bowdoin.

During the Fall semester of my second year at Bowdoin, bolstered by the accolades and recognition I received from the faculty in the Mathematics Department, I went to the off-campus apartment of a young professor one Saturday, intending to discuss some insights I gained in my study of a specific mathematical problem. After I rang the doorbell, he opened the door, looked surprised as well as annoyed, and told me that I should never show up at someone's home without an appointment. I was totally humiliated, crestfallen and left in dejection.

In Chinese society, it was normal for people to call on each other without prior notice. In fact, a whole family might show up at the door of a friend's home without forewarning, and the surprised host would always be delighted to welcome them with open arms, invite them in, serve up tea and treats. In Xi'an, the old capital of Qin, Han, Sui and Tang dynasties, where contemporary tourists from all over the world flock to see the life-size terracotta soldiers in the first Qin emperor's tomb, there usually hangs a huge banner on the ancient city wall. Written in large Chinese logographs are the well-known words of Confucius,

"Friends visiting from afar, how delightful!"

It is a famous adage deeply imprinted on the Chinese mind for millennia. Needlessly to say, it was practically impossible to send notice of a visit to a faraway host ahead of time before the invention of modern communication technology.

In the process of self-examination brought on by my new awareness of the gulf separating China and the Western world with respect to the concept of personal space, I began to think that some of the hostile and abusive behavior of the Kappa Sigma brothers at Bowdoin could very well be a consequence of my ignorance and Chinese mindset, even though I never intended to provoke.

"Oh, well! At least that was in the past." I tried to seek relief from my self-criticism and refused to dwell on it.

Many decades later, in 2001, I went on a personalized tour of the Silk Road in western China, visiting the cities, ancient ruins, cave art, historical sites and natural wonders along the route through the Gobi Desert and the Taklamakan Desert. In the city of Kashgar overlooking Afghanistan, I bought a large antique Baluchi rug woven by artisans in present-day Pakistan at a bazaar which, at that time, drew merchants from all over Central Asia, just as it had for thousands of years. Dirty and dusty, the rug was fraying on the fringes. But there was no question that it was a rare find in terms of its design and quality. I had it folded and tied into a solid cube, like a medium-sized bundle of garbage to bring back to America. At the airport of Ürümqi, the capital of the Uighur Autonomous Region, a Chinese lady sitting next to me, curious at the bundle I was lugging, asked me what it was. I told her that it was an old rug that I purchased in Kashgar.

She looked at me, wide-eyed, and said, "You bought an *old* rug?"

"Yes," I responded matter-of-factly.

"Are you crazy?" She exclaimed, "You have been ripped off!"

Just as I was about to take offense, I caught myself with the awareness that I was interacting with a Chinese in China. Her questions and comments were perfectly reasonable from the Chinese perspective because she was trying to warn me against flimflam merchants. So, I thanked her and reassured her that I was quite knowledgeable about old rugs from Central Asia and therefore, I didn't get ripped off. If I had shown irritation at her, she would have been taken aback and most likely thought of me as one of those "foreign devils" who happened to look like a Chinese. Then I remembered what one of my acquaintances, who had lived several years in America, warned me about before I left Hong Kong:

"Foreign devils don't criticize each other and don't make friends. They are very self-centered. Prepare yourself for loneliness in America!"

I couldn't make much sense of what he said at the time. Now I know that he conflated the Western sense of personal space with "self-centeredness."

The concept of personal space is at the core of the immense gulf that separates China from the Western world in human interaction. In the

West, personal space is all-important. Everyone, even among family members, honors each other's personal space, physical as well as psychological. In China, personal space is minimal, and the closer the relationship, the less it matters. In fact, to the traditional Chinese mind, personal space is a barrier in close human relationships. The rationale is simple: If you care for each other, why do you need personal space?! You want to be as close to each other as you can, physically and psychologically.

During my senior year in high school, as graduation approached, the entire class took a celebratory four-day trip to a Buddhist monastery on a faraway island, called Lantau Island, which today houses Hong Kong's ultra-modern posh airport and links to the city by a bridge more than twenty miles long. At the time, the island was completely isolated. At twenty nautical miles from the hub of Hong Kong, Lantau stood for a faraway place to the residents of Hong Kong. In fact, some of the monks in the monastery on Lantau had never set foot in Hong Kong.

After the trip was planned, everyone in my class was excited. For weeks, I suffered intense anxiety because I didn't know if my father would pay for me to go. The trip didn't cost much, but Father loathed spending money on me in spite of the fact that he had a reputation for generosity in his circle of friends and associates. On this occasion, much to my relief, he granted me permission to take the trip and paid the $20 fees to my school. Happiness enveloped me as I looked forward to the first pleasure trip of my life.

At the monastery on Lantau island, the teachers assigned our sleeping berths. Every two boys and every two girls, all in their late teens, shared one small bed and slept under the same quilt. Each student was allowed to choose his/her best friend to be the bedmate. I still have a photo of my friend and me under the same quilt, with our heads perched on two small pillows. Nobody considered the sleeping arrangement strange or felt an iota of sexual innuendo. It was natural for good friends of the same gender to sleep in one bed if only one bed happened to be available.

Before I met Yuha, I, like most Chinese people, also believed that friendship did not exist among Westerners, and the so-called "friendship" in the Western world was, at best, paper-thin, superficial and devoid of loyalty or devotion.

It is not surprising that the Chinese rendition of the term "individualism" implies self-centeredness, and Ralph Waldo Emerson's philosophical musing on self-reliance is practically anathema to most people in the East Asian cultures influenced by Confucian ethics.

In Ürümqi airport, after the Chinese lady and I ended our conversation with pleasantries, I thought to myself, "Gee! I have become a Westerner."

The first time Yuha and I had dinner together in a casual restaurant, I hastened to pay the bill because I appreciated his friendship, and it was a longstanding tradition in China that one should always strive to be generous to one's friends.

Generosity toward friends has always been extolled as a basic and essential virtue in Chinese folklore and legends. In my generation, every high school student read *Water Margin*, a captivating 14th century Chinese novel about the brotherhood of 108 Chinese outlaws, each with a unique personality, distinct physique and a set of special skills unduplicated among the brotherhood. All of them shared the spirit of the legendary Robin Hood in the sense that they rebelled against a corrupt authority and empathized with the poor and downtrodden. (The book has been translated into English as *All Men Are Brothers*.) I read it five times in high school. A glorified trait of all the 108 outlaws was their generosity. They were all generous to a fault in their interactions with others, not just in terms of material goods, but also in terms of devotion and courage.

Another influential novel that teenagers of my generation read repeatedly was *The Romance of the Three Kingdoms,* in which the 3rd century battle at the Vermillion Cliffs of the Yangtze River gorge was described in detail. This historical novel was also written in the 14th century. The three main characters, who lived in a tumultuous era of war during the late 2nd century and the early 3rd century A.D., were celebrated for their generosity, loyalty and devotion to each other. One of them, Guan Gong (Lord Guan), had been repeatedly deified by different emperors after his death on account of his virtues. Temples in honor of Guan Gong were popular in every Chinese city and village until the Communists came to power. He was much more important to the general populace than Confucius ever had been. Even today, merchants in Taiwan and overseas Chinatowns typically keep a small shrine of Guan Gong on their premises seeking his blessings. Americans often mistook those little Guan Gong shrines in the shops and restaurants of a Chinatown as miniature ancestor worship platforms.

The impact of the values extolled in these novels on young Chinese of my generation was immeasurable. Those values were further fortified by instructions in schools and various social conventions. My two roommates in Hong Kong and I, for example, never hesitated to pay for each other's meals, depending on who happened to have money in his pocket that day. We considered a miser to be a social pariah. In my Hong Kong high school, a stingy person would be a constant target of ridicule and contempt, earning nicknames that were equivalent to cheapskate and scrooge. The Cantonese word for "stingy," pronounced *Gu-hoen*, literally means "friendless-frigid." The Mandarin Chinese word for "stingy," pronounced *lìn-sè*, means "excessively in love with one's own possession." Both words offer a glimpse of the ostracization a stingy person might suffer in a traditional Chinese society. (There is a more frequently used colloquial expression in Mandarin Chinese for "stingy," pronounced as *xiao-qi*. Its first component, *xiao,* means "picayune, petty, small" with a pejorative implication. For example, *xiao-zi*, literally, "small-son," is a pejorative way of referring to a man, equivalent to the English expression, "shit head.")

When I paid for the first dinner Yuha and I had together, I was just behaving normally according to my Chinese worldview. Yuha was a little surprised. But he accepted my generosity graciously and thanked me for it.

The second time Yuha and I dined together, I tried to pay the bill again. As I took the bill in my hand, Yuha said very seriously,

"No, no, no! You cannot do this."

He went on to explain to me that in the Western world, "Dutch" would be the proper social etiquette in our situation. That was the first time I heard the expression "Dutch." It appeared totally bizarre to me, as if the practice would erect a barrier between my friendship with Yuha. But I acquiesced because Yuha was all serious and business-like. It took me many years to understand that while "Dutch" was the norm when a group of friends incurred an expense, generosity was not unappreciated in America and Europe. If a person offered to pay for everyone's expense in a social gathering, there would be some reason for that act of generosity, and those who benefited from the generosity would usually know about it beforehand.

Several years later, I had to enlighten my very close friend Jean-Marie Hombert, a French linguist in Berkeley, about what Yuha had taught me. Jean-Marie grew up in a village in Picardy, an agricultural region in northern France, where people held generosity in great esteem. At Berkeley, Jean-Marie lived on a meager graduate student stipend. But when he went out to eat with his fellow graduate students, he always offered to pay the entire bill because he wanted to be generous. The other students readily accepted his offers, assuming he was rich. In time, he became baffled that they never reciprocated until I explained to him the practice of "Dutch" as a norm in America.

As the year progressed, I made other friends, all of whom were political dissidents. Yuha supported our politics but didn't participate in our demonstrations against the Vietnam War. The dissidents began organizing antiwar activities earnestly in the Winter quarter of 1964. Yuha thought it would be inappropriate for a Fulbright Fellow to protest against the government of the host nation.

In the summer of 1964, Yuha returned to Finland just as the antiwar movement in America began to gather strength, and Barry Goldwater, the Republican candidate for presidency, suggested the use of nuclear weapons against North Vietnam. I was sorry to see Yuha leave, but the antiwar activities kept me from feeling the blues.

After moving to Berkeley in 1966, I lost touch with Yuha; I was preoccupied with navigating a new academic discipline and engaging in daily antiwar protests. By happenstance, we re-established contact forty-some years later, in 2007, through a Finnish linguist who, after receiving her Ph.D. from my department at the University of California, Santa Barbara, took the professorial Chair of Linguistics at the University of Helsinki. She told me that Yuha was not only a renowned scholar on the social and psychological study of addiction, but also an important public intellectual in Finland.

A few months after the Finnish linguist put me in touch with Yuha, he notified me that he had a one-week layover in Los Angeles during one of his round-the-world voyages on a freighter. After retirement, his favorite activity was to travel around the world by freighter, where he had a spartan suite. Bringing scores of books on board to read, he lived in solitude during the two-to-three-month voyages, except at dinner, when he broke bread with the senior officers of the ship at the captain's table. When Yuha's freighter stopped at a port, he disembarked and did whatever struck his fancy, depending on the location. In spring of 2009, I picked him up at the Los Angeles harbor and brought him to my home in Santa Barbara to meet my family. A few years earlier, he had retired from an illustrious career as a world-class scholar on addiction. He retained his signature trait, the radiant smile that was infectiously cheerful.

The next spring, I took him on a long camping trip to a series of spectacular national parks in the southwest, which he enjoyed immensely, in spite of his physical handicaps caused by a lifelong habit of chain-smoking and alcohol consumption. One year later, my daughter and I visited him in Helsinki and met his daughter. There was never a dull moment during the days and weeks we spent together. Our conversations ranged from history, politics, art, native cultures of Africa and American Indians, fiction, film to behavioral studies, biological sciences and the human condition. The only interruptions were his cigarette breaks, which he took by walking thirty or forty yards away from me. Both of us were partial to gourmet dining. While camping, we ate simply. Once we reached a city such as Santa Fe or Las Vegas, we dined in the best restaurants. Much to his delight, I brought along a case of outstanding merlot and syrah from the wineries in the Santa Barbara region for his consumption while we camped in the wilderness. For him, the good wine made up for the absence of gourmet food in national parks.

Five years after our reunion, Yuha's daughter wrote me to announce that Yuha had succumbed to lung cancer after rejecting all medical interventions, including chemotherapy. He did not think it was ethical to use the medical benefits of Finland's social security system to prolong his life, because he had brought on the lung cancer with his chain-smoking.

He was a remarkable individual.

KEITH

A SHORT MAN WITH COPPER BROWN SKIN, CURLY BLACK HAIR, almond eyes and a round face, Keith looked like a miniature Kublai Khan or a diminutive sumo wrestler. The opposite of Kublai the warrior, Keith was patient and nonviolent. Never in a hurry and always thoughtful, he spoke gently and moved slowly. We met in February of 1964 at a conference in Monterey, California, for Danforth Fellows organized by the Danforth Foundation. Conferees came from various universities in the western United States. Some were first-year graduate students, like Keith and I; some had already completed two or three years of work toward their doctoral degree. Freshly recovered from my brain injury, I felt exceptionally energetic at the conference and volunteered to make a presentation on the "mystery" of mathematical education. My presentation focused on the nature of mathematical thinking: in particular, how a student approached and tackled a mathematical problem worthy of a Ph.D. dissertation, an issue that preoccupied every Ph.D. student in mathematics.

By tradition, mathematical education at all levels remains exclusively confined to formal derivations of theorems and corollaries on the basis of clearly defined mathematical constructs such as set, group, field, tensor, polynomial, etc. That was and still is how mathematics courses are taught in schools, undergraduate colleges and graduate schools. In other words, the instructor demonstrates to the students, given A, B and C ... how one derives, through logical reasoning, D, E and F. Every textbook in mathematics consists of a series of formal derivations from which lemmas, theorems and corollaries arise.

This educational process has created a popular misconception that mathematical research *is* formal derivation. In reality, formal derivations come only after a mathematician has thought through a problem creatively in his/her research, which involves issues such as how to approach a mathematical problem, what machineries to use, and so on. This process of "thinking through" a problem constitutes the bulk and the creativity of each mathematical research project. At the highest level of achievement, a mathematician establishes new concepts and creates hitherto unknown mathematical tools to achieve his/her goal of proving a hypothesis, a conjecture or an intuitive claim.

What inspires or enables a mathematician to "think through" a problem? This question was never explored in mathematical education at the time I was a student of mathematics, not even at the Ph.D. level.

Nor has it ever been made clear that finding a solution to a serious mathematical problem is NOT the discovery of a process of step-by-step formal derivation on the basis of what is given. Indeed, some of the more challenging mathematical problems have almost nothing as "given."

Consider a sample problem:

What is the distribution of prime numbers among all the integers?

Everyone knows that prime numbers (e.g., 2, 3, 5, 7, 11, 13, 17, 19) are integers that can only be divided by themselves or the number 1 in order to yield another integer. The number 6, for instance, is not a prime number because it can be divided by the number, 2, to yield the integer, 3.

Most integers are not prime numbers, but many integers are. The questions then arose: Are prime numbers bunched together in the set of integers? Are they randomly distributed among the integers? Are there some regularities or patterns by which prime numbers are distributed among all of the integers? It is obvious that one cannot answer those questions by listing all integers, because there are an infinite number of them. It is also easy to see that the properties of primes, i.e., integers which can only be divided by itself or the number 1 to yield another integer, provide hardly any substance or hint for one to begin the process of formal derivation.

If one wishes to find the answers to those questions, one must first find an entry or a door to tackle the issue of the distribution of prime numbers among integers. "Finding a door" to solve a problem can be very challenging and difficult. The process of formal derivation is irrelevant during this initial stage of research, because the given definition of primes and integers does not allow one to derive anything.

Finding a door to tackle a deep mathematical problem is akin to the discovery of a hidden entry to an enormous edifice. It calls for insight, ingenuity and luck. Yet, finding a door is just the first stage in a creative process of solving a deep problem. Using the same metaphor, the next stages, which also require ingenuity, involve outlining the entire edifice, leading to a sketch of its structure. None of those stages of creative thinking are formal derivations. Formal derivations come into play only after the overall framework of a solution to a problem has been mapped out, i.e., the structure of the edifice has already been elucidated.

I am not denigrating the importance of formal derivation, which often can be difficult and challenging. What I emphasized in my presentation at the Danforth Conference was that formal derivation did not constitute the fundamental creativity in mathematics, nor was it the way by which a mathematician solved a problem. It was the discovery of an entry or a door to a problem and then arriving at a sketch or a framework for the solution that constituted the essence of mathematical thinking.

Even a trivial problem may require some ingenuity to solve. Consider, for example, that we want to prove the imaginary number, i, equals its negative inverse, $-1/i$, where the imaginary number is defined as the square root of negative one.

The proof of $i = -1/i$ entails a single step of multiplying the imaginary number, i, with i/i. (Dividing a number, even an imaginary number, by itself equals 1, and multiplying any number by 1 yields the same number.) The rest of the proof involves trivial derivation.

The step of multiplying the imaginary number with i/i does not require a great leap of imagination, but it represents a small token of creativity.

One of the best nontrivial examples illustrating mathematical thinking is the elegant and celebrated Galois theory, which was sketched out by the French mathematician, Évariste Galois, at age 20. It is always taught in mathematics graduate programs as a semester-long course of arduous formal derivations, beginning with the definitions of such concepts as "group" and "field," and ending with theorems and corollaries. It would be much more illuminating to the students if a course on Galois theory began with examining the problems (the roots of polynomials) Galois tried to solve, and then followed up with the "how and why" he arrived at the concepts of "group" and "field," two of the most important concepts in mathematics.

The great algebraic geometer, John Tate, once described mathematical research as mental yoga. Yoga, executed at a high level, implies fluidity and a spontaneous, unpredictable sequence of movements. Tate's analogy suggests that mathematical research is much more than logical derivation on the basis of what is given. But that "much more" substance of mathematical research is never explored or even mentioned in any graduate curriculum of a mathematics department!

I remember during orientation, on the second day of my arrival at Stanford to begin my Ph.D. program in fall, 1963, Professor Shatz—a tall, intimidating algebraic geometer—told the eight new graduate students including me in the Department of Mathematics:

"Mathematics *CANNOT* be taught! You've got to learn it by yourself! If you get it, you move ahead. If you don't get it, please leave ASAP."

It was a shocking and intimidating initiation for the new students.

Years later, I came to understand that what Shatz meant by "mathematics" was the creative process of mathematical thinking.

It is true that creativity cannot be imparted. It is also true that there is no algorithm for creativity. A novelist can attest to it; a painter is intimately aware of it. But it does not alter the fact that mathematics students cannot infer mathematical creativity by taking courses that only present formal derivations, which is all that traditional mathematic curriculum offers at every level of education. Going through such a curriculum, a student might be misled into equating mathematical thinking with formal derivation.

In the 1960s, among the top mathematics departments in U.S. universities, more than 70% of the ABD's (All But Dissertation), i.e., students who had fulfilled all the requirements except the production of a dissertation, failed to earn their Ph.D. degree. The statistics were shocking. No other discipline had such abysmal statistics in the success rate of its Ph.D. students working on their dissertations in top-ranked universities. The reason for the high failure rate could not be the quality or the mathematical aptitude of the students who had competed successfully to gain admission to the best departments of mathematics in the nation and subsequently passed all the requirements, including the Ph.D. qualifying examinations. The large proportion of ABD's in mathematics failed because graduate education in mathematics never introduced them to research methodology, namely, the nature of mathematical thinking.

For a mathematics graduate student, advancing to the stage of Ph.D. dissertation research was akin to being tossed into an Olympic-size swimming pool without ever having a swimming lesson. Some, by hook or crook, and with the help of their dissertation advisor, if the advisor happened to be a gifted and dedicated mentor, managed to stumble upon a way to stay afloat. The majority sank into oblivion.

Even though Keith never studied mathematics beyond high school, he thought my discourse on the shortcomings of mathematical education illuminating. After my presentation, he sought me out and we had a long conversation.

He smiled gently. "I am glad you were challenging the authority."

"I didn't think I was doing that," I responded. "I was just trying to point out some inadequacy in mathematical education."

Our conversation soon drifted from challenging the authority in mathematics toward the general issue of the oppressors and the oppressed in societies. It was an issue that had lurked in the back of my mind throughout my life: My father was an authoritarian figure with an explosive temper, Communist China was a totalitarian state where the government terrorized the individual, the colonial government in Hong Kong stood for oppression in order to exploit the natives. Even in graduate school, I felt that my professors wielded tremendous authority over me. Keith was the first person who brought out this significant aspect of my existence in an open discussion. He believed that questioning and challenging authority could stimulate social progress. But he also thought that all challengers of authority should take an oath never to be a bully, so that when they became invested with authority, they would always give first priority to the welfare of their subordinates. That was one of Keith's essential ethical principles. I had never read or heard of such a principle of morality before. It made perfect sense to me. Usually a bully is also a sycophant, not a rebel. Sycophants/bullies are people to be shunned. But it would be an outrage as well as a disgrace if a rebel, who challenged his or her oppressor, were to end up as a bully.

At the Asilomar Conference, Keith's presentation on his three years of experience in Africa was as fascinating as it was baffling. At the time, I was absolutely ignorant of Africa, its people, its cultures, even its geography. It was a distant world, as far away from the environment in which I grew up as another planet. During all those years in China and Hong Kong, I had never met or seen an African. It was not surprising that when Keith reflected on his experience in Ghana and his travel in Africa, my interest was piqued, as if he had inadvertently led me to recognize an enormous lacuna in my knowledge. I listened to him attentively as he spoke haltingly and thoughtfully. But his presentation ended with more questions than answers. In particular, he betrayed a tinge of anguish that I couldn't grasp. Was he disappointed or thwarted in his pursuits in Africa? Identity politics, which had never been important to me, loomed large throughout his life. I never reflected on who I was. It was not one of my existential problems. For Keith, his identity has always been center stage in his life. That came through clearly in his presentation. But I couldn't grasp why identity had been a crisis in his African sojourn. He didn't say so. I inferred it.

In the ensuing months, as we became close friends and organizers in the antiwar movement at Stanford, I slowly uncovered his past. The similarity between his background and mine was fascinating, yet not as striking as our differences. Getting to know him shed light on his identity issues, his rebellion, his anguish, his love and ultimate abandonment of Africa. He was a brave fighter, overcoming enormous odds and misfortunes in life with grace and spunk. I want to tell his story in detail because not only was he an interesting person in his own right, but our development and fate became closely intertwined after we met.

The son of a Chinese immigrant and his three-quarters-Chinese, one-quarter-mulatto wife in Kingston, Jamaica, Keith stood out among his peers in secondary school with his intellectual gifts and scholastic aptitude, passing multiple A-level subject examinations with distinction before his graduation. The British colonial government of Jamaica awarded him a Queen Elizabeth II Fellowship to attend Oxford University, funding all of his tuition and living expenses, including transportation between Jamaica and England. It was a great honor, not to mention a golden opportunity for a young Jamaican to escape a penurious colonial existence and seek higher education in one of the great universities in the world.

But Keith had other ideas.

During the first eighteen years of his life in Jamaica, Keith had witnessed and endured plenty of abuse and discrimination at the hands of the British colonialists. Now he was awarded a Queen's Fellowship to Oxford. A free education at Oxford University would appeal to any young person, including him.

He was flattered by the award, but couldn't help asking himself, "Do I want a life serving the British?"

"After Oxford and postgraduate education, am I heading to a career of a rich comprador, a second-tier professor in a British commonwealth university on account of my ethnicity, or a subservient functionary in a colony?"

Long before the award of the Queen Elizabeth II Fellowship, he had learned in his secondary school that America was different from western European countries. America began as a colony and successfully fought for its independence from the British in the 18th century. Keith thought that Americans, given their history, would understand the cruelty and humiliation of colonial life. Influenced by the ubiquitous radio broadcast of the Voice of America and a stream of information distributed through the offices and reading rooms of the USIS (United States Information Service), Keith bought the idea that America represented hope and progress—a nation dedicated to freedom, democracy and meritocracy! Gradually but surely, he dreamed of an education and a life in America.

One day, Keith learned serendipitously from the Kingston office of USIS that as a graduate of a secondary school in the British educational system, he could apply for admission and scholarship to any universities in the United States. He understood that application did not imply admission and financial award. But armed with a sterling academic record, he thought he should try his luck.

Try, he did, and lucky, he was, even though he received no advice or counseling on how and where he should send his application. Among other Ivy League schools, Harvard University came through with a four-year fellowship covering his tuition, room and board plus a small stipend, which would pay for his travel from Jamaica to Cambridge, Massachusetts.

Jubilant and triumphant, Keith Lowe went to Harvard.

That was fall, 1957.

After settling in Cambridge, Keith noticed that many people, including some of his fellow students and residents of Cambridge, often looked at him in a strange way. It wasn't the condescending or contemptuous look of a British colonial officer in Jamaica. He would recognize that in an instant. Neither was it a look exuding warmth and goodwill or proffering friendship. The look cast in his direction was just a tad longer than the fleeting glance strangers in the street gave each other. It held an element of surprise, as if they were wondering, "Why are you here!?" or "What are you doing here?"

But they were not rude, although their body language communicated a reluctance to approach or get acquainted with him, which fell perfectly in the realm of a normal reaction to a stranger. Other than thinking those people were a bit reserved, Keith did not dwell on it. He certainly did not attribute their way of looking at him as a reaction to his bronze skin, kinky hair, Kublai Khan eyes and short stature. He chalked it up to being an alien, a new arrival from a foreign country, speaking with a lilting Jamaican accent.

He came to America to arm himself with knowledge and skills and prepare for a career. Socialization did not rank high on his priority list. If people were not warm and open, he reckoned, he would just keep to himself and plunge into his studies.

"Perhaps Americans are just less outgoing than Jamaicans," Keith thought to himself.

But he didn't become a hermit, burying himself in books.

A humanist deeply interested in the human condition and the socio-political factors affecting it, he wanted to understand American society, familiarize himself with American history, get a handle on American politics, and find out just what made America the most powerful and, in his mind, the most attractive nation in the world.

Barely a day after settling into his dorm room, he went out on foot to explore his environment.

―――――――――――――――――

The city of Cambridge was unlike any place Keith had ever seen in Jamaica, the only country he had known. In tropical Jamaica, the sweltering sun, rendered more oppressive by the ambient humidity, felt like it could melt you if you strained yourself. In defense, Jamaicans spoke to each other and conducted their activities at a slow pace.

Even the young men at the Kingston International airport, trying to hustle a buck or two out of newly arrived tourists by carrying their luggage from the curbside to a taxi or a waiting limo, took their time to cover the ten or twenty paces. The young hustlers chatted jovially as they ambled toward the automobiles, while the luggage owners waited impatiently.

Why rush or hurry!? Life was short enough!

Here in Cambridge, the opposite way of life held sway: people rushing everywhere, hurtling from one place to another, speaking at a breakneck speed, sometimes wolfing down their sandwiches while walking. To Keith, the street scenes of Cambridge looked like a sped-up movie.

Keith soon learned that in America, time was money, even though "time" and "money" did not share any semantic features that placed them in a natural category. After all, one is a measure, the other a commodity. But in America, time and money were inseparable, bordering on being equivalent if not identical.

Even the speech of Americans reflected the coalescence of time and money. People spoke of "investing" time, "donating" time, "borrowing" time, "saving" time, "wasting" time, "spending" time, being "stingy" or "generous" with time, just as they spoke of money. The adage "time is money" had taken on a substantive existence beyond its metaphorical function in America!

Of course, expressions like "wasting time" or "saving time" also existed in Jamaican English. But one rarely heard them in ordinary, day-to-day speech. Definitely not "investing" time or "donating" time. Why should they? Time did not carry much significance in the typical Jamaican worldview, and life provided little impetus for people to hurry.

In the sweltering heat of a poor tropical country, "slow" was the mantra. Everyone had time to spare.

The hurried way of life in Cambridge contrasted so sharply from the slow tempo in Kingston that it was at once baffling and amusing to Keith.

But he did not dislike what he saw, even though he did not change his way of life. The fast pace may have been a little jolting, but he appreciated the purposeful pursuit that drove people to the fast lane of life. Americans seemed to always chase after something in earnest.

"Perhaps the fast pace of life is what makes America rich!" Keith mused as he described his first impressions of America to me.

He also noticed that in Cambridge, a great number of people, young and old, carried book bags or held books in their hands as they walked. Many wore horn-rimmed glasses. They all looked like students or professors. But there couldn't be so many students and professors living there, he reckoned. It took until graduate school for him to realize that every prominent American university employed more staff and researchers than it did faculty and students to take advantage of the synergy and interface between research and teaching.

Keith liked the physical make-up of Cambridge.

It was small yet vibrant, crowded yet orderly, prosperous yet not ostentatious: an alluring new world to a young man who grew up in a dirty, chaotic neighborhood of the sprawling Kingston, Jamaica.

In fact, he liked Cambridge so much that he would have been content living there for the rest of his life. From parts of the city, he could see the skyline of Boston across the Charles River, which he knew was a major metropolis. But it didn't pique his interest at all for many months after his arrival. He wanted to absorb what Cambridge had to offer.

Walking around Harvard, the nearby MIT campus and the city of Cambridge, Keith admired the diverse architecture displayed by a great collection of imposing buildings. The campus of Harvard alone contained many architectural gems. His favorites were the Hellenistic

Widener Library, a veritable temple, which stood majestically with its colonnades at the geographical center of the campus, and Memorial Hall, a jewel of Victorian Gothic design immediately north of Harvard yard, colorful and picturesque. Cambridge City Hall and the historic public library were no less impressive, as was the Great Dome overlooking Killian Court at MIT.

During the first few weeks after his arrival, the architectural monuments in Cambridge kept him entertained. He walked around each of them, took in the different perspectives from different angles, and reveled in their splendor. Now and then, as he explored the city, he would unexpectedly come upon a new architectural marvel, not necessarily as famous or important as the Widener Library, but in his view, equally beautiful and appealing.

To Keith, walking around Cambridge was as rewarding as visiting a conglomerate of great outdoor museums, where one could indulge the senses in the beauty of diverse design.

Before listening to his recollections of Cambridge's architecture, I had never thought of architecture as an art form. Hong Kong in the 1950s was full of grey, three-story, nondescript concrete buildings. Shops and restaurants on the street level, apartments, offices or factories on the second and third levels. A few Victorian government buildings stood out on the waterfront of the Hong Kong island. They were modest in size and ho-hum in design, not architectural showpieces. The most attractive buildings at the time were the ancient Hakka villages hidden in the mountains of the New Territory. Rectangular in shape and long as a football field, each village was a single structure nestled in an evergreen foothill facing a valley of rice paddies. With its simple geometric design, gabled roof covered with black earthenware tiles, stone-framed windows, white-washed brick walls, two-to-three huge parabola-shaped wooden doors framed by granite columns and slabs, a Hakka village looked charming, elegant and picturesque in its bucolic setting. I loved those villages, particularly from a distance. They looked like they had jumped out of the scrolls of fabulous Chinese brush paintings. But I was unschooled in architectural designs. Keith was my gateway into this domain of fine arts and, in due course, introduced me to the master architects of the Western world, from Andrea Palladio and Christopher Wren to Le Corbusier and Walter Gropius.

But I learned much more than architecture from Keith's account of his early experience in America.

As Keith wandered the streets of Cambridge, he discovered that even more pleasurable than examining some of the great buildings was the opportunity to browse the bookstores surrounding Harvard and MIT. I was envious when Keith described his adventures in the bookstores in Cambridge. Brunswick, Maine was too small a town to sustain a bookstore. Of course, Bowdoin had its own campus bookstore, but it carried primarily textbooks. Neither were bookstores common in Hong Kong or Kingston during the 1950s, and those in existence did not welcome browsers. If you wished to purchase a book, you were, of course, welcome. But if you looked like a pauper or a poor student intent on browsing, you would be asked to leave.

Not in the bookstores in Cambridge.

All browsers were welcome, no matter how you dressed or what you looked like. Even better than this open-door, welcoming policy, many of the bookstores carried books that Keith could never find in Jamaica.

In one store, he accidentally found Ludovico Ariosto's epic Italian poem *Orlando Furioso* in masterful English translation, a scintillating book of war, fantasy and romance, and Lucretius' *De Rerum Natura* in Classical Latin, a book of immense influence among the au courant in Classical Rome and centuries later in Renaissance Florence. Keith had learned Latin studiously for five years in secondary school. The language of Cicero was practically his second language.

He had read excerpts from both *De Rerum Natura* and *Orlando Furioso* in his high school. They were part of his curriculum in literature and Latin for good reasons:

Orlando Furioso, because of its widespread influence on European literature ranging from Shakespeare's *Much Ado About Nothing* and Edmund Spencer's *Faerie Queen* to Cervante's *Don Quixote*, Byron's poetry and the work of the 20th century Russian poet, Osip Mandelstam;

De Rerum Natura, because of its enlightened philosophical musing, in addition to its superb diction and impeccable style, both of which rivaled Cicero's oration.

Back in Jamaica, the excerpts Keith studied gave him only a glimpse of those two books. Yet, even a glimpse had captivated him and filled him with questions:

How could the Epicureans (of whom Lucretius was a devoted follower) know that matter was made of atoms, even though the Classical Greek notion of the atom doesn't bear much resemblance to that of contemporary physics?

What gave the Epicureans the courage to renounce religion and superstition, constructs that had held sway over human beings since the dawn of civilization?

What prompted their categorical dismissal of God and an afterlife two millennia before modern science demonstrated that life originates from self-assembling molecules (which, in turn, gave rise to living organisms through evolution and symbiotic combinations), that seasonal changes result from the earth orbiting the sun and the tilt of the earth's rotational axis, that earthquakes stem from the movement of tectonic plates, that infectious diseases are caused by microorganisms invisible to the naked eye, that hominids originated in Africa six to seven million years ago, and that water, the fundamental element of life, is made of two parts hydrogen and one part oxygen.

A committed Catholic, Keith had been haunted by those questions ever since he encountered *De Rerum Natura* in his high school Latin classes.

Orlando Furioso, an epic poem of war, fantasy and romantic love between protagonists belonging to opposing religious groups, was less thought-provoking but more entertaining than *De Rerum Natura*. Being exposed to a segment of a thrilling story about romance between men and women of different religions at war was like watching a trailer for a suspense movie, only to be told that the movie would never be shown, or like catching a whiff of delicious food, only to be denied an opportunity to eat it.

Keith wanted to know how the romantic attraction between the pagan Ruggiero and the Christian woman warrior Bradamante would unfold, as well as the real cause of Orlando's madness.

With all the questions churning in his mind, he wanted to read those two books in full when he was a student in secondary school.

In Jamaica, Keith couldn't find either of them. His Latin teacher didn't have them. The school library didn't carry them.

Finally, at a bookstore in Harvard Square, both books unexpectedly came into his hands. He was overjoyed and started reading immediately. For several weeks, in late afternoon of each day, he would show up at the bookstore and read five to ten pages while standing. He knew those books would be in the Harvard library. But he felt elated when he read them in a bookstore. Unlike going to the library, signing out a book and putting it in your backpack, all of which constituted a part of the academic pursuit, reading books in a bookstore was a form of entertainment. To a penurious student like Keith, browsing in a bookstore was equivalent to breaking life's routine and going out to have fun. It was recreation and exploration. The page limit he imposed on himself served to prevent the ire of the bookstore staff, as Keith had no funds to purchase the books. He didn't know if the staff would kick him out if he stayed longer than fifteen minutes, as he would have been in a Jamaican bookstore. Being cautious, he didn't want to take a chance. It was an exciting few weeks as he voraciously devoured the two books. He didn't find answers to all the questions that jumped at him when he first encountered a few excerpts of the books in high school. But it was gratifying to fulfill an important wish.

During his three years at Harvard, even though he could ill afford to buy books, go to a movie or attend a concert, the bookstores, the plethora and diversity of their stock, made life in Cambridge luxurious and exciting for Keith. Going to bookstores in town was his way of stepping out of the academy to explore the unknown and be surprised by new discoveries of gems in the world of knowledge, similar to stumbling upon beautiful seashells along a beach.

As the school year progressed, he found another source of recreation by hanging around the bustling center of Harvard Square.

The center of Harvard Square had a slightly sunken arena, in which a subway station marked by a quaint but well-stocked newsstand served as a landmark. The arena looked like a veritable open theatre with pedestrians hurrying in all directions, musicians performing for donations, chess players hustling gullible novices, youngsters hanging about, and tourists meandering around as they paid homage to Harvard and MIT. On weekends, walking slowly up and down Massachusetts Avenue or Brattle Street, with Harvard Square as a point of reference, pausing here and there, watching people go by, taking in the scenery, browsing in stores of African folk art, Keith enjoyed what he saw. It was grand entertainment.

He noticed that Cambridge had very few dark-skinned people. Caucasians dominated, especially among the students and faculty at MIT and Harvard. One day, not long after his arrival, he heard someone referring to him as "that Negro boy" when he walked by. He didn't take it as an insult, although it surprised him.

He thought Negro, in the English language, referred only to people of African descent. In Jamaica, everyone identified him as a Chinese, copper skin and kinky hair notwithstanding. Most Jamaicans were dark-skinned to some degree. For sure, the British colonialists had pale skin, roasted into a shade of pink by the tropical sun. But they, being capos and bosses and vastly outnumbered by the plebeians, didn't count as part of the general populace of Jamaica. Neither did the tourists, who were typically people of European descent. They were transients confined to tourist ghettos like Montego Bay.

From the perspective of the natives, all of the people of European descent in Jamaica constituted a special stratum, institutionally, economically and socially removed from the natives through an unspoken, mutual consent. Some of the Caucasians owned valuable properties, commanded political and economic power. Some even lived permanently in Jamaica. But they were not Jamaicans, neither did they see themselves as Jamaicans. To the natives, they might just as well be extraterrestrial humanoids sent by a wrathful God to rule and plunder their homeland, whereas to the colonialists and most tourists, the natives were, at best, heathens and, at worst, barbarians.

Among Jamaicans, the color of skin did not determine a person's identity or ethnicity. Many Jamaicans were of East Indian origin, mostly members of the Dravidian ethnic groups from south India, who were as dark as some of the people of African descent. Jamaicans considered them East Indians, not Negros. In lumping people into groups, Jamaicans relied on their ancestral lineage. Keith was considered a Chinese because his father was a Chinese and his mother's father was a Chinese, although Keith didn't speak a word of Chinese, couldn't write his Chinese name and knew very little about China and Chinese culture when he was growing up. Even after he came to America, he didn't have the faintest idea of what his Chinese heritage meant. But Jamaicans considered him Chinese. The mulatto component of his maternal grandmother merely added some exotic elements to his bona fide Chinese identity.

Even the Chinese in China, contrary to popular misconception around the world, constitute a mosaic of many ethnic groups, among which the dominant one consists of the descendants of the early agriculture settlers in the Yellow River basin, later known as the Han ethnic group. They represent the stereotypical Chinese to the rest of the world.

The Han people constituted the majority in China, but they descended from scores of ethnic groups. For many thousand years, the Han people intermarried with members of other ethnic groups who made their home in what is known as China today. Among them are the Tibeto-Burmans; the Tai-Kadai people; the Hmong-Mien tribes, also known as Miao-Yao ethnic groups; the Altaic pastoralists (divided into three major branches, the Turkic, the Mongolic and the Tungusic), who conquered and ruled all or parts of China more often than any other ethnic groups, including the Hans, during the past two millennia (the imperial household of the last dynasty, the Qing, which ruled China from 1644 to 1911, was Manchurian, a branch of the Tungusic pastoralists); and the Austronesians, who, inhabiting China's coastal region about ten to fifteen thousand years ago, sailed into the Pacific

Ocean and produced generations of irrepressible, intrepid seafarers in the Pacific and Indian Oceans, colonizing eastward all the way to New Zealand, Easter Island, and westward all the way to Madagascar, a few hundred miles from Mozambique along the coast of Eastern Africa. Today, the total population of officially recognized ethnic minorities in China exceeds 120 million. They constituted a much larger percentage of China's total population in the dynastic days.

In addition, there were also the well-documented, smaller ethnic groups joining the "Han Chinese" melting pot throughout the past two millennia:

A band of Roman legionnaires named by the Han as the "tortoise shell people" because, when they faced a fusillade of arrows from the nomadic marauders of Asiatic steppes, they collectively crouched under their Roman shields, raised upward to form a protective cover like a tortoise shell. Those legionnaires were the survivors of a crushing defeat of the Roman army in 53 B.C. by the Parthians in present-day Turkey, in which the commanding Roman general, Marcus Crassus, Julius Caesar's fellow consul of the Republic of Rome, was killed. In defeat, some of those surviving legionnaires chose to march eastward instead of turning back to the Roman Empire to face humiliation. They ultimately settled in Western China. Over time, they were gradually absorbed into the Han ethnic group through intermarriage. Some of their descendants today have blonde hair, and some have blue or green eyes, but they are considered members of the Han ethnic group.

There were the Tocharians, an old Indo-European tribe whose language was closely related to Hittite, Sanskrit and Classical Greek. One wonders how they interacted with Alexander the Great when his army arrived in present-day Western China, the home of Tocharians in the 4th century B.C. By the 7th century A.D., the Tocharians vanished into the Han ethnic group through inter-ethnic marriages when climatic change desiccated their homeland and expanded the Taklamakan desert.

There was a contingent of Hebrew immigrants who took up residence in Eastern China in the 18th century, in addition to an on-and-off influx of Arabs, Middle Easterners, Persians and Indians settling in

China from the silk road throughout the last two thousand years. All of these people melted into a sea of Han Chinese. They intermarried at one point or another with the Hans and members of other ethnic groups, and their progeny belong to the present-day Han Chinese majority.

Given the heterogeneous complexity of the ancestry of Chinese, dark skin and kinky hair do not undermine a person's Chinese identity at all. Not in China, and certainly not in Jamaica.

The novelty of being considered a Negro in America didn't last long for Keith. He soon found out that everyone at Harvard regarded him as a Negro. As time passed and he became informed of racial prejudice in the United States, especially prejudice against Blacks, he proudly held up his new identity as a badge of honor, joining the Black people of America. He followed the civil rights movement assiduously, participated in civil rights marches whenever he could, and read extensively in African-American literature ranging from the slave narratives of the 19th century to the non-fiction writings of W.E.B. Du Bois and Booker T. Washington. He planned to spend time in Africa to learn more about his cultural heritage, to establish for himself a firm footing for his new identity: Black American.

Keith attained senior standing two years after his arrival at Harvard. That senior year dawned with a cascade of honors and awards that took him by surprise. In the fall, he was elected to the Phi Beta Kappa honor society. He won the Boylston oratorical prize twice. His prize-winning play was performed at Sanders Theater in Memorial Hall. His short story won a top prize and was published in an anthology. Harvard University, at the recommendations of his professors in the English Department, nominated him for a National Danforth Fellowship to pursue a Ph.D. degree and professorial career. He won it handily through a national competition. Finally, to cap all of the surprises, he was told toward the end of that year that as the top student of his graduating class, he had been chosen to be the valedictorian.

Unlike many of his classmates, all the honors and recognition did not entice him to pursue a financially rewarding life. Instead, he quietly applied for high school teaching posts in Accra, the capital of the Republic of Ghana in West Africa.

Trying to go to Ghana was his major strategy for the purpose of understanding and bolstering his "Negro" identity. Being partly African, he reckoned, meant that he ought to experience Africa firsthand, not as a transient tourist, but as a resident and educator, which would allow him to immerse himself in African life and culture.

He felt that Ghana would be an ideal choice to begin the consolidation of his African identity. A former British colony like Jamaica, Ghana became independent in 1957. In 1960, the year Keith graduated, Ghanaians approved a new constitution as the prime minister, Kwame Nkrumah, became the first popularly elected president. Nkrumah was respected throughout the world as an intellectual, an author, a leader of the non-aligned nations consisting of 120 nations of the developing world. He was also the founder of Pan-Africanism, an intellectual movement to unite the people of Africa with people of African descent who have come to inhabit the entire American continent, including the Caribbean islands, over centuries of a diaspora created by the cross-Atlantic slave trade.

When one of the high schools in the capital of Ghana offered him a teaching post for two years, Keith was overjoyed. The offer came in late spring of 1960, a few days before he was scheduled to deliver his commencement speech. He accepted the offer immediately, even though the English Department at Stanford had expected him to begin his Ph.D. studies in the coming Fall. In response to Keith's request, both the Danforth Foundation and Stanford University granted him a three-year delay to begin his graduate studies.

Commencement events at Harvard have always been an upbeat and festive affair attended by the graduates, their family members, friends, professors, alumni, honorary degree recipients, members of the Governing Board and an assortment of luminaries. It is a celebratory event, replete with fanfare and pageantry. For Keith, the 1960 commencement marked the culmination of three years of hard work. There was much to celebrate.

But he was by himself, in the midst of a cheerful and spirited crowd.

Keith's parents didn't stand a chance to travel from Jamaica to Boston to attend the commencement.

For his father, such a trip would not only be financially ruinous, but also logistically and psychologically onerous, if not overwhelming. He nearly lost his life during the long, hazardous ocean voyage from Hong Kong to the Caribbean in the 1920s to seek a new life among Chinese settlers who had escaped penury in their native villages. When he finally set foot on terra firma in Jamaica at the end of that voyage, he swore that he would never again trust his life to a man-made vessel that rocked and tumbled unpredictably up and down, left and right, day and night in an open sea. As for airplanes, which had become the popular mode of long-distance travel by 1960, he preferred to look at them from a safe berth on earth. He felt strongly that trusting one's life to a huge metallic vessel flying through thin air was nothing but a fool's challenge against the specter of death. He knew that in the struggle for survival, death ultimately held the upper hand. Why should a man flirt with a dangerous journey, even if the adventure meant seeing his son graduating with the highest honors at a preeminent American university?

His foremost duty in life was to postpone the inevitable end with all his power. After all, he was a reserved and prudent man in the sixth decade of his life by 1960. In addition, he couldn't fully grasp the significance of his son's achievement. Like any Chinese father, he wanted his son to attain the highest level of education and excel in the process. In his scheme of the world of education, postgraduate studies did not exist. According to his Chinese language, tertiary education is called "Big Learning," secondary education, "Middle Learning," and primary education, "Little Learning." Now that Keith had completed "Big Learning" splendidly, it meant the son had met the father's expectation. In other words, it was done, finished, like the END of a movie. From the perspective of the father, what was the point of making a big fuss of it?

For Keith's mother, the thinking was just the opposite. She would have given anything to attend her son's commencement. An intelligent autodidact, she had followed Keith's academic progress assiduously ever since his days of "Little Learning." After Keith went to Harvard, she was both happy and sad. Happy because her son had embarked on a path to a promising future, sad because he had left home. Her beloved son was gone! In his absence, she comforted herself by reading and re-reading his letters. Often tears welled up in her eyes when she did.

Unlike her husband, who was nearly thirty years her senior, she rejoiced in her son's achievements and wanted to attend his graduation. But she couldn't find a way to finance a trip to Boston. She even explored the possibility of borrowing money from the loan sharks in the tongs of Kingston's Chinatown. Without her husband's backing, the tongs would not grant her a loan. When the tongs rejected her application, she could hardly hold back her tears. The rejection deprived her of the opportunity to witness the most important event in her life.

But she never cried in front of her husband for fear of annoying him. Seeking comfort in the pride she felt for Keith, she secretly hoped that Keith would eventually bring her to America when he became a professor. Each letter he wrote to her was safely stored away in a metal English cookie box, which she kept in a secret nook in her kitchen.

To Keith's mother, her marriage didn't mean much of anything. At sixteen years old, her father offered her to his newly widowed friend as a bride—a gesture of friendship not uncommon between traditional men in pre-modern China. For twenty-some years, she had endured a meaningless and loveless marriage, imposed on her against her will. By 1960, she was in her late thirties, yearning for a new life, a life beyond her boring and empty role as a perennial maid and cook to an old man who rarely had anything to say to her and rarely provided any meaningful companionship.

At commencement, Keith was not just without any family members. Hardly anyone among a crowd of thousands paid any attention to him. He was friendly with some of his classmates in the English Department. But they were preoccupied with their families and friends. Keith didn't want to intrude. Several English and Classics professors knew him well. But they were nowhere to be found in that huge crowd.

For the first time in three years, he felt overcome by solitude. The throng of thousands of cheerful people and the celebratory atmosphere further magnified his loneliness.

Of course, he had been alone most of the time during the past three years. But the pressure and stress of studying and surviving as a penurious foreign student didn't leave much time and energy for him to feel lonely. Now that the pressure and stress had lifted, at least for the day of the commencement, he felt out of sorts.

To counter his melancholy mood, he decided to silently rehearse his valedictorian speech. But his mind soon began to wander.

Taking stock of the past three years in America as if he were both the psychiatrist and the patient, he felt he had definitely made the right choice by coming to America, a nation, in spite of its defects and pitfalls, that had granted him free rein with full financial support to develop intellectually and emotionally. Yes, at that moment in the commencement, he felt like a Martian, alone and without a family member or friend; yes, he experienced some racial prejudice, if not outright discrimination, in America; yes, he had been working or studying most of his three years with little entertainment or relaxation. Yet those three years were filled with excitement:

Excitement from attending novel classes; from discovering new knowledge; from reading fabulous literature; from being lauded by his professors for his poems, plays and essays; from seeing the spectacle of the flaming foliage in autumn; from experiencing the beauty of his first snow storm and glistening icicles; from earning some Yankee dollars to buy books and clothing; and above all, from a new life brimming with hope and the freedom to pursue it.

At that moment of self-examination, he focused on a future that gave him hope: the opportunity to explore his African roots in Ghana and earn a Ph.D. in American literature at Stanford. He had already chosen the novels and short stories of Flannery O'Connor for his research, and he was ready to embark on a professorial career that, most importantly, would allow him to fight against any authority that promoted bigotry and social injustice. That fight had been his commitment since his teens.

In the midst of his reverie and self-examination, Keith was jolted by the sudden appearance of McGeorge Bundy, Dean of the Faculty of Letters and Science, in front of him. The Dean would be the Master of Ceremonies at the commencement.

"Mr. Lowe, I am delighted to meet you!" Dean Bundy spoke with an unusual crispiness, projecting both authority and confidence. "Congratulations on your academic achievements."

"Thank you, sir," Keith responded humbly.

Looking Keith in the eyes, Bundy asked for his input, even though he had already prepared a short introduction of Keith. "How would you like me to introduce you?"

"A Black man from Jamaica," Keith replied without hesitation.

Surprised, Bundy had no intention of bringing up Keith's skin color. A cerebral and liberal scholar, he considered identifying a person by the color of his/her skin an affront, if not a gross travesty.

"Thank you, Mr. Lowe," Bundy responded before walking away. "I will not do that. But I will say that you are an admirer of Dr. Martin Luther King Jr. Looking forward to your speech."

Bundy had read Keith's mind. He knew exactly what Keith was thinking. Keith was impressed.

Because Bundy mentioned Martin Luther King Jr., Keith wanted to ask him a question about a recent event in the civil rights movement. But before Keith could utter his question, Bundy had already left. He seemed to be in a hurry to join a small group of people standing nearby. In fact, he almost loped over. Keith looked at the group and spotted

Nathan Pusey, the President of Harvard, and two of the four Rocke-feller brothers, John D. Rockefeller III, whose son John D. Rockefeller IV (Jay Rockefeller) was one of the graduates, and David Rockefeller, President of Chase Bank. There they were, members of the ruling class of the United States standing right in front of him, commanding all the attention of the academic elite.

Keith wasn't upset, nor did he feel slighted by Bundy's abrupt depar-ture. He knew his station and understood he wasn't a VIP. But what he had just experienced reaffirmed the naivete of his earlier view of American meritocracy when he was a teenager in Jamaica. As a newly minted gradu-ate of Harvard, he understood that meritocracy did not trump everything. Class difference and income disparity took priority in social preference.

In recounting his experience at Harvard, Keith unintentionally reminded me of my ignorance of America at the time of my graduation from Bowdoin. I wouldn't have known the Rockefeller name, let alone be able to identify any of them in a crowd. I had barely heard of Martin Luther King Jr., although my aborted automobile trip to the South awak-ened me to America's racial prejudice and segregation. The fundamental difference between Keith and I was that during our undergraduate years, I sequestered myself in the study of mathematics and physics, while Keith blossomed as a humanist. Paradoxically, Keith's three years in Cambridge also created an identity crisis that evolved into a devastating calamity, which Keith couldn't have anticipated.

In July 1960, with great expectation and excitement, Keith arrived in Accra, Ghana. He was looking forward to immersing himself in Nkru-mah's Pan-Africanism, acquiring some understanding of African cul-ture, and seeking an answer to the question that had been gnawing at him since Harvard:

What did it mean to be a man of African ancestry?

Teaching at a high school in Accra was pleasant enough: the local coastal climate was similar to that of tropical Jamaica; the students were motivated to learn; the school provided him a comfortably furnished apartment on campus; people were courteous and friendly to him. He liked the Ghanaian cuisine with an emphasis on spicy seafood soup and stew; he took to traditional Ghanaian tunics and robes made of sturdy, bright colored fabrics with embroidered or hand-printed Adinkra symbols, each of which served as a stylized representation of a traditional concept or cultural entity of the Ashantis (Akans), the major ethnic group of Ghana.

Those were niceties of life in Africa. But Keith didn't come to Ghana for niceties. He came to embrace Pan-Africanism.

Much to his chagrin, most Ghanaians paid little attention to Pan-Africanism. Even the students in the University of Ghana, who were being groomed to join the elite of the nation, did not show much enthusiasm. Keith came to that conclusion when he gave a presentation at the university on English literature. Most of the Ghanaians Keith interacted with knew about Pan-Africanism. Few took it seriously. They paid lip service to it because Nkrumah was their president and Pan-Africanism was Nkrumah's pet ideology that provided him with an international following. But it remained an abstract ideology with little or no relevance to the life of Ghanaians. The truth, as Keith found out, was that there was no such thing as "African Culture." Instead, there were hundreds, if not thousands, of ethnic groups, cultures and languages in Sub-Saharan Africa alone, all of which differed dramatically from those of North Africa. Ghana, a Sub-Saharan African nation, was on the Atlantic coast, over 4,000 miles from the East African coast on the Indian Ocean. As a continent, Africa accounted for more than twenty percent of the earth's total land mass, equivalent to 1.7 times the size of South America. It was not surprising that such an enormous continent was home to an immense variety of people and cultures. Some African people, like the Bantu agriculturalists living in rural villages across Sub-Saharan Africa, shared certain cultural characteristics; some, like the Ituri rainforest hunter-gatherers in Central Africa, bore little resemblance to the sedentary agriculturalists in terms of language and culture until their assimilation into the Bantu world during the last century.

African unity, let alone the unification of Africans with the Black people of the American continent, was just a dream, Kwane Nkrumah's dream, adopted by other ambitious African leaders like Patrice Lumumba as a convenient political platform to attract the attention of the international media and create a following in the American continent. It was not on the radar screen of most Ghanaians, whose primary concern remained survival and economic development. After winning freedom from the yoke of colonialism, their priority shifted to achieving a better life. While they were united in their effort to oust the British colonialists, nationalism remained, at best, a nascent sentiment among the people of Ghana. A Ghanaian's loyalty belonged first to his/her clan, and secondarily to his/her tribe. Even in Accra, Ghana's capital and a sophisticated metropolis, where English served as the lingua franca, tribalism and ethnicity tended to trump nationalism. The Akans, speaking Ashanti, for example, preferred to form social groups with other Akans, not the Ewes, not the Mole-Dagbani, not even the Akans who spoke Fante.

By the end of his two-year stint in Accera's high school, Keith came to the conclusion that Pan-Africanism served primarily as an ideology of African-American identity politics, with some spillover in the Caribbean islands. It had little or no relevance to the vast majority of Africans.

But the most important lesson Keith had learned in Ghana was that Ghanaians never considered him an African. The Ghanaians he interacted with respected him. His colleagues liked him. They treated him with great courtesy. But he was not one of them, and there was no chance of him becoming an African. He knew it, and the Ghanaians knew it. When he became better informed of Africa and its history, he realized that he could not possibly discover his maternal roots anywhere in that enormous continent of Africa. There were thousands of tribes with a diversity that far exceeded that of other continents. He found most Ghanaians firmly grounded in their pursuit of the materialistic improvement of life, which was understandable. Some of them, especially the better-educated and the privileged urban citizens, shared his values, worldviews and devotion to Pan-Africanism. Many Ghanaians considered political ideology abstract and ponderous. If Keith chose to be a Black man, he would have to forge his identity in America. Nevertheless, Keith left Ghana on a high note after taking a one-year tour of the continent after fulfilling his teaching contract. He had learned a great deal about Africa and understood the challenge faced by Africans.

Keith returned from Ghana to the United States in the Winter of 1963 and settled in Palo Alto to begin his Ph.D. studies at Stanford University. As we became friends after the Danforth Conference in winter, 1964, we discovered that we had a similar path of development of our political knowledge and awareness of America.

As teenagers, Keith and I, ten thousand miles apart, chafed under British colonial rule, yearned for equality, freedom and a decent, compassionate society. We both came to the United States by happenstance. After arriving in America, we both suffered social isolation, if not discrimination, during our undergraduate years. Seeking refuge in learning and academic advancement, we both felt a deep gratitude to America for the superb educational opportunities it granted us.

Our first image of the United States, conceived in our teens, was overwhelmingly positive and favorable. That favorable image, partly enhanced and buttressed by the wealth of America in contrast to colonial Hong Kong and Jamaica, started with the fact that the United States did not seize territories of the Third World during the 19th and early 20th centuries, when European countries were colonizing and plundering Asian, African and American continents with alacrity. (The Portuguese, the Spanish and the Dutch pioneered the colonization of the Third World three hundred years earlier.) The absence of U.S. colonies during the 1950s had a profound impact on us, since Keith and I both resented British colonialism. We admired America for her lack of colonies.

We became further enamored with America when we learned that, at the end of World War II, the U.S. government granted independence to the Philippines, while Britain, Holland and France were desperately holding on to their colonies with military campaigns against local independence fighters.

The U.S. inherited the Philippines from Spain as a colony in 1898 for taking the side of the Philippine independence movement against the Spanish colonial rule. By 1899, the United States betrayed the Philippine independence movement and made the Philippines its own colony through military campaigns against the independence movement. But in the ensuing decades, America gradually granted an increasing degree of autonomy and self-rule to the Philippines. This autonomy ultimately led to independence in 1946. However, there was a hitch to this magnanimous deed of the United States, which I did not discover until the mid-1960s. That hitch involved the CIA control of the Philippine government. During the first twenty years of Philippines independence, the American head of the CIA station in Manila dictated every major policy decision of the Philippine government to such an extent that on one occasion, a CIA station chief allegedly assaulted the Philippine president for not following his directive.

But the most impressive action of the United States, for both Keith and me long before we met, occurred in 1956 during the Suez Canal crisis, when the Egyptian president, Gamal Nasser, nationalized the Suez Canal. In response to Nasser's nationalization move, Great Britain and France, the two bastions of colonialism, immediately invaded Egypt and occupied the Canal with the collaboration of Israel. It was a crisis that could have triggered a nuclear war between NATO and the Soviet Union, if it were not for the United States, which prudently pressured Britain, France and Israel into withdrawing their army from Egypt to allow the Egyptian nationalization of the Suez Canal to proceed. At the time of the crisis, both of us, as teenagers, interpreted America's response to the crisis as a sterling example of U.S. actions championing democracy and anti-colonialism. We didn't fully understand that the action of the United States was, in part, motivated by the need to avoid a third world war.

The first international incident that cast a shadow over my glowing impression of the United States occurred in early 1961, when I was still in Hong Kong, preoccupied with the tests and interviews required by the competition for a World University Service scholarship to study in an American liberal arts college.

The incident was the U.S. invasion of Cuba at the Bay of Pigs.

The invasion failed and marred the presidency of the popular and charismatic John F. Kennedy. It raised many questions in my mind:

How could the United States justify invading a country just because it disagreed with the U.S. on ideological grounds? After all, Cuba, a small impoverished nation, was far from posing a military threat to the United States.

Didn't the world condemn the Soviet Union for invading Hungary and Poland in the mid-1950s when those countries decided to change tack in pursuit of a different political system?

Even though the U.S. did not mount a full-scale invasion of Cuba as the Soviet Union did in Hungary and Poland, the U.S. intention of toppling Fidel Castro, the popular leader of Cuba, was unmistakable. Wouldn't this incident give credence to the Chinese and Soviet propaganda that the U.S. was imperialistic?

After arriving at Bowdoin College in 1961, I did not notice anyone talking about the Bay of Pigs incident or showing any interest in Cuba, even though the aftermath of the failed invasion (namely, the execution of U.S. citizens and Cuban exiles who were captured by Castro's army, and America's ransom payment to repatriate some surviving captives) continued to unfold. I never revealed my sentiment on the Cuban situation while at university and was not aware of any negative reaction to the Bay of Pigs incident in the Bowdoin community.

As for Keith, who was in Accra, the capital of Ghana, at the time, he was swept up by the Ghanaians' strong anti-American demonstrations in protest of the Bay of Pigs invasion. The left-leaning Kwame Nkrumah was Ghana's President. He spared no words in his repeated condemnation of the United States for invading Cuba. Keith agreed with Nkrumah. The incident opened Keith's eyes to America's aggression, which appeared just as insidious as the behavior of the Soviet Union in Eastern Europe. Sadly, several years later, Kwame Nkrumah fell victim to a CIA-engineered coup d'état. A senior operative revealed the CIA covert operation and its execution in later years. His account was subsequently corroborated by the investigative reporting of Seymour Hersh in *The New York Times*.

After Keith and I met in 1964, we went on to independently learn a trove of damning information about America's imperial activities abroad and the full range of atrocities within America itself. On the domestic front, we had already witnessed the prejudice against Black people, learned about the slaughter of Native Americans on top of the eradication of their social and cultural identities, saw the exploitation of Mexican-American farm workers, and became familiar with a history of discrimination against new immigrants, European as well as Asian. In short, we woke up to an America which, on the one hand, presented unparalleled opportunities for life improvement to some hard-working immigrants like us, and, on the other, festered with bigotry and injustice within while bristling with imperialistic ventures abroad.

It wasn't the curriculum at Harvard, Bowdoin and Stanford that led us to our new understanding of America. Driven by our quest for knowledge, we read voraciously. Our reading had informed us that the absence of U.S. colonialism in the Third World during the 19th century did not stem from any lofty moral principle on the part of the American people and their government. The U.S., after the Civil War, was preoccupied with colonizing territories in the western region of what is the United States today.

That process of colonization of the North American continent by the descendants of European immigrants was just as brutal as the European colonization of large swaths of Asia, Africa and Central/South America, if not more so.

Scores of books documented the killings of the Native Americans as American colonizers swept westward. In 1881, the Bishop of Minnesota's Episcopal Church, H. B. Whipple, observed in his introduction to Helen Jackson's book, *A Century of Dishonor: A Sketch of the United States Government's Dealings with Some of the Indian Tribes*:

"We have not a hundred miles between the Atlantic and Pacific which has not been the scene of an Indian massacre."

Some massacres, like the slaughter of hundreds of Lakota men, women and children by the U.S. cavalry at Wounded Knee Creek on the Lakota Pine Ridge Indian Reservation, have become public knowledge. By the late 20th century, there are monuments, books, films, poems and songs commemorating the Wounded Knee massacre, although few people are aware that shortly after the incident, the U.S. Congress awarded twenty Medals of Honor to members of the cavalry who took part in the massacre, as if their killing of the Lakotas required exceptional courage, deserving the highest military honor in America.

Other killings, like the ethnic cleansing of Native American tribes in California, where cultural and linguistic diversity exceeded that of all of the United States prior to the arrival of Caucasian Americans, were conducted without any public fanfare or remonstration. Today, that ethnic cleansing is mostly forgotten. One can hardly see any Native American in the most populous state of the union, unless one takes the initiative to visit a poverty-ridden "reservation" of some tribes which are "lucky" enough to have been granted them. Most of the California Indians, such as the Yuki, the Atsugewi and the Ohlone (Costanoan), have been wiped out, relegated to the past.

Before the arrival of Caucasian Americans, the Yuki lived peacefully in Mendocino County, the Atsugewi thrived near Mount Shasta, and the Ohlone people's homeland covered the entire San Francisco Bay Area, extending all the way through Salinas County. Nowadays, Yuki, Atsugewi and Ohlone are names of exterminated ethnic groups that exist primarily in academic books on Californian Indian languages and cultures.

In the 19th century, the words of Peter Burnett, the first elected governor of California, summed up the sentiment of the Caucasian settlers toward native Indians. In a State of the State address of 1850, he declared that:

"A war of extermination will continue to be waged between the races, until the Indian race becomes extinct."

Burnett correctly described the action of Caucasian Californians as a "war of extermination." But he was absolutely wrong about the "war between the races." The ethnic cleansing of native Californians was a one-sided affair carried out by newly arrived Caucasian immigrants. The overwhelming majority of the California Indians never fought back even after many new settlers from Eastern America started hunting them down as a recreational activity. Unlike the Nez Perce, the Apache or the Sioux Indians, most Californian Indians did not have the tradition of engaging in warfare against other people. Governor Peter Burnett's "war between the races" was a fantasy, an exculpatory euphemism for ethnic cleansing.

I witnessed some of the consequences of the cultural and psychological devastation of the remaining California Indians during the 1970s when I befriended an elderly lady of the nearly extinct Wappo ethnic group. Being the only surviving speaker of Wappo, she allowed me to study and analyze her language for several years. Whenever I was not teaching, I drove up to her trailer in the Pomo Reservation in Alexander Valley to study her language. During those years, I met and became familiar with many members of her extended family, their plight and suffering.

For more than a century, the U.S. Bureau of Indian Affairs forcibly whisked pre-teenage Native American boys and girls away from their parents, families and tribes, placed them with Native American children from other parts of the United States in special "boarding schools" in Alaska, ostensibly to give them an "American education."

This practice of the American Bureau of Indian Affairs was as insidious and brutal as the 21st century Chinese "re-education" camps for the Islamic Uighurs. It was cultural and psychological annihilation of the Native Americans.

One can hardly imagine the trauma inflicted on those Indian children, torn away from their families and tribes to be confined in frigid Alaskan camps with other American Indian children, most of whom did not even share a common language. By the time they returned to their reservations in their late teens, they had lost their native languages and forgotten their ancestry, tribal history and cultural practices. Like war veterans suffering from severe post-traumatic stress disorder, they were psychologically and emotionally devastated. Many became listless and semi-catatonic, wasting their life on drugs and alcohol. Some committed suicide in the prime of their life.

The elderly lady who taught me Wappo, Laura Somersal, was an exception among her people. Indeed, she was an exceptional person among any people. At the beginning of the 20th century, she was spared from being taken to Alaska because she served as her blind mother's eyes. The Bureau of Indian Affairs took the humane decision to allow a young daughter to stay with her blind mother, a single woman whose family members had either been killed or died at a young age from infectious diseases. Growing up with her mother, Laura spoke Wappo, her mother's native tongue, as well as Pomo, the language of her father's ethnic group. In the Russian River basin near Clear Lake, she mastered the Pomo craft of weaving intricate baskets from roots dug up along the banks of Russian River (her baskets are on permanent display in many museums, including the Smithsonian); learned how to collect acorns, leach them and cook them into mush over heated stones in baskets woven with her own hands; knew where and how to harvest edible seaweed from the shores of the Pacific Ocean; and acquired the skill of trapping rabbits with devices she made from pliable tree branches. She was a fountain of knowledge of how to survive in the wilderness of California. In her eighties when I met her, she remained nimble enough to climb large live oak trees to pick the best acorns from the treetop.

Good-natured, generous and full of vitality, she counseled, supported and provided for a good number of youngsters on the Pomo reservation where she lived—the Wappo people were never granted a reservation. All the anthropologists and linguists who worked on Wappo or Pomo knew her as a bright light on her reservation in Alexander Valley of Sonoma County, a one-woman rescue mission for her devastated people. She is featured in a book entitled, *The Wappo: A Report* by Yolande S. Beard, Malki Museum Press. In 1990, at more than one hundred years of age, Laura died tragically as a consequence of the invasion of a gang who sprayed automatic gunfire at her trailer.

By the time Keith and I met at the Danforth Conference, we had all but abandoned our original view of the United States as the champion of democracy, justice and freedom. We had learned independently that after World War II, the CIA repeatedly engineered regime-changing coup-d'états against democratically elected governments in the Third World for the purpose of advancing U.S. economic gains and strategic dominance. In those countries where the CIA was successful, it established puppet governments that were corrupt, inept, autocratic and dependent on American aid. The toppling of the Iranian government of Mohammad Mosaddegh and the Guatemala presidency of Jacobo Árbenz during the 1950s stood out as two of the most egregious examples, although Keith and I didn't learn about those facts until the early 1960s.

In 1954, the U.S. ousted Jacobo Árbenz, the democratically elected President of Guatemala, because he espoused socialism and tried to nationalize Guatemala's meager resources, the mainstay of which consisted of the banana plantations, a single highway and a single harbor, all of which belonged to the United Fruit Company of America. Beyond Guatemala, the United Fruit Company also monopolized the banana plantations in other Central American countries. (The Chiquita brand of bananas, ubiquitous in American supermarkets today, are renamed from the United Fruit brand.) During the 1940s and 1950s, whenever resistance to its grotesque exploitation of the Central American nations arose, whether in the form of plantation workers' protest or strike, the United Fruit Company bribed or paid the corrupt local army or government to quell and stamp out the resistance, often murdering hundreds, if not thousands, of people. One example of the atrocities orchestrated by the United Fruit Company was the massacre of the Columbian banana plantation workers who went on strike demanding a living wage. (The incident is immortalized as the climax of Garcia Márquez's celebrated novel, *One Hundred Years of Solitude*.)

After Jacobo Árbenz was elected by an overwhelming majority of Guatemalans, he instituted a program of agrarian reform to redistribute land to poor agricultural laborers while seeking negotiations with the United Fruit Company in his attempt to reclaim what belonged to Guatemala. Immediately, the CIA and the State Department orchestrated a coup d'état to oust him. At the time, Allen Dulles, the Director of CIA, and his brother, John F. Dulles, the Secretary of State, were two of the most senior and influential cabinet members of the U.S. government. They had a long history of association with the United Fruit Company before becoming Dwight Eisenhower's cabinet secretaries.

Since the CIA coup against the popularly elected Árbenz, Guatemala has been plagued by a series of incompetent, corrupt dictatorships. Paramilitary death squads have murdered countless students and Mayan villagers over half a century. Today, Guatemala remains a dangerous and politically unstable country.

When Keith and I delved into America's dirty tricks in Iran, we didn't need to dig into the U.S. Congressional records or consult Noam Chomsky's exposé of illicit American foreign policies to understand that the Iranian situation revolved around the strategically important commodity of petroleum.

Mohammad Mosaddegh, the popularly elected prime minister of Iran from 1951-1953, appeared to be a threat to American and British oil companies, which controlled access to Iran's petroleum reserve, because he was leaning toward nationalizing Iran's oil fields. Iranian oil belonged to Iran. It was and remains under the ground in Iranian territory, not in U.S. or British territories. If a popularly elected government of Iran wished to nationalize its own petroleum resources, no matter how unpleasant it might be for Chevron and British Petroleum, it was a choice to which Iran was entitled. Of course, Chevron, British Petroleum and other oil companies, which had invested in developing the Iranian oil field, deserved compensation in case of nationalization. But the U.S. response to the Iranian attempt at nationalizing its oil industry was to have the CIA orchestrate a coup against the Mosaddegh government in 1953 and install the Shah as a puppet autocrat who was unfit to govern and, later in his years, proved to be delusional. Under the Shah, U.S. and British oil companies were able to continue monopolizing the extraction of Iranian oil.

In addition to CIA-implemented regime changes among Third World countries after World War II, the United States maintained a policy of supporting dictatorships in many nations in exchange for the protection of American interests. Most of those dictatorships involved corrupt military strongmen who plundered their own countries and murdered their own citizens. Propped up by American military and economic aid, those dictators ranged from Ferdinand Marcos in the Philippines, Park Chung Hee of South Korea, to Suharto of Indonesia and Manuel Noriega of Panama.

I could never forget a wealthy Iranian student at Stanford in 1965, notorious for ostentatiously gunning his expensive sports car around campus. He boasted that he could kill anyone in Tehran with impunity, as if killing people were a casual recreational activity he indulged in periodically, because his father was a powerful general in the Shah's secret police, the Savak, established and sustained with the advice and guidance of the CIA.

One month after Keith and I returned to Stanford from the Danforth Conference in 1964, the U.S. government dramatically escalated its military intervention in the war between the "Viet Cong" and the South Vietnam government. Many people were alarmed by the policy of President Lyndon B. Johnson. On campus, Keith and I met at the Tresidder Union most afternoons to discuss political issues and current affairs in the world. The war in Vietnam was a recurring topic. Our discussions galvanized a group of like-minded people: Anatole, Rudy, Francelle, Jim, Ira, Pinkus, Risco, Morty and others. Several of them became my close friends.

Besides our concern with the Vietnam conflict, all of us found the Marxian utopia of equality, freedom and justice appealing. We had lost faith in capitalism.

But there was a hitch to our youthful romantic yearning for Marxian utopia. The two major countries where Marxist revolutions occurred were both totalitarian. They were the Soviet Union and China. As much as we wished for Marxian utopia to be the ultimate goal of evolving political systems in human society, we did not support totalitarianism.

We were aware of Stalin's atrocities and his reign of terror in the Soviet Union. All of us had read Issac Deutscher's multi-volume biographies of Trotsky and Stalin. But we dismissed Stalinism as a Marxist experiment gone awry. In our view, the pursuit of the utopian dream shouldn't be abandoned because of the crimes of Joseph Stalin supported by his lackeys in the Soviet politburo.

I need to digress momentarily from my narrative to point out that it was easy for me, being far away from Stalin in time and space, to dismiss his politburo members as lackeys. A little vignette amplifies my point:

In 1956, during the 20th Congress of the Communist Party of the Soviet Union, the Soviet leader Nikita Khrushchev gave an epoch-changing speech, denouncing Stalin's reign of terror and ushering in a new era of moderated government control of the population in the Soviet Union. After his speech, Khrushchev allowed a question-and-answer session. Staff members of the 20th Congress collected written questions from the delegates and read them out loud one by one for Khrushchev to answer.

One question jolted the Congress and stunned Khrushchev as a staff member read it aloud:

"Secretary General Khrushchev, why did you obediently carry out Stalin's criminal orders during the past twenty years?"

Khrushchev stared at the delegates with steely eyes, bit his lip, and barked into the microphone, "Who asked this question?"

There was no response. The Congress was silent.

Khrushchev leaned into the microphone, ponded the lectern, and screamed, "Who asked this question? Raise your hand!"

The hundreds of delegates sat rigidly in their seats, their faces contorted with fear. Nobody moved. The silence in the cavernous Kremlin Hall was deafening.

In the midst of unbearable tension, foreshadowing cataclysm, suddenly and unexpectedly, Khrushchev switched his angry face into a benevolent smile, and said gently, "Now you understand why I did not disobey Stalin's criminal orders."

This story is hearsay from a friend who happened to be studying rocket science in Moscow at the time. Since he was not at the Congress, I cannot vouch for its veracity. But it should enlighten those who instinctively condemn or seek vengeance from people who have been complicit in a political regime deemed immoral or criminal.

As for the other major totalitarian communist power, China, which professed to uphold Marxism, I had experienced some of the consequences of Chairman Mao's folly and mayhem. But none of my friends, including Keith, shared my disillusion with Mao's China. On the contrary, most of them admired Mao as a visionary leader serving the people of China and striving to build a society free of inequality and capitalistic exploitation. At the time, China was in the throes of Mao's Cultural Revolution, which claimed hundreds of thousands of victims and destroyed China's economy.

I thought those American Mao worshippers were fools, not knowing what they didn't know.

They thought my condemnation of Mao stemmed from my inability to come to terms with the rejection I suffered in China in 1958.

Throughout the 1960s, the standing of Mao and the assessment of the political system in China constituted a major schism between me and the other antiwar activists. Even though I was the minority of one, neither side compromised. Fortunately, China was not at the center of our political concern, and the schism did not cause a ripple among the Stanford activists. At the time, it surprised me that Keith didn't side with me in the dispute. I had thought of him as a Chinese because of his identity in Jamaica. But I was wrong. During the three years at Stanford when he and I were close friends and fellow dissidents, he never mentioned his Chinese identity, except at the Danforth Conference in Asilomar when we first met. To faculty, students, fellow antiwar demonstrators and other citizens at Stanford, Palo Alto and Berkeley, Keith was always a Black man from Jamaica with an Anglo name, Keith Lowe.

Our diametrically opposite opinions of Mao still loomed large forty-some years later when I visited Keith in Toronto. By then, his private and public persona had transformed from a Black American into a Chinese Canadian. We fell into a long and heated argument about the merit vs. evil of Chairman Mao. Long after the atrocities, mayhem and enormous death toll of Mao's mass campaigns, such as the Great Leap Forward Movement and the Cultural Revolution, had come to light in the West, and in spite of the tacit acknowledgment of Mao's "mistakes" by the Communist Party of China, Keith continued to put Mao on a pedestal as a great proletarian revolutionary. We argued passionately. But he was irrevocably entrenched in Mao's merit while I was thoroughly convinced of Mao's evil.

Keith fired his final volley in our debate. "I'm not the only one who considers Mao a great revolutionary. He has admirers all over the world."

"Yes, I know," I retorted. "It is easy to be a Maoist if you have never lived in Mao's China!"

The Toronto argument did not dent our friendship. But it revealed a chink in Keith's rationality: He held certain beliefs, which, in one way or another, were connected to his identity, and those beliefs, like religious canons, were inviolate.

When we held up the Marxian utopia as our social and political dream in the sixties, I wondered how Keith reconciled his Catholic faith with his Marxist belief. The two systems of faith were diametrically opposed to each other. After all, Marx had put it in black and white that religion was the opiate of the people, not to mention that the cornerstone of Marxism is materialism, whereas religious faith is all about spiritualism. After our Toronto reunion, I came to understand that Keith would never question his own beliefs. If those beliefs were contradictory, he would sequester them in different compartments of his mental world.

In later years, as I tamed my impetuosity and grew intellectually, I woke up to the fact that my subscription to the Marxian utopia in my twenties was also a blind belief, not unlike Keith's religious faith. During the early 1960s, I castigated my fellow radicals as fools not knowing what they didn't know for their admiration of Chairman Mao. By the late 1970s I realized that I was as much a fool in my belief of the Marxian utopia as they were in their belief that Mao was a great revolutionary. I was unaware of my ignorance about human nature and the human condition.

The Marxian utopia presupposed perfect or near-perfect human beings, even though Marx and his followers had never explicitly stated that presupposition. In reality, all human beings, plagued by a deeply entrenched potential for greed, avarice, fear, aggression, not to mention a strong penchant for revenge, are far from morally perfect. The Marxist ideal of "taking what you need and giving what you can" amounted to an empty dream, appealing but unrealistic. After I learned more about Greek mythology in the 1970s, I even doubted the originality of the Marxian utopia because of its resemblance to the Golden Age of harmony and prosperity told by Hesiod. A major difference between the two idealistic constructs is that Hesiod's Golden Age was ruled by the god Kronos, whereas god was anathema to Karl Marx. But in Hesiod's time (7th to 8th century B.C.), people believed that gods presided over everything and all human affairs. It would make sense that Hesiod had a god for each of his "Ages."

Worse and more alarming than human imperfection, which made Marxism an empty dream, a normal person can become evil in certain political, social and economic contexts. In short, a socio-political circumstance can induce, lead, even coerce people into any direction of the moral compass, often without their awareness. One may be a perfectly normal human being while living in one socio-political context, only to become villainous or evil in a different context. A well-known experiment conducted at Stanford University in 1971 on the psychological and emotional states of male graduate students role-playing prisoners and prison guards unexpectedly revealed the fickleness of an individual's moral principles. The experiment had to be aborted prematurely because some of the students playing the role of guards had dangerously veered toward using torture against the students who played the prisoners. The students acting as prison guards allowed themselves to descend into abominable behavior. They defended themselves by claiming they were merely doing their best to play the role and execute their duties, not different from many people who embrace irrationality and believe exclusively in selected facts, lies and misrepresentations that they can use to support their behavior.

The potential for ordinary folks to become evil led Hannah Arendt to her concept of the "banality of evil." She came to the conclusion that Adolf Eichmann, the Nazi organizer/manager of the Holocaust, was merely a mundane, ordinary bureaucrat, unaware of the monstrosity of his work in Nazi Germany. During his trial in Israel, where Arendt was an observer, she concluded that Eichmann was neither a sociopath nor a deranged fanatic. I am not convinced by her conclusion. In her final two books, *The Life of the Mind* and *The Human Condition*, she further compounds this questionable conclusion with the hypothesis that evil comes from a person's inability or failure to think critically. It is debatable, for example, whether the influential philosopher, Martin Heidegger (who was a mentor and lover to Arendt), and the eminent conductor, Herbert von Karajan, should be denounced as evil. But one cannot deny that both Karajan and Heidegger were among many highly educated thinkers who willingly served the Nazi regime in Germany. It matters not that Heidegger and Karajan collaborated with the Nazis in a very different capacity from that of Adolf Eichmann, a mid-level bureaucrat who orchestrated a genocide. They were thinkers who became a part of Hitler's evil empire.

It is true that people who are not well educated and cannot think or reason deeply are more likely to fall prey to the mendacity and manipulation of a cunning propagandist like Joseph Goebbels or a skillful demagogue like Benito Mussolini. It is also true that the same people are more susceptible to the herd mentality, a Homo sapiens propensity with a strong phylogenetic root—our hominid ancestors escaped extinction only by banding together, strengthening their herd mentality after they descended from the relative safety of the forest canopy to Africa's savannas, the habitat of predators much bigger, faster and stronger than hominids. Nevertheless, the capacity for thinking does not offer immunity to evil as Arendt hypothesized. Neither do erudition and the ability to engage in deep thought prevent a person from becoming evil. In the end, I believe the most important defense against encroaching evil, when evil makes its appearance, hinges on the strength of an individual's moral character. That strength is forged by nature as well as nurture during the life span of each individual. There is no evidence to support a generalization about the origin or the source of evil in Homo sapiens. Arendt was barking up the wrong tree.

In a different venue, *The Battle of Algiers*, a dramatic film so realistically constructed that it could be mistaken as a documentary, addressed the complex and thorny issue of good vs. evil during the same period Hannah Arendt was grappling with it.

The film depicts a savage, protracted battle in the city of Algiers between a French paratrooper regiment commanded by Colonel Mathieu, who was a heroic Resistance fighter during World War II, and a secretive underground cell of Algerian National Liberation Front fighters led by Ali La Pointe, who was a former petty criminal. Ali had morphed from a petty criminal into an effective urban guerrilla leader, fighting to liberate his country from French colonialism. His favorite tactic was terrorism against the French civilians, while his archenemy, Mathieu, received a mandate from the French government to destroy the urban guerrillas in the city of Algiers by whatever means he wished to employ—a desperate decision by France in her attempt to hold on to her colonies in the 1950s.

During the battle, Mathieu used torture to extract information from captured Algerian fighters in order to penetrate the secretive organization of the National Liberation Front. Torture turned out to be an effective tactic that ultimately resulted in the killing of Ali as well as the capture of his mentor, a high-level leader of the Algerian National Liberation Front. Ali's mentor died under torture, refusing to yield any information about NLF, as Mathieu and his troops eliminated Ali and his NLF fighters in the city of Algiers. Yet, in Mathieu's press announcement of his triumph over the NLF independence fighters, he paid tribute to Ali's mentor as a brave soldier, a man of principle and integrity, and a heroic, admirable fighter for his cause.

Was Mathieu evil for using torture against the Algerians fighting for the independence of their country, or was he merely a good soldier implementing the wish of the French nation to retain Algeria as a French colony and executing the French government's order to fight a war as effectively as possible?

In a similar vein, one might wonder if Ali La Pointe was a martyr fighting for a noble cause or a petty thief turned terrorist who maimed and killed innocent civilians.

The Battle of Algiers brought into focus the blurry boundary separating good from evil. As diametrically opposed as "good" and "evil" are in theory, they can be difficult to tease apart in real life.

I have digressed from my narrative because the abhorrence of evil was an overwhelmingly important motivation in my life and Keith's life. Both of us found it difficult to understand how human beings, with all of our introspective capability, could become evil. In the 1960s, the ethologist Konrad Lorentz searched for the origin of human aggression and violence, a common manifestation of evil, from the phylogenetic perspective. As in other members of the animal kingdom, competition for resources, territory and reproductive opportunity often engenders aggression and violence among humans. Lorentz suggested that humans had an innate propensity for aggression. In my opinion, humans have compounded, if not enhanced, that innate disposition. With unprecedented brainpower, humans have created ideology and belief to facilitate, promote and justify aggression. In fact, many ideologies and beliefs have become a much more potent source of evil than the competition for resources. Examples abound in human history. One does not need to look beyond the Inquisition, the burning of infidels on stakes, to see the evil potential of an ideology. Ironically, the Inquisition was couched in the name of the merciful, benevolent and all-loving Jesus Christ.

To a large extent, it was our abhorrence of evil that drove Keith and me to become political activists in America during the 1960s. We saw the American persecution of the Vietnam War as evil. We perceived racial discrimination as evil, and we considered gross exploitation of the underprivileged and poor as evil. Our sensitivity was forged during our upbringing in British colonies, even though what we suffered was insignificant in comparison to the discrimination against Jews and Blacks, the plight of Native Americans, the agony of Stalin's prisoners in the gulag, or the sacrifice of the Chinese people during Chairman Mao's campaigns.

In opposing U.S. intervention in South Vietnam, Keith, I and our friends knew that North Vietnam supported the "Viet Cong" and that North Vietnam, under the leadership of Ho Chi Minh, was, in turn, supported by China and the Soviet Union, casting the military conflict in South Vietnam under the shadow of the Cold War. But we had also learned that the division of Vietnam into two countries, North Vietnam and South Vietnam, was a compromise foisted on the Vietnamese people in 1954, after the Vietnamese had defeated the French colonialists in a horrendous independence war that lasted more than seven years in Indochina, the former French colony in Southeast Asia since 1887. The defeat of the French colonialists led to the 1954 Geneva Conference, which carved the former French Indochina into four nations: North Vietnam, South Vietnam, Laos and Cambodia. The creation of Laos and Cambodia was based on historical, ethnic, linguistic and cultural grounds, but the partition of Vietnam into two countries, North Vietnam and South Vietnam, was a political compromise between the opposing superpowers of the Cold War in their quest for spheres of influence. There was no linguistic, cultural, ethnic, historical or economic justification for the partition.

After the partition, North Vietnam, as expected, fell into the communist bloc, while South Vietnam was placed in the orbit of the Western nations. By the early 1960s, the North Vietnam government was an unadulterated communist autocracy, while the South, dependent on military and economic aid from the United States, devolved into a corrupt and inept dictatorship by the Ngo family. At the time, leaders of the U.S. government could only see the conflict between the North and the South Vietnam from the perspective of the Cold War. They refused to recognize that most Vietnamese people viewed the American presence in their country as a continuation of European colonialism. It was true that the American government never intended to turn Vietnam into a colony and, because of that, Americans couldn't understand why the Vietnamese considered them colonialists or neo-colonialists. What the Americans failed to grasp was that the Vietnamese people preferred a Vietnamese autocracy to colonial rule, even though an autocracy might not be the most desirable form of government. In the early 1960s, French colonial brutality and exploitation remained fresh and vivid in the minds of the Vietnamese people, even though they had already won their independence from France. It was their fear and hatred of that primitive and violent kind of colonialism that made the Vietnamese fight so fanatically against American intervention.

Primitive and violent colonialism belongs to an era that ended in the 1960s, when almost all colonies in the Third World had become independent nations. It differed significantly from the cultural colonialism so eloquently expounded by the American-educated Palestinian intellectual, Edward Said, in his book *Orientalism*, a study of how the Western perception of the Eastern world dominated cultural studies, even among indigenous scholars of the Third World. Cultural colonialism outlasted primitive colonialism by decades. In fact, the vestige of cultural colonialism remains alive today in some forms of Eurocentric dominance in cultural studies. Scholarly descriptions and interpretations of social and cultural phenomena in the Third World are typically couched in the perspective of Western civilization, presenting a distorted view and evaluation of human behaviors, social constructs and linguistic structures outside the Western world. An example familiar to me as a linguist is the "completion aspect marker" that appears in most languages of the world, whereas the "past tense

marker" appears only in some languages of the world, most prominently within the family of Indo-European languages.

Because the study of grammar began with scholars of Indo-European languages, grammars of non-Indo-European languages tended
to follow the Indo-European model until the late 20th century. When
early linguists came upon completion aspect markers in languages such
as Chinese, Japanese, Tagalog and hundreds of other languages, they
equated completion aspect with past tense. But completion aspect is
totally different from past tense. The former indicates the completion
of an activity or event, independent of the time of speech. The latter
indicates that an event/activity conveyed by a phrase/sentence occurred
prior to the time of that phrase.

In other words, past tense relies on the time of utterance or speech as
a point of reference. If an activity or event has occurred prior to the time
of utterance/speech, that event or activity will be marked with past tense.

Unlike past tense, the completion aspect marker signaling the completion of an activity or event is independent of the time of utterance.
One can communicate the completion of an event/activity in the past,
present or future. For example, the Chinese phrase:

Ta shao - le fan cai kanshu

S/he cook (Completion Aspect) food then read

signifies the completion of "cooking" before "reading." If the speaker
wishes to provide a time frame for the activities of "cook" and "read,"
time words such as *zotian* (yesterday) or *mingtian* (tomorrow) can be
added to the phrase. For example:

Mingtian ta shao - le fan cai kanshu

Tomorrow s/he cook (Completion Aspect) food then read

This means, "Tomorrow, s/he will read upon finishing cooking."

Because the study of language is dominated by scholars from the Western world, the completion aspect marker is typically interpreted as the past tense. Today, most language textbooks on Chinese, Japanese, Thai, Korean and numerous other languages continue to follow the old Indo-European tradition of equating the completion aspect in those languages with the past tense of Indo-European languages.

When Keith and I criticized American policy in South Vietnam, we were mystified by the strategic decision of the American government. We couldn't see any good reason for America to be involved in a domestic war in South Vietnam. It did not enhance the reputation of the United States; it didn't help the people of Vietnam; it didn't reduce the tension of the Cold War; it was morally and economically ruinous to the United States.

Why would such brilliant presidential advisors as Robert McNamara, Dean Rusk, Maxwell Taylor, McGeorge Bundy, George Ball and Dean Acheson lead President Johnson down a war path in South Vietnam?

The only possible answer we could come up with was that those presidential advisors, having never experienced the pathetic life of a downtrodden colonial subject, couldn't grasp the simple fact that the colonial subjects of the Third World wanted to eradicate generations of colonial rule *AT ALL COST*. They wouldn't hesitate to sacrifice their lives fighting against any colonialists, and they were unified in their desire to expel the colonial overlords from their country.

In addition to that oversight, the Cold War had circumscribed the American perspective and worldview. Since World War II, American leaders considered every conflict in the world as part of the global Cold War between the Communist nations as a unified, inseparable block and the Western alliance of democracies. They ignored the strategic and political significance of the historical antagonism between Vietnam and China and ignored the deeply rooted distrust between the Soviet Union and Communist China.

Throughout history, the Vietnamese people had fought for their independence from the Chinese, their bigger and more powerful neighbor, who invaded and occupied Vietnam repeatedly. The first Chinese invasion and occupation of Vietnam occurred in 111 B.C., when Emperor Wu of the Han Dynasty conquered Vietnam. The first rebellion against Chinese colonization took place in A.D. 40. That rebellion was led by the celebrated Vietnam heroines, the Trung sisters. They secured Vietnam's independence from China for several decades. As a consequence, the Trung sisters have been revered in Vietnam, North as well as South. They were the symbol of national independence for all Vietnamese. Temples and monuments have been dedicated to them; schools, streets, an entire district in Hanoi are named after them; and a national holiday commemorating their death has been observed throughout the history of Vietnam.

The enshrinement of the Trung sisters as heroes in Vietnam makes it clear that a fierce determination to expel foreign domination, especially a domination of Chinese origin, has always been deeply embedded in the culture and psyche of the Vietnamese people.

American foreign policy makers in the 1950s and 60s paid no attention to this important tradition of Vietnam, a tradition that had a longer history than the struggle of the Finnish people against their more powerful and often invasive neighbor, the Russians. Yet, Western leaders had no difficulty understanding the negative sentiment of Finnish people against the Russians. Winston Churchill and FDR tolerated Finland's alliance with Nazi Germany at the beginning of the Second World War. After World War II, Truman, Eisenhower, Dean Acheson, John F. Dulles never took any hostile action against Finland for her erstwhile alliance with Nazi Germany. They understood that the Finnish-Nazi alliance had the function of expelling the Soviet Union from Finnish territory. Yet, twenty years later, Western leaders refused to take into account the long history of Vietnam's antagonism toward China.

The bad blood between the Soviet Union and China has its roots in the late 19th century, when Czar's Russia and China's Qing (Manchu) Dynasty vied for control of Mongolia as the Qing Dynasty's hold on the

Central Asian steppes weakened. By the mid-20th century, the Chinese resented the Soviet Union for incorporating the Republic of Mongolia into its sphere of dominance. Even today, China continues to refer to what is now the Republic of Mongolia as "Outer Mongolia," hinting that it ought to belong to China because "Inner Mongolia" designates a Chinese province.

In addition to the conflict stemming from control and influence over Mongolia, Chinese leaders and Chinese people harbored a serious grudge against the Soviet Union. That grudge began when Chairman Mao traveled to Moscow, shortly after the founding of the People's Republic of China, the only foreign trip Mao had ever taken. As the founder of a newly established communist country, he had high hopes that the Soviet Union would renounce the claim on a vast territory in southeastern Siberia that the Czarist Russia acquired through an unequal treaty with the Qing Dynasty in 1860, shortly after Qing was defeated in the Opium War against Britain. That territory was the Maritime Province, including the city of Vladivostok and the Sakhalin island. Chairman Mao and his colleagues naively expected that the Soviet Union would be, at a minimum, amenable to some sort of compromise settlement as a gesture of goodwill among two sibling communist countries. But they were dead wrong. Stalin refused to discuss the issue with the Chairman. The Chinese leadership was taken aback by Stalin's uncompromising stance. Thus, the alliance between China and the Soviet Union under the banner of communism was fraught with animosity and mistrust from the very beginning. Over time, the relationship between the two communist regimes worsened and deteriorated into a so-called ideological dispute in the late 1950s. By 1961, the ideological dispute erupted into a border war along the Amu River. It was obvious that the alliance between the Soviet Union and China on the international stage was, to a large extent, forced on them by American hostility.

After the unrealistic partition of Vietnam by the great powers of the world and the subsequent effort of North Vietnam to undermine the corrupt government of the South, American political leaders insisted on seeing the conflict between North Vietnam and South Vietnam through the lens of the Cold War, sweeping aside the history of antagonism between Vietnam and China as well as the Sino-Soviet split. Believing that all communist countries were united to vanquish the Western democracies, American strategists viewed the world like frogs dwelling in a deep well. With its eyes located on top of its head, a frog living in a well can only see a small patch of sky through the well's opening. The tunnel vision of American foreign policy experts unwittingly helped to strengthen the alliance between the communist countries.

By spring 1964, Keith and I decided to take direct action against the U.S. involvement in Vietnam. We felt the United States' action in Vietnam did not differ from what it had done in many other Third World countries, propping up inept and corrupt regimes against the wish of the majority of the native population. We also felt that it was time to expose the hypocrisy of proclaiming America to be the champion of freedom and democracy. Instead of staying on the moral high ground, the richest and most powerful nation seemed determined to implement a form of neo-colonialism to dominate and control Third World nations through subterfuge and outright military intervention. Vietnam was a prime example.

But protest against the Vietnam War in early 1964 was not popular in America. Most Americans didn't even know that the United States was slowly getting mired in a brutal war in Vietnam.

With the collaboration of many other left-leaning dissidents at Stanford, we became active in two organizations: The Stanford Committee for Peace in Vietnam, established by David Ransom, and the newly founded chapter of the Students for Democratic Society (SDS) at Stanford. SDS began at the University of Michigan in 1960. We admired SDS's 1962 political manifesto, the *Port Huron Statement*, which criticized U.S. foreign policy, condemned racism within the United States, and urged fundamental reform of the operation of business corporations that polarized the distribution of wealth in the nation.

Following the example of the student activists at University of Michigan, David Ransom, Keith and the activists from those two organizations staged a teach-in on campus to disseminate information about America's unethical and impractical policy of sustaining the government in South Vietnam. The teach-in did not draw a large crowd. But it was a good clarion call.

In the end, the driving force that grew the antiwar sentiment among the people at Stanford and its neighborhood was not the teach-in and protests organized by a few dozen dissidents. It was the unceasing escalation of American military intervention and the growing casualties among American soldiers fighting a guerrilla war against an enemy supported by the majority of Vietnamese.

Originally, the American military was advising and assisting the South Vietnamese army, a policy formulated during John Kennedy's presidency. But the role of U.S. forces in South Vietnam expanded steadily due to the ineptitude of the South Vietnamese government and the determination of Vietnamese people to resist foreign domination. By late 1964, the American military was the main fighting force on the ground. Ground forces needed air support, and air support led to the bombing of rural civilians and the defoliation of jungles with the toxic chemical Agent Orange. The American military then succeeded in persuading President Lyndon Johnson to take the war to North Vietnam, because it was the source of supplies and fighters for the Vietnam Liberation Front (Viet Cong) in the South. In order to win the support of Congress and the American people for bombing North Vietnam, President Johnson, in late 1964, accused North Vietnam of attacking American warships in the Gulf of Tonkin without provocation. Gunfire was exchanged between warships of the two sides in the Gulf. What really happened remained murky. There were serious questions about the version of the Gulf of Tonkin incident presented by the U.S. government to Congress and the American public.

The expanding and intensifying war began to have an impact on life everywhere in America as more and more young Americans were drafted into the army and sent to Vietnam. Many of them perished there for reasons that they, their families and friends couldn't fathom.

By 1965, while the war was slipping into a grisly quagmire, President Lyndon Johnson insisted on a face-saving "victory." He was the leader of the free world, and fighting the Vietnamese to a stalemate would, in his mind, shatter the image of the United States as the most powerful nation. Although he began to see that an ultimate communist takeover in Vietnam might be inevitable, he wanted a short-term military victory by sending more and more American troops to fight in Vietnam. But American military victory was never a possibility, because the Vietnamese would endure any hardship, any deprivation and any sacrifice to drive out the Americans.

In lockstep with the U.S. escalation of its war effort in Vietnam, the antiwar movement took off, winning more and more popular support in America.

I remember the first demonstration the Stanford activists staged in the Town and Country shopping center of Palo Alto in the spring of 1964. It hardly roused any interest among the shoppers. Around fifteen Stanford dissidents walked in a small circle, with raised placards denouncing U.S. intervention in Vietnam, at a corner where Embarcadero Street intersected El Camino Real. We chose that corner because it appeared to be the most visible spot for shoppers and drivers in a town with few pedestrians. We also tried to pass out information leaflets explaining the reasons for our action. It was a one-hour, midday demonstration. The city of Palo Alto had officially approved our application to stage it at the specified location. The only memorable event of the demonstration was that a Palo Alto police car drove by and a policeman sitting inside tossed two bags of horse dung at us.

One year later, in 1965, President Johnson authorized Operation Rolling Thunder to deliver saturated bombing in the dense tropical jungle along the Ho Chi Min trail in Laos and Cambodia, a supply line from North Vietnam to the South Vietnam insurgents. The number of American soldiers fighting in South Vietnam surged toward two hundred thousand—it ultimately exceeded half a million. The demonstrations organized by the Stanford activists in Palo Alto began to attract hundreds of participants from all walks of life.

In one year, the escalation of the American war effort increased the number of participants in our antiwar demonstrations by ten to twenty-fold.

More heartening than the steady growth of popular support of our antiwar protest was the presence of veterans in rallies and marches. By spring of 1965, fresh from their tours of duty in Vietnam, they began to show up in demonstrations at Stanford and elsewhere. Dressed in military fatigues, some on crutches after having lost a leg to improvised explosive devices (I.E.D.), some in wheelchairs because of devastating injuries, they recounted their harrowing experience of fighting in remote jungles, unfamiliar paddy fields and hostile villages. They were the most persuasive voices conveying the futility of American intervention in Vietnam, which was clearly, as Keith and I had long ago suspected, to the detriment of U.S. interests.

"On the basis of my experience battling the Viet Cong, it's obvious that we don't have the support of the Vietnamese people." One veteran, whose name I did not record in my journal, articulated his opposition to the war in simple words at a demonstration on Stanford campus. "Our military intervention in Vietnam is foolish and doomed. What will determine the outcome of the war is not who triumphs on the battlefield, but who wins the heart of the Vietnam people. Imagine yourself as an apolitical and uneducated Vietnamese peasant, eking out a living on a small plot of land without any ideological convictions. You have never heard of such highfalutin concepts as democracy or capitalism, and you couldn't care less about them. Preoccupied with survival, you barely grow enough food to have a roof over your head and keep your family alive. One day, while working in your paddy field with your son and daughter, you are startled by several deafening helicopters descending from the sky onto your rice paddy field, ruining your crops for the season and disgorging scores of heavily armed American soldiers. Your young son and daughter, frightened and disoriented, start running back toward your village. Then, a burst of automatic gunfire, and your children lie dead in pools of blood."

The veteran paused for a moment. Then he asked, "What would you do? Yes, what would you do? Wouldn't you join the Viet Cong and fight against the invaders with fury and determination? Wouldn't you accept wholeheartedly Viet Cong's ideological propaganda, whatever that might be?"

"Well," he continued, "that, in a nutshell, is what the American G.I.s face in Vietnam! There is no hope and there is no end, unless we, the people of America, end it!"

It was the most stirring antiwar speech I had heard. Contrary to the belief of those brilliant American policy makers, the Vietnam War was not a war between democracy and communism. It was not an extension of the conflict between the Communist bloc and the Western Alliance. It was a war between the Vietnamese people that no longer wished to submit to colonialism and an American juggernaut who unwittingly took on the role of a neocolonialist.

Along with demonstrations and teach-ins, Keith, I and other activists at Stanford University organized a "free university" in Palo Alto and Berkeley, where we held discussions on topics such as the Non-Aligned Movement, the history of Vietnam, Frantz Fanon, Patrice Lumumba, Sukarno's Guided Democracy in Indonesia, neo-colonialism and U.S. foreign policy, and theory and reality of socialism, offering information and analyses rarely found in the curriculum of American universities. Each course met once a week for ten weeks. The course instructors prepared a list of readings, which could be augmented at the suggestion of anyone who attended the class. They served as moderators of the weekly meeting that took place in some volunteer's living room.

In the class on Patrice Lumumba taught by Keith, most participants had never heard of Lumumba, the first prime minister of the Republic of Congo. He was assassinated in 1961 with the complicity of Belgium, which ruled Congo as a colony from 1908 until it became an independent country under the leadership of Lumumba in 1960. Prior to 1908, Belgium Congo belonged to King Leopold II of Belgium. It was his personal property for more than two decades. During those two decades, his agents plundered the area with unprecedented rapacity, looting everything of value and exterminating people as well as wildlife who stood in their way.

Leopold II never fought a war to conquer the tribes and ethnic groups in Congo. He did not negotiate with any African agency, organization or governing entity or obtain permission from any African nation in claiming ownership of Congo. Nor did he purchase the land from anyone. He simply laid claim to this enormous region with the geographical information provided to him by Henry Morton Stanley, a Welsh explorer financed by Leopold in search of the source of the Nile. (Stanley also coined the term "Dark Continent" for Africa.) Even more brazen than Leopold's audacious act, the colonial nations of Europe "authorized" his claim. That "authorization" was a chilling demonstration of how Europe's ruling class at the time viewed Africa and Asia. From their perspective, the billions of people and the multitudes of cultures in those two largest continents of the world were not only irrelevant and expendable, but also constituted a God-given largess for Europeans to enslave and plunder.

The Belgian Congo that Leopold II arbitrarily claimed as his personal property covered more than nine hundred thousand square miles of land with more than 16 million inhabitants. It is more than three times the area of Texas.

It was in this "free university" class that I learned of the provincial and insular nature of America and most Americans. Many members attending the class couldn't identify Congo on a map of Africa. They pointed out in class discussions that most Americans were not interested in the affairs of the world outside of the United States. To bring into focus the insular mentality of most Americans at the time, one member of the class cited a study conducted by the Department of War during World War II. The study revealed that, as America was waging a bloody war against Japan in the Pacific Ocean, battling fanatic Japanese soldiers from island to island, more than 60% of Americans didn't know where Japan was located on a world map.

The opposite of America's insular attitude was the Chinese Communist Party's edict during the 1950s that all Chinese had to learn the censored international news delivered on a weekly basis by the government propaganda machine. (The Chinese government maintained a Ministry, blatantly named Ministry of Propaganda, in those days.) I still remember an utterly esoteric piece of information I had to learn in 1957 that had no relevance to my life whatsoever: The people of the province of Kerala on the southwestern coast of India elected a communist government that year. (Until that time, I had never heard of the province of Kerala in Southern India.)

In organizing the two free universities, Keith and I strove to bring forth political and cultural information about Third World countries that rarely reached the general public, including the antiwar protestors. Our effort endured a little longer than one year. One year later, the participants of the free universities voted us out of the steering committee and installed courses like "The Alternative Universe," "Psychedelic Explorations," "Timothy Leary and his View of Life" instead of the ones we thought were relevant to a better understanding of the geopolitical world. We were deeply disappointed.

Keith and I never took part in the drug culture that became popular among young Americans as the antiwar activities intensified. We also never discussed other people's desire for LSD, marijuana and other hallucinogens. Coming from an upbringing in which even alcoholic beverages were taboo, I was scared to death of mind-altering drugs. My brain had been the strength and the inviolate final resort in my struggle for survival. I would never mess around with it.

But I didn't condemn people who used drugs. At the same time, I didn't care to find out why they were attracted to mind-altering substances. Some of them told me that drugs served as an escape hatch, allowing them to transcend the world that upset them. That sounded to me like a lame excuse for surrender in the face of hardship. But I kept my opinion to myself, because I didn't wish to antagonize my friends and fellow activists. It was a bit of déjà vu from my life at Kappa Sigma fraternity at Bowdoin college, which at that time had begun to fade from my thought.

On the personal side, the free university affirmed my desire to pursue a career as a teacher and scholar. Teaching brought up issues and questions that I could not have thought of by myself. Those issues and questions drove me to seek new knowledge. Most importantly, continuous learning made me feel that I was doing something worthwhile. Even though the free universities of Keith's and my design lasted only one year in Palo Alto and Berkeley, they were a valuable experience.

By spring, 1966, antiwar protests occurred regularly on university campuses and the streets of many cities all over the country. The size of the demonstrations grew by the week, and their composition became increasingly diverse. At the beginning, in 1964, protestors were primarily college students. Now, there were "Mothers Against the War," who showed up in demonstrations with their babies in strollers; "Veterans Against the War" often in their military fatigues; "Faculty and Teachers Against the War," who tended to be clean-shaven and over thirty years of age; "Longshoremen Against the War," "United Auto Workers Against the War," "Plumbers Against the War," and so on . . .

Many demonstrations were peaceful. Many ended in violent confrontations between the police and the protestors. In those confrontations, some protestors threw rocks. But the law enforcement officials often engaged in extreme, egregious violence. In the end, the over-zealous response of law-enforcement officers against protestors led to the shooting of thirteen unarmed students (four dead, nine seriously wounded) by the Ohio National Guard at Kent State University on May 4, 1970, and, ten days later, the shooting of another fourteen peaceful protesting students (two dead, twelve wounded) at Jackson State University by the police of Jacksonville, Mississippi. Richard Nixon, who ascended to the presidency in 1968, encouraged violence against student protestors, publicly calling them "bums." He rewarded a right-wing local hardhat union boss in New York, Peter J. Brennan, with the U.S. Secretary of Labor cabinet post for organizing a violent attack against a crowd who declared their solidarity with the Kent State victims in downtown Manhattan. During the melee, the hardhat union members inflicted severe injury on scores of peaceful antiwar protestors.

In the Bay Area, the most violent and notorious segments of the law enforcement force were the Blue Meanies of the Alameda County Sheriff and the Tactical Squad of San Francisco Police. The Blue Meanies always wore light blue overalls. Members of the San Francisco Tactical Squad, equipped with face masks, helmets, leather gloves, high boots, bulletproof vests and weapons, appeared in pitch-black uniforms. They all looked like Darth Vader, minus his flowing cape. Both Meanies and Tact Squad members were large, barrel-chested males who couldn't wait for an order from their commander to charge the demonstrators. They relished and savored the assignment to inflict physical harm.

When they charged antiwar protestors, the Blue Meanies swung extra-long, lead-laden truncheons to bludgeon anyone who happened to be in their path; members of the SF Tact Squad wielded long, hardwood swords carved in the form of the signature weapon of Japanese samurai, sharp on one side of the wedge. The lead-laden truncheon could inflict life-threatening damage on a victim's head. But the curved hardwood sword was a much more vicious weapon. One sweeping blow on a limb would break a femur or an ulnar. If the blow hit the torso, it would inflict serious internal injury.

Many nonviolent marchers received a bloody beating at the hands of the Blue Meanies and Tact Squad members. One of my friends sustained a ruptured spleen after a Tact Squad member hit her with the hardwood samurai sword. She had to have her spleen removed in an emergency operation and was hospitalized for more than one week.

In an emotional meeting between the Stanford activists and the Berkeley activists on the issue of strategy in our antiwar protests, many participants broke down in tears when they recounted how members of the Tact Squad and the Blue Meanies broke their limbs, split their scalps, knocked their teeth out, and stomped on them even after they had collapsed in pain.

Keith, I and other activists from Stanford drove to Berkeley most days to support our fellow protestors there in 1965 and 1966. At mid-day, people gathered at Sproul Plaza on the south side of campus, where speakers railed against U.S. atrocity in Vietnam, many bearing personal grudges against the Blue Meanies and the Tact Squad. After the speeches, protesters began to march from Sproul Plaza southward about two hundred meters to Telegraph Avenue, an avenue filled with stores and eateries abutting the campus. There, the demonstration inevitably morphed into a tense, angry confrontation between the protestors and the goon squads. The confrontation soon became a pitched battle between sworn enemies.

Each side sought revenge as if they were two opposing tribes with a long history of grudges and hostility against each other in the highland of Papua New Guinea. The antiwar chant, the tension in the air, the ebb and flow of the two hostile groups on Telegraph Avenue resembled the Papuan warriors fighting against each other in their arena, an open space in the rainforest not belonging to either of the warring hamlets. One such battle was captured in the celebrated documentary film, Dead Birds, made by a team of anthropologists led by Robert Gardner of Harvard University's Peabody Museum.

Whereas the Papuan tribal battle was fought by two tribes equally armed with spears, bow and arrow, the confrontations on Telegraph Avenue told a vastly different story:

One side consisted of a ragtag crowd, chanting antiwar slogans, carrying placards denouncing American atrocity in Vietnam. Many looked physically unfit, with legs like stilts, arms like broomsticks. Wearing grungy clothing, many sported long hair and unkempt beards. Some wrapped handkerchiefs around their nose and mouth in preparation to ward off tear gas. Some had a small peace sign painted on their fore-heads. Those who sported a large iridescent peace sign on the back of their denim jackets reminded me of the soldiers of the Chinese Boxer Rebellion at the fin-de-siècle, who wore traditional Chinese Boxer jack-ets adorned with a bright red disk at the front. Following the Empress Dowager of the Manchu imperial family, the Boxers bought the lies of a charlatan who claimed that the painted red disk on their jacket, rein-forced by his secret mantra, would render their chest bulletproof. When the Boxers faced the Joint Expedition Force of Europe and America, the red disks became the God-sent targets for the Expedition soldiers, and the Boxers were slaughtered like ants.

The other side of the confrontation on Telegraph Avenue looked like a modern infantry platoon, loaded with equipment and weapons, usu-ally in wedge formation. Each member of the platoon in the front line held a transparent plastic shield, shoulder high, to protect them from projectiles. Some of the policemen behind the front line held teargas guns that looked like sawed-off bazookas. Most of the police in those confrontations resembled former amateur weightlifters or aspiring foot-ball players who had gained weight as they advanced in age. Their torso and limbs bulged in their uniforms, muscles rippling under a layer of fat.

At the beginning of each battle, a neutral zone about half a block deep separated the two sides somewhere along Telegraph Avenue. The demonstrators, halting at the neutral zone, chanted the usual antiwar slogans. The police, holding their line, stood in silence with hands on their weapons.

At some point, a captain of the police began to order the protestors to disperse. Speaking through a bullhorn, he typically announced:

"This is a thoroughfare. You are blocking traffic. If you don't stay on the sidewalk, we will commence actions to arrest you."

The antiwar demonstrators reacted by shouting insults and calumny, all anger and fury.

"Down with the pigs!"

"Fascists!"

"Fuck you!"

"Go to hell!"

As soon as some protestors lobbed bottles and garbage in the direction of the police, Telegraph Avenue began to reverberate with the sound of explosions as the police fired teargas canisters at the demonstrators. At this point, most protestors scattered from the street in all directions, like the panicked dispersal of Formicine ants suddenly exposed beneath an overturned rock.

A few daring protestors would pick up the gas-spewing canisters and throw them back at the police. Some rocks and flaming objects might follow. Those projectiles would trigger a charge by the police who held their transparent plastic shields in front of them, raised their wooden swords and batons, ready to exact blood from anyone in their path.

Now the panic dispersal of the protestors morphed into a full-speed running retreat. Those who foolishly sought safety on the sidewalk would receive a solid beating. Some would be handcuffed and taken away for allegedly resisting arrest. Those unfortunate souls were often novices at these "battles." They failed to understand that the initial command of the police captain to stay on the sidewalk was no longer operational as soon as the violence began. When the police charged, the sidewalk was no longer a safe haven. It mattered not to the police that people on the sidewalk might be innocent passers-by who got caught in the melee or sworn pacifists who had never raised a hand against anyone. Those who were arrested would be handcuffed and transported to the Alameda County jail, where they would be forced to lie face-down on the sharp gravel of a parking lot for hours before being processed through the prison bureaucracy.

The psychological impact of those battles on me was dreadful. I slept fitfully every night, haunted by nightmares of being crushed by an enormous boulder, a recurring nightmare that plagued me for years shortly after I arrived in Hong Kong the first time in 1950. It stopped after I graduated from high school. Now it began to haunt me again as violence escalated in the antiwar demonstrations. Sometimes I dreamt of defending myself against a Blue Meanie or a member of the Tact Squad, only to wake up screaming and drenched in sweat. When I was awake, the fear of succumbing to my own emotional need for violent retaliation in the face of an assault was even worse than the fear of being beaten.

The police violence caused some war protestors to question the validity of the nonviolent principle advocated by the organizers. Some had already violated our nonviolent principle by throwing projectiles at the police. Some wanted to further escalate the violence by starting a war against the Tact Squad and the Blue Meanies.

"Why shouldn't we use weapons against them?" one protestor asked in a meeting held at an organizer's Berkeley home.

"Well," the host, a veteran of Berkeley activism, responded with an inscrutable smile. "If we use weapons, whatever they might be, the police will use more powerful weapons, and we'll be killed. From a tactical point of view, we would have committed a foolish mistake. But more important than the tactical choice, if we fight the police with weapons, the news media and people sitting on the sidelines will turn against us. Let's not forget that our goal is to stop the war in Vietnam. We are not trying to start a war against the Blue Meanies and the Tact Squad in America."

"Yes," one participant voiced his approval of our host's admonition. "The Fascists are trying to provoke us into making mistakes so they can justify killing us. Let's not fall into their trap."

After the meeting, as I drove from Berkeley back to Palo Alto with Keith, he asked, "Do you know the guy who brought up the use of weapons?"

"No, I don't know him."

"Hmm," Keith mused, "I wonder if he is a provocateur working for the FBI."

The possibility of having provocateurs among the protestors sent chills down my spine. I had read about the use of provocateurs by the Czar's secret police in Imperial Russia to quell dissent and by the Nazis during their quest for power. I never thought that American authorities would stoop so low as to employ such abominable tactics against antiwar demonstrators.

"Could that be true?" I wondered out loud. "I thought only totalitarian governments use provocateurs. Not the United States."

"You are naïve, Charles!" Keith retorted. "Power does funny things to people's minds. When people feel that their power is being challenged, they might use any means to vanquish or destroy their opponents. The only difference between a democratic government and a totalitarian government is that a democracy has built-in mechanisms, such as a legal system to check and hem in the exercise of power, and a free press that may expose illegal or unethical activities of the authorities. But that doesn't preclude powerful people in a democracy from engaging in unlawful activities against their opponents. Of course, if they do, they know that they are taking the risk of being exposed."

I wasn't convinced by his stated difference between a democratic government and a totalitarian regime, because I felt the exercise of power by the authority, especially in a local situation, could easily get out of hand.

Before I voiced my objection, he continued, "In the case of the FBI, if an agent employs provocateurs to incite antiwar demonstrators to riot, so that law enforcement agents could arrest and prosecute them, I don't think such an agent would face any retribution. The chief of the FBI, J. Edgar Hoover, will not hesitate to use any means, legal or illegal, against people he considers communists. In fact, I'm sure there are FBI informants everywhere around us, even in the Berkley and Stanford chapters of SDS."

"That sounds like China's approach to any citizen who happens to be labeled a counterrevolutionary, with or without evidence," I said dreamily.

The thought of U.S. suppression of political dissent with vile tactics unsettled me. I had learned in Hong Kong and subsequently at Bowdoin College that the U.S. Constitution guaranteed freedom of speech. Had I constructed an imaginary America that didn't exist?

"Well," Keith jolted me from my thoughts, "in America, 'communist' is a pejorative word designating any evil, undesirable person who deserves to be destroyed. It's become a convenient tag for some politicians to pin on any person they wish to get rid of. I bet, in J. Edgar Hoover's view, you and I are communists."

Keith was agitated once he brought up J. Edgar Hoover.

"Yes, power spurs people to commit evil in their quest for more power," he went on. "Sometimes, evil can also help unscrupulous politicians accrue power. Joe McCarthy was a good example. Simply by pinning the label 'communist' on anyone who might thwart his political ambition, he cowed his colleagues in the U.S. Senate and corralled immense power, until, carried away by his success, he took on the institution of the U.S. Army and tried to destroy it."

Keith's words instilled fear in me because I began to suspect that he and I could very well be the targets of a conspiracy designed by some zealous government agents. When I drove back to my apartment after depositing Keith at his place in Palo Alto, I began to have a premonition that there would be serious trouble ahead.

Not long after Keith and I started our antiwar activities, Keith became a spokesman and leader of the dissidents at Stanford. Unflappable and articulate, he did not advocate violence, nor did he demonstrate any hostility toward an institution or individual. He was always patient, projecting a willingness to listen, negotiate and take a rational approach to issues at stake. Arguing from the premise of economic egalitarianism, he presented the views and positions of the Stanford dissidents to the public with reasons buttressed by logic and empirical facts. Academics appreciated him. Professors and university administrators knew that they could always have a dialogue with him.

I admired Keith's measured and methodical approach to all problems in all situations. I did not have that quality. Impetuosity was part of my DNA. There was nothing that I wanted more than to overcome it. Yet no matter how hard I tried to emulate Keith, I was never fully successful.

In a press conference announcing the formation of the Committee on Medical Aid for the Vietnam National Liberation Front on Stanford Campus, one journalist asked Keith, "Mr. Lowe, did you establish the Medical Aid Committee to provide support to the Viet Cong?"

"I am one of many people who took part in establishing the Medical Aid Committee after some soul-searching deliberation among us," Keith answered. With an impish smile, he continued speaking at his usual snail-like pace, syllable by syllable, "I wish you wouldn't use the term 'Viet Cong' to refer to fighters of the Vietnam National Liberation Front. In Vietnamese, Viet Cong is an acronym for "Communist Traitor of Vietnam." They may be communists. But if you consider them traitors of their own country, you are presupposing the legitimacy of the Ngo Dinh Diem regime and its successors currently headed by General Minh, who, a little more than one year ago, led a military coup with the tacit support of the United States, and murdered Ngo Dinh Diem and his brother Ngo Dinh Nhu."

The journalist who queried Keith did not try to conceal his antagonism as he carried on with his next question, "How can you, in good conscience, justify your support of the Viet Cong? The United States is at war with them."

Annoyed with the journalist's insistence on using the derogatory term, "Viet Cong," Keith stared at him for a split second before firing his riposte.

"The United States Congress has not declared war against Vietnam, has it? Neither has President Lyndon Baines Johnson, has he?"

He paused for a moment to let his rejoinder sink in. Then he continued, "That is a separate issue. We can parse it another time. As for your challenge about my conscience, let me just say this." With a raised voice, he intoned, slowly, "A WOUNDED MAN IS A WOUNDED MAN, and a wounded man deserves medical attention. Even a wounded enemy soldier, left behind on a battlefield, gets medical aid from his captors."

The room exploded into applause, and the journalist left in anger.

People who liked Keith interpreted his cautious and measured manner as prudent and thoughtful, a valuable trait, especially in the academic world during the era of protests and demonstrations as emotionally charged university students rebelled against the draft, opposed the Vietnam war, adored Martin Luther King Jr., glorified Cesar Chavez and took direct action against social injustice.

Those who disliked Keith, especially the security agents of the U.S. government, considered his manner an unmistakable sign of a deeply conspiratorial personality. To them, he was a dangerous adversary plotting to undermine the security of the United States. I inferred their view from an FBI agent who was assigned to watch Keith, my roommate, Anatole, and me for several months in 1966.

The agent never strayed more than twenty feet from us when we sat around Tresidder Union shooting the breeze. Tresidder Union was a new, architecturally bland student cafeteria on campus where the antiwar dissidents rendezvoused. On the patio outside the building, most of us would be sipping American coffee if we had money in our pockets, or guzzling water if we didn't.

The agent was also "surreptitiously" recording our conversation, as if we were some important conspirators plotting an insurrection. ("Surreptitious" because the tape recorder hidden in the inside pocket of his jacket bulged out.)

One day, I was sitting alone at the Tresidder Union, waiting for my friends to drop by. The agent sat at a table next to me. In a very friendly tone, I asked him why he was monitoring us. He told me that he was merely doing his job.

"We are not criminals and we don't engage in any illegal activity," I pleaded gently. "You and your agency are wasting time and money."

"Well, we will see." He smiled. Then, much to my surprise, he went on to claim that some of my friends were dangerous subversives.

"No, no, no," I protested. "None of us is subverting anything. We have neither the power nor the capability of subverting anything. We don't use incendiary rhetoric, we don't brandish weapons, we are not extremists. In fact, we are peaceniks. Our motto is nonviolent dissention. We protest against the Vietnam War in part because we think it's detrimental to the interest of the United States."

"Perhaps you are, perhaps you aren't," he said. "But some of you are more dangerous than people who advocated armed confrontation against our government. Some of your friends are conspiratorial. They spread Marxism. They may look peaceful, but they are not."

I didn't know whom he was referring to among the dissidents at Stanford. But I suspected Keith was one and my roommate, Anatole, was another.

The government surveillance did not stop with that one FBI agent shadowing us for several months. Letters sent to Keith, me and Anatole were routinely opened and re-sealed sloppily before their delivery, as if the law enforcement agents wanted us to know that they read the letters from our friends and members of our families. The message of the government agents came across clearly:

"We are watching you, and we will pounce on you as soon as we find an excuse."

One day, my roommate Anatole announced that our telephone was bugged. He claimed that he could hear a click, the sound of a recording machine being activated, every time he answered or made a call. Being a prankster, he started the practice of intoning into the phone with a monotonous voice, "Fuck you, fuck you, fuck you. This is a recording," every time he heard a click. In the end, we disconnected our phone.

In April 1966, an FBI agent and an immigration agent kicked down the door of my Palo Alto residence shortly before 6 a.m. and came into my living room with guns in their hands. Anatole, I and another friend, Pepe, were renting the house together. When the noise of the agents crushing the door woke me up, I jumped out of my bed and went to the living room to find out what had happened. In the living room, both the agents and I were stunned.

I was stunned because I couldn't believe the scene in front of my eyes: Two government agents wearing trench coats and holding handguns were facing me in my living room.

"Is this a dream or is this real?" I asked myself.

Those agents were also stunned because they didn't expect a bleary-eyed man without any clothing in front of them.

I rubbed my eyes and said, "Are you going to shoot me, or is this a Humphrey Bogart movie?"

They responded, "We are here to check your legal papers."

After I showed them my Stanford student identity card and my Hong Kong identity card with the U.S. visa, they left. Only then did I feel shaken, realizing that they could have shot me.

Sometimes, the government harassment of dissidents could be comical.

One of our friends, a French national studying African linguistics at Berkeley, attracted the attention of the FBI because he volunteered to teach Swahili, without remuneration, to the Black inmates in the Alameda County jail. The teaching of Swahili was petitioned by the inmates themselves who wished to acquire an African language. Their petition came to the attention of the Linguistics Department of the University of California at Berkeley. In a gesture to help the down-and-out prisoners, our French friend thought he should volunteer as an instructor. His name was Jean-Marie Hombert, pronounced as "Shawn Ma-Ree Om-Bare" in French. Everyone who knew him in Berkeley called him "Shawn Ma-Ree" because that was how he introduced himself. He was not involved in any protest movements.

One day, two young FBI agents showed up at the door of Shawn Ma-Ree's apartment while he was working on campus.

His roommate answered the bell.

One of the agents, in his dark suit, white shirt, nondescript tie, with a serious demeanor and trademark conservative crew cut in an era when most young people in the San Francisco Bay Area kept their hair long, flashed his badge and announced, "We are FBI agents looking for Miss

Jean Mary Hombert, a Negro woman who teaches Swahili to inmates of the Alameda County jail."

To which Shawn Ma-Ree Om-Bare's roommate responded, "She doesn't live here. My roommate is a male."

The agents were mystified and taken aback.

One of them decided to take a crack at the mystery. With a menacing look, he barked, "Are you sure? Our information indicates that she lives here. You're not lying to us, are you?"

The roommate looked the agent straight in the eyes and responded calmly, "Yes, I am sure, and I have no reason to lie to you. My roommate is a WHITE MALE. One-hundred percent white and one-hundred percent male! He happens to be on campus. You might find him in the Linguistics Department in Dwinelle Hall on campus."

The agents didn't appreciate the "one-hundred percent male" comment. They looked at each other and, sensing that Shawn-Ma-Ree's roommate was telling the truth, decided to leave.

A few days after the incident, Shawn Ma-Ree Om-Bare, somewhat concerned that the FBI was looking for him, asked Keith and me, "Why does teaching an African language to jail inmates warrant the FBI's attention?"

I threw my hands up.

Keith muttered, "They are crazy. In their obsession with communists, they see devils everywhere."

In spring of 1966, I decided to abandon mathematics at Stanford and transfer to Berkeley to pursue a Ph.D. degree in linguistics, even though I had been attending mathematics classes for three years and hardly knew anything about linguistics. I had wanted to live in Berkeley ever since I started going there regularly with Keith and other Stanford activists in 1964.

There were good reasons.

Berkeley was the hub of the student antiwar movement and protest. That reputation gave Berkeley a halo effect in the eyes of many political activists, including myself. But the attraction of Berkeley went far beyond its reputation as a center of political dissent.

To begin with, Berkeley was a city of many bookstores. The most celebrated ones included Cody's Books, Moe's Bookstore, Shakespeare & Company along Telegraph Avenue on the south side of the campus, and Black Oak Books on the north side. Friendly and accommodating, these bookstores created a welcoming atmosphere for browsers, offered an enormous inventory of new as well as used books, provided sofas and armchairs, and served as pleasant rendezvous spots. They were large bookstores, occupying multiple rooms and floors, making the little bookstore in Boston, where I worked during my first Christmas vacation in America, feel like a Ma-and-Pa corner store operation. Each time I went to Berkeley, I spent hours browsing in those bookstores. It was always edifying and delightful.

Right around Moe's and Shakespeare, there was Cafe Mediterranean, where the café latte was created. It was rumored that the Italian barista/owner got fed up with the customers' endless demand for extra milk in the cappuccinos brewed from a dark roasted blend of coffee beans, which, at the time, remained novel for the taste of American coffee consumers. So he invented a separate drink, called it café latte and charged 50 cents more than a cappuccino. Cafe Mediterranean was always lively, filled with loquacious customers engaging in animated conversations about art, music, philosophy, literature, politics and daily events. The place had a magical effect of mood-lifting on its customers. If you were haunted by loneliness, jilted by your lover, or bereaved of a loved one, you might seek relief at the Cafe. As soon as you stepped into the establishment, you became engrossed in its boisterous and vibrant atmosphere, as if you had been teleported to a different universe where everyone appeared like-minded, friendly and supportive. At the time, Cafe Mediterranean was the only establishment that served cappuccino, espresso, and café latte in the Bay Area and probably all of California outside of the small Italian community in the area of North Beach in San Francisco. Left-leaning intellectuals, raconteurs, pseudo-intellectuals, artists, writers and aspiring writers, Bohemians, student activists from the entire Bay Area flocked there during the sixties just to enjoy the tasty coffee, converse with like-minded people and revel in its vibrant ambiance.

Then, there were the movie theaters: one on the north side of the campus and one on Telegraph Avenue. They were not the usual movie theaters that served up the normal fare produced by Hollywood studios. Foreign films were their mainstay. There, one saw movies by Akira Kurosawa, Sergei Eisenstein, Federico Fellini, Vittorio De Sica, Roberto Rossellini, François Truffaut, Luis Buñuel, Tasujirō Ozu, Jean Renoir, Michelangelo Antonioni, Ingmar Bergman, Axel von Ambesser, Luis Buñuel, . . . influential filmmakers and directors who transformed movies into an art form that rivaled the great novels written by Tolstoy, Dostoevsky, Balzac, Hugo, Joyce, Proust, Murasaki, Cao Xueqin . . . They produced a body of riveting and thought-provoking movies which led to the establishment of Film Studies as a standard academic discipline in most institutions of higher education.

The films of those directors and producers did not merely entertain and captivate, they probed the essence of what was human—emotions, death, aspirations, conflicts, morality, sociological phenomena, political issues—and confronted the viewers with existential questions and philosophical conundrums. Like great novels, those movies made viewers think of what might have never occurred to them.

In hindsight, I must admit that pondering existential questions was not always beneficial and confronting the dark side of human nature could be depressing. During those years, I met many people who lost their bearings in their existential despair and sought relief from drugs. It was sad to see them becoming dysfunctional and turning into addicts.

(I must not create the false impression that those theaters only showed foreign films. They also showed American classics, mostly made in the 1940s and 1950s, like the Bogart movies, the films directed by Alfred Hitchcock, the Marx brothers, W. C. Fields, etc.)

Another unique feature of Berkeley was a number of casual and inexpensive eateries that catered to the needs of busy and impoverished students. Unlike "fast food," which had not yet become an American vogue, those Berkeley eateries served simple but wholesome fare with none of the additives, like MSG, designed to enhance the taste and wreck your health. They were typically family-owned, strategically located and offered food with an exotic touch long before foodies existed. La Val's Pizza, an Italian sandwich and pizza joint on Euclid Avenue, north of the campus, was next door to the movie theater that showed foreign films. One could sit on an outdoor bench at La Val's and enjoy a sandwich before watching a scintillating film like The Bicycle Thief, directed by Vittorio De Sica. On the south side of campus, within a couple of blocks from Cafe Mediterranean, there were ethnic eateries serving inexpensive Chinese, Mexican, Thai and Indian dishes on Durant Avenue and Channing Way. The food wasn't gourmet, but it was diverse long before diversity became a code word for a progressive social agenda.

Finally, Berkeley was a town where people walked, not just walking purposely from one place to another, but walking leisurely to see what was going on. Sauntering along the sidewalk, one had the sensation of being a member of a lively and active community. The ambiance wasn't the nerve-wracking hustle and bustle of a city like New York, nor was it the comatose and tomb-like feeling of a typical American suburban town where the landscape was dominated by car dealerships, gas stations, Levitt homes and automobile traffic. The streets in Berkeley always had pedestrians, morning, afternoon and evening. They were diverse not just in ethnicity but also attire, hairdo, facial expression, movement, language, what they held in their hands and what they wore on their feet. No matter how outlandish or unconventional a person might appear, people did not look askance at him or her. Of course, there were always some eccentric characters parading down Telegraph Avenue and displaying themselves like the Papuan New Guinea male birds of paradise in their attempt to attract a mate. Sometimes half-nude and bare-footed, they glided along the concrete pavement begging for attention: a segment of free public entertainment.

My friends and I loved Berkeley.

We felt alive there, especially in contrast to Palo Alto, which, in those days, was an anemic, homogenized suburb, and the campus of Stanford

University, where the Quad, with the Memorial Church as its center-piece, looked like a deserted movie set in the glaring California sun when you drove toward it on University Avenue. There were reasons for us to call Palo Alto "Pallid Alto."

All of Berkeley's attractions notwithstanding, I was making a bold and potentially risky move when I decided to abandon mathematics to pursue linguistics as a career. Before the 21st century, nearly all the Chinese students who came to the United States for graduate education specialized in science, engineering and mathematics. I was no exception.

Linguistics, the study of language, does not fall within the domain of humanities disciplines. It is interdisciplinary, because language permeates every aspect of human existence. Besides communicating through language, humans use language to cogitate, create, analyze and accumulate knowledge. There is a neurological and evolutionary aspect of language, just as there is a sociological dimension of language use and an aesthetic arena in the language of literary descriptions. The former is clearly related to biological science, whereas the latter crosses over to social sciences and literature. The multi-faceted nature of language appealed to me. But the attraction did not diminish my fear of abandoning a discipline in which I had done well and stepping into a new discipline without knowing much about it. In making the decision to switch my area of specialization, I was encouraged by a good friend, Rudy, who was a junior faculty member in mathematics at Stanford at the time. In fact, he had planted the idea in me long before I entertained any thoughts in that direction. He felt strongly that mathematics, beautiful and challenging as it might be, was too restrictive to a person with as broad a spectrum of interests as I had.

While I was studying linguistics at Berkeley in 1967, Keith became an Assistant Professor at Howard University in Washington, D.C. After two years, much to the regret of his students and colleagues at Howard, he accepted a faculty position at the newly founded University of

California, San Diego, where he was slated to be the provost of the soon-to-be-established College of Third World Studies.

Then, a bomb dropped on Keith and me.

In winter, 1968, the U.S. Immigration and Naturalization Service informed us separately that we would be deported from the United States. Without any explanation, INS refused to extend my student visa and revoked Keith's work visa.

At Berkeley, a Boalt Hall law professor learned of my plight and decided to take up my case pro bono. He immediately filed a motion in a federal court challenging INS's decision and demanding to know the reason for their action. The federal court referred my case to a quasi-judicial hearing at INS as the first step of a legal process. Several months later, INS informed my lawyer of the reason for my deportation:

"Charles N. Li advocated the violent overthrow of the government of the United States."

When my lawyer told me the reason for the INS action, I could hardly believe what I heard. How ludicrous! A graduate student trying to become a university educator harboring the ambitious thought of overthrowing the U.S. government?!

I was flabbergasted.

The "violent overthrow of the U.S. government" was such a novel, absurd and outlandish idea that it didn't occur in my wildest imagination. Anyone in my position—a position without wealth, power or following—entertaining such a thought would have to be suffering from some form of grand delusion, if not outright schizophrenia. Perhaps INS thought I had a god complex, a phenomenon not uncommon in the academic world. Some academicians believed that their research was epoch-changing and earth-shaking. They spoke, walked and acted as if they were shouldering the most important task or solving the most difficult problem that would transform the world. Arrogance was too benign a word to characterize them, even though most of their work ended up as moldy tomes in university libraries only to be consulted by other academicians. Even this god complex did not lead those academics to advocate the violent overthrow of the U.S. government; neither were they causing harm to their institutions other than occasionally being a nuisance to their colleagues. They suffered from a disease which I called "Infantile Disorder." It seemed endemic in academia. As for myself in 1968, I was not yet an academic. Just an aspirant.

While my pro bono lawyer from Boalt Hall was litigating my deportation case, the University of California at San Diego (UCSD) mounted a major campaign to defend Keith. They deployed lawyers to question INS's action and sent lobbyists to seek intervention from California's congressional delegation to obtain permanent resident status for Keith. UCSD considered Keith a highly valuable asset. In the age of Huey Newton's Black Panther Party and Elijah Muhammad's Nation of Islam, not to mention Malcolm X's fiery Black Nationalism, Keith stood out as a sensible, rational and accomplished Black leader who could attract minority students to UCSD and promote their cause without riots and violence. In addition, he had already proven himself to be a popular teacher and a good academic at Howard University. In short, he was a treasure for UCSD.

A few months later, INS surprised Keith and me with another unexpected action.

Without offering any reason, INS aborted the procedure to deport Keith, while my case remained ongoing. Appearing conciliatory and helpful, the INS bureaucrats further informed UCSD that they would grant permanent residency to Keith, i.e., issue him a green card, so that he could legally work in the U.S. But they pointed out that U.S. immigration law required a person from the American continent pursuing an education in the U.S. on a student visa to return to his/her home country to receive a green card.

Much to the relief of UCSD's lawyers and lobbyists, the INS bureaucrats told Keith and UCSD that they would facilitate the process of getting him a green card by setting up an appointment for Keith at the U.S. Embassy in Kingston. They ascertained a date that would be convenient to Keith in consideration of his teaching duties so that he could fly to Kingston for the appointment. All he had to do, they assured the concerned parties, was to show up at the Embassy where his green card would be waiting for him.

During Spring break, 1969, Keith flew to Kingston. The morning after his arrival, he went to the U.S. embassy at an appointed time. There, a U.S. consul, upon verifying Keith's identity by his passport, pulled out a document and read from it aloud:

"From this day on, Mr. Keith Lowe is prohibited from entering the United States."

Then, looking at Keith in the eye, he said officiously, "Mr. Lowe, you are dismissed."

As composed and unflappable as Keith was, the incident shocked him to the core and upset him profoundly. His whole life had just been turned upside down through treachery and deceit by the U.S. government. Worse still, his identity as an Afro-American was abruptly terminated.

UCSD pulled out all stops to reverse the unlawful action of the Immigration and Naturalization Service with the help of lawyers, lobbyists and publicly elected officials. The University held Keith's position for him for six years, trying to reverse INS's action before giving up their effort.

Thus, Keith was forced to start afresh and forge a new life in Jamaica, his country of birth, which had gained independence from England in 1962. He took comfort in the departure of the British colonialists and decided to dedicate himself to help building a new Jamaica. Two years later, I went to Jamaica to visit him and lend him my support. Calm as usual, he accepted his fate with aplomb and showed no trace of bitterness.

Shortly after his return, he became a high-ranking official in Jamaica's Ministry of Education, in charge of shaping the curriculum of schools in the country. He found his work meaningful and stimulating because he was not only improving the curriculum of primary and secondary schools, but also helping the underprivileged Jamaicans gain access to education. He appointed councils of scholars to help him choose suitable and edifying textbooks for Jamaican children and slowly raised the standard of primary and secondary education in underprivileged communities. He introduced affirmative action policies in the distribution of school funding and the recruitment of better-qualified teachers.

In the midst of his self-imposed heavy work schedule, he also found time to marry and become the father of two sons.

By the mid-1970s, Jamaica had sunk into economic chaos under the premiership of Michael Manley, an inept and opportunistic politician. The country quickly devolved into political violence. Bloody struggles between different political parties plunged the nation into anarchy. Some politicians resorted to fanning ethnic conflicts and racial riots for political gains. Since the majority of the population in Jamaica consisted of people of African descent, and the Chinese minority tended to be well-placed economically and socially after Jamaica's independence, inciting pogroms against people of Chinese descent became a useful political strategy for unscrupulous demagogues. The day the massacres of Chinese Jamaicans began in 1978, Keith was working in the Ministry of Education. Upon hearing the news, he had less than one hour to collect his family and drive to the airport through mobs, mayhem, looted stores and burning homes, abandoning everything he had earned in the past ten years: his house, his car, his books, his bank accounts, not to mention his career and livelihood. At the airport he bought one-way tickets for himself, his wife and children to Toronto, Canada, where his sister was residing. As a man who gave the highest priority to who he was, he had been robbed of his identity twice in his adulthood. The first time, the U.S. government took away his identity as an Afro-American. The second time, the machination of unscrupulous politicians and an inept government deprived him of his Jamaican identity.

Uprooted once again, Keith started afresh as a political refugee in Canada. He and his wife made Toronto their home, became Canadian citizens and raised their two sons there. When I visited him in Toronto, he had a civil servant post in the government of the Ontario province. While stabilizing his life in Canada, he began a quest to embrace yet another identity: the identity of a Hakka Chinese, his paternal heritage. He took several trips to China, bringing his family with him, visited his father's ancestral Hakka village in the southern Guangdong province, which remained the home base of the Lowe (Luo) clan, and organized Hakka conferences in Toronto for Hakka Chinese in the diaspora. He even volunteered to teach English in a secondary school in the Guangdong province for one year after he retired from his civil service job in Ontario.

Few people, with the exception of some double agents in espionage who survived liquidation, have experienced the erasure of their identity. In his adulthood, Keith suffered two traumatic identity erasures: his identity as a Black American and his identity as a native-born Jamaican. In each case, the erasure was equivalent to psychological assassination in addition to financial devastation. Not only was his identity erased, but he also lost his professional career and material possessions. The first time, he was well on his way to becoming an important Black American educator in a major research university. Then, suddenly the U.S. Immigration and Naturalization Service expunged him. The second time, he fell victim to the racial violence instigated by unscrupulous politicians in his native country, Jamaica. This time, he barely escaped with his life. One could hardly imagine the trauma and anguish visited upon him by those identity erasures. But Keith bore his fate stoically, never losing his calm, patience and gentleness.

While the INS pulled a trick on Keith that removed him from the United States in 1969 without due process, my deportation case advanced to a quasi-judicial hearing. My lawyer told me that I didn't need to show up to the preliminary hearing, during which he would file motions to challenge the INS action. I am taking the liberty of reconstructing the critical part of the hearing according to what my lawyer told me.

At the hearing, my lawyer demanded to know the evidence that INS used for charging me with the crime of advocating the violent overthrow of the U.S. government. He wanted to know if INS had a recording of a speech of mine or a slogan or pamphlet written by me that constituted proof. The INS representative responded by citing a memo from the FBI accusing me of being a communist. When the presiding judge asked for evidence that backed up the FBI accusation, the INS representative said:

"A congressman of the House Un-American Activities Committee has charged that Mr. Li was an agent of Communist China."

I had known of that charge from HUAC, an off-the-cuff accusation by a congressman without any evidential support. It happened in 1966 when HUAC held a public hearing on antiwar protests in the country. More specifically, HUAC wanted to investigate the Medical Aid Committee for the South Vietnam Liberation Front at Stanford University. The head of that Medical Aid Committee, Stuart, was a volatile firebrand undergraduate antiwar protestor. HUAC subpoenaed him for his testimony.

In the course of the hearing, a Texas congressman by the name of Poole on the HUAC panel asked Stuart, "To what extent are you influenced by the Chinese agent, Charles Lie, who is a graduate student at Stanford?"

Because Congressman Poole's question presupposed that Stuart was "under the influence of Charles Lie" and therefore implied that he was incapable of thinking and acting independently, Stuart was enraged. He was so incensed that he shouted into the microphone:

"First, my friend's name is not Charles Lie—it's pronounced Charles Lee! Secondly, I refuse to answer your question on the grounds that it nauseates me."

At that moment, pandemonium broke out in the spectators' galley where antiwar protestors approved of Stuart's irate riposte with wild applause and loud catcalls. Immediately, the Chair of HUAC terminated the hearing.

The incident was reported in *Time*. But it didn't carry any weight in the quasi-judicial hearing of my deportation, because it did not constitute any evidence in support of INS's charge that I advocated the violent overthrow of the U.S. Government.

After noting that both the FBI agent and the Texas Congressman were merely accusing me of being a Chinese communist, the judge pressed the INS prosecutor for substantive evidence in support of the charge leveled against me.

"Well, Mr. Li is a founding member of several socialist organizations at Stanford University," the INS man said, "and he regularly participated in antiwar demonstrations in Palo Alto and Berkeley. In addition, he picketed the Dow Chemical's napalm factory south of San Jose many times."

"Those activities fall under the aegis of free speech, a privilege we extend to all people living in the United States, citizens as well as visitors," the judge lectured the INS prosecutor. "Now, has Mr. Li ever been arrested or charged with any crime?"

The INS prosecutor answered with a sheepish "no."

At that point, my lawyer informed the court that the Chinese government considered me a reactionary in 1957, and I was denied the right to higher education in China.

"Furthermore," my lawyer continued, "Mr. Li was not entitled to a Chinese passport. He came to America after winning a scholarship from the World University Service that administered a fund provided by the U.S. State Department in recognition of the World Refugee Year. Mr. Li entered the U.S. as a stateless refugee without a passport."

The judge shook his head in dismay, dismissed INS's case, and ordered the INS to grant me a green card as a remedy for bringing a groundless charge against me.

So, an ominous cloud gathering over my head for almost three years came to a happy ending, thanks to my brilliant lawyer who never charged a penny for his work.

But the INS agents did not take kindly to their humiliation at the quasi-judicial hearing.

Several years later, when I began to receive invitations to lecture in European universities, I found it nearly impossible to travel as a stateless person without a passport. For a professional trip to Holland, Switzerland and France in 1974, I had to fill out reams of applications and paid exorbitant fees to the embassy of each of those countries to obtain a visitor's visa. The process took several months before I could embark on my journey to my first destination, Amsterdam, Holland.

After three pleasant days of lecturing and visiting museums in Amsterdam and Leiden, I boarded the overnight Rhinegold express train for Geneva, where an old friend from California teaching at the University of Geneva would meet me. No sooner had the train left the station, I fell sound asleep in my seat.

Hours later, the train stopped and someone tapped my shoulder. I opened my eyes and saw two uniformed officials standing in front of me.

"Passport, please," they said in their thick German accents.

I handed them all of my papers: my green card, my visas to Holland, Switzerland and France.

"Where is your passport?" one of them demanded.

"I don't have one."

"Do you have a visa for visiting the Federal Republic of Germany?"

"No," I was surprised and alarmed, "I am not going to Germany."

"You are in Germany!" the same officer said dryly.

"No, no, no," I protested. "I am not! I'm on a train from Amsterdam to Geneva."

"Yes, but the train is in Germany," he responded matter-of-factly.

"Well, that's unfortunate," I said. "Nobody told me that. I don't want to be in Germany and have no intention of getting off the train."

"You will have to get off the train with us here at the border, because you don't have a visa," the police officer said officiously.

Thus, I was yanked off the Rhinegold express just before it crossed the border to Basel, Switzerland, taken to a German border police station, given several forms to sign and fined 40 Deutsch marks before I was allowed to get on the next train to Geneva. By the time I arrived in the Central Railway Station in Geneva, my friend was no longer there. With great trepidation, I managed to find my way to the Biochemistry Department of the University of Geneva and got hold of him.

That experience taught me that I needed a passport if I were to travel around the world, an activity high on my priority list of things to do in life. In addition, my professional activities required more and more overseas travel. So, I applied for U.S. citizenship.

Now INS had me at their mercy.

For two years, my application simply vanished into the INS bureaucracy. No response, no acknowledgment, no action from INS. I could not accept any invitation or attend any scholarly conference overseas unless I was willing to navigate the same bureaucratic maze and risk suffering the same kind of nightmarish experience of my first European venture. INS neither denied nor approved my application for U.S. citizenship. They simply ignored it, a stance they didn't have to defend.

Fortunately, my employer came to my rescue.

In 1976, the University of California, through its government relations office in Washington D.C., secured the assistance of Alan Cranston, the senior senator from California and, at the time, the senate's majority party whip, to pressure INS into responding to my application.

After repeated prodding from Senator Cranston's office for several months, INS finally sent an attorney to interview me in Santa Barbara for my application to become a U.S. citizen.

My appointment with the U.S. assistant attorney at the Santa Barbara courthouse was a unique experience, different from any interview or any encounter I had ever had.

After making me swear on a Bible that I would tell the truth and nothing but the truth, which seemed strange to someone who was not a Christian, she asked the first question:

"Have you ever been a prostitute?"

Stunned, I thought for a while, fully aware of the fact that I was under oath and mindful of my knowledge that during the McCarthy era witch hunts, many naturalized U.S. citizens sympathetic to socialism were deported after the INS revoked their citizenship on the grounds that they committed perjury during their interviews for citizenship, even though those interviews took place decades earlier. I wanted to be very cautious in answering the attorney's questions.

"If by prostitution, you mean selling my body, the answer is NO. But I know of many academicians who prostituted themselves in order to seek professional advancement."

She glared at me and fired off the next question, "Have you ever committed adultery?"

"Interesting question." I was cogitating. "I graduated from Bowdoin College. More than one hundred years ago, a Bowdoin graduate wrote a great novel, *The Scarlet Letter*. You must know from my record that I have never been married. But *The Scarlet Letter* never clarified for me the question: If an unmarried man sleeps with a married woman, has he committed adultery?"

She was visibly angry at my response. But she moved on, "Have you ever associated or affiliated with communists?"

"Oh, my God!" I exclaimed. "Up to my neck! I spent 1957 and 1958 in Communist China where communists lurked everywhere and reported on everyone to the authority. They controlled every aspect of the lives of every Chinese in those days. People couldn't marry and married couples couldn't divorce without the prior approval of the Chinese Communist Party."

So, the questioning went on. Some insulting, some frivolous. After a while, the U.S. attorney switched to factual questions such as:

"What is the Second Amendment to the U.S. Constitution?"

"Who was the most recent appointment to the U.S. Supreme Court?"

"What are the two branches of the U.S. legislature?"

"How many U.S. senators are there?"

"Who was Ulysses Grant?"

And so on.

A dozen questions later, she seemed pleased with my knowledge of the United States. With a wan smile, she said, "Now I am going to ask you a couple of hard questions. Do you know the number of U.S. representatives in the Congress?"

I admitted that I didn't know the answer but ventured to say that it was probably in the low hundreds.

"Okay, one last question," she said. "Who was President Eisenhower's Secretary of Defense?"

"Charles Wilson," the answer leaped out of my mouth. "He was the CEO of General Motors, famous for his statement during his Senate confirmation hearing for the Secretary of Defense, that 'what's good for the United States is good for General Motors, and what's good for General Motors is good for the United States.'"

"Well, Mr. Li," she said as she collected her papers, "you are a knowledgeable person."

"Thank you," I responded politely. "I am in the business of acquiring and disseminating knowledge."

Six months after the interview, I received a notice from the U.S. government informing me that I should go to the Santa Barbara Court Building for a swearing-in ceremony to become a U.S. citizen. It was 1978.

ANATOLE

I LIKED ANATOLE THE MOMENT WE MET. HE EXUDED KINDNESS, honesty and a forthright personality.

Wearing horn-rimmed glasses, he looked a little disheveled, like an absent-minded philosopher, which was not quite in congruence with his looney laugh and strong torso shaped like a wine-barrel. Although a little clumsy in his movements, he emanated vitality, affability and goodwill. With fair skin, a round face, wide lips, and a head of straight blond hair thinning in the front, he could have passed as a Russian. In fact, he was Russian by lineage. Both of his parents came from the Jewish enclave in Odessa on the coast of the Black Sea. But as soon as he spoke, you knew he hailed from New York. His accent was so thick that there was no need for even a fraction of the sensitive ear of the legendary Professor Henry Higgins (in G.B. Shaw's *Pygmalion* or the Hollywood film, *My Fair Lady*) to infer where he came from. Not only was he born in New York City, he spent his youth living in a dilapidated flat in Manhattan above a rowdy bar in Greenwich Village. The flat was his home until June 1963, a few months before he came to Stanford to enroll in the Ph.D. program in the Philosophy Department. The very first venture away from home and New York City took him to Cuba with a group of people from the Progressive Labor Party, in defiance of the State Department's edict prohibiting American citizens from visiting that newly minted communist nation.

When we met at the Tresidder Union on the Stanford campus, he was regaling the assembled dissidents with his encounter with Che Guevara in Havana. Among other activities, Che Guevara entertained that group of American visitors with a yacht trip in the Bay of Pigs to show them the spot where the CIA-organized invasion force landed.

We became good friends shortly after meeting each other. By Winter quarter of 1964, we shared a rental house in south Palo Alto, the house that an FBI agent and an INS agent broke into during Spring 1966.

Anatole was a core member of the dissidents at Stanford and a faithful participant in all protests, teach-ins and demonstrations against the Vietnam war from the beginning. Even though he visited Cuba with members of the Progressive Labor Party, he didn't belong to it. (A splinter group from the American Communist Party (ACP), the Progressive Labor Party consisted of no more than a few dozen intellectuals. They formed their own political organization because they were tired of the undercover FBI agents embedded in the ACP. It was rumored in the early sixties that the number of undercover FBI agents exceeded the number of true believers in communism in the American Communist Party. Although no one knew who the undercover agents were, the mere knowledge of their presence within the Party induced nerve-wracking paranoia and suspicions among party members.)

Anatole never thought highly of the ACP. Its subservient relationship with the Soviet Union grated on him. A political party in America, in Anatole's opinion, should be capable of formulating its own agenda suited for America, not toeing the line of another country. In 1963, the ACP, still functioning in a fantasy world of international communism created by Lenin and Trotsky, was incapable of independence from the Soviet Union, even after Stalin's great purges in the 1930s; his embarrassing, short-lived peace treaty with Hitler; the invasion of Poland and Hungary in the 1950s; and the ideological dispute with Tito of Yugoslavia, all of which exhibited Stalin's totalitarian rule and outright Soviet imperialism.

Shortly after we began sharing a house in South Palo Alto, Anatole asked me to teach him how to drive a car. He preferred not to drive or own a car. But in 1964, municipal buses did not constitute a practical or useful system of public transportation. It was common for a person to wait for an hour or more for a bus to go to a place. Growing up in New York, Anatole was used to public transportation and walking. But the campus was several miles away from our rental home. He didn't mind the walking. It was the amount of time he had to spend to get from one place to another that irritated him. His attire and manners already made him a misfit in affluent Palo Alto. In addition, he felt weird walking alone on the streets and boulevards under a hot sun, not to mention the expression of consternation on the faces of people who saw him from their automobiles. Reluctantly, he decided to abandon his New York way of life and seek driving lessons from me.

One Sunday morning, I showed him the essentials of automobile operation: the steering wheel, the brake, the gas pedal. Then, we got into the front seat of my Buick, the pale green tank. He sat behind the wheel and started his first driving lesson.

As I closed the car door on my side, the car suddenly shot forward with its tires screeching, followed by a violent abrupt halt as Anatole slammed on the brake. I barely managed to brace myself with extended arms against the dashboard as Anatole crashed into the steering wheel, his horn-rimmed glasses flying to the windshield. Luckily his wine-barrel torso absorbed the impact from the steering wheel without any serious injury, and his glasses remained intact. He was contrite, apologetic and embarrassed. I brushed off the inauspicious start and told him to be gentle on the gas pedal and the brake. Then, we took off again.

In less than a block, he stopped the car and asked, "Why am I sitting on the left? Shouldn't I sit in the middle of the front seat in order to have a better sense of the road as the car moves forward?"

"You sit on the left because that's where the steering wheel is, and you are the driver," I told him.

"Yeah, I see that," he responded. "It's the tradition, but this tradition does not seem logical. The driver should sit in the middle to have a balanced and commanding view of what's in front of him. Do you mind if I try sitting in the middle of the front seat?"

I hesitated, but decided to let him experiment with his preferred way of sitting, thinking that he would soon adopt the traditional practice out of inconvenience, if nothing else. He edged toward the center of the front seat, extended his left arm and left leg diagonally to reach the steering wheel and the foot pedals. It seemed to work for him. After driving around the block a few times, he went onto the six-lane El Camino Real, cruising for a mile without a hitch. Drivers on El Camino Real who passed by our car cast puzzling looks at us, wondering what in the world was going on.

After one week of practice driving in his unique and bizarre manner, Anatole, pleased with himself, bought an old Ford. Without my knowledge, he took his Ford all around town, doing errands and going to campus. One evening, when I was reading at home, the telephone rang. It was Anatole.

"Hi, Charles." He sounded nervous and distraught. "This is embarrassing. I have been arrested. Can you come to the Palo Alto Police Headquarters to bail me out?"

I had never been to a police station, let alone bailed someone out of jail. It was a bureaucratic nightmare, answering question after question, signing paper after paper. Both Anatole and I were concerned about the bail because we were living on meager stipends. Luckily, it was $100, a significant but not ruinous sum, given that my fellowship stipend as well as Anatole's Teaching Assistant salary was pegged at $200 per month. Upon being released from jail, Anatole told me that he had never been jailed before. In this case, he was confined in a holding cell at the police station, not a real prison.

"It was shockingly depressing," he said in a subdued voice. "The people in the holding cell were down and out."

The next day, we had to negotiate another bureaucratic maze and pay a bundle of money to retrieve his impounded car.

The incident precipitating his arrest occurred on El Camino Real, the major north-south thoroughfare that linked Palo Alto with nearby towns like Mountain View, Meno Park and Redwood City along the San Francisco Bay. The morning he got arrested, Anatole was cheerfully heading north to campus in his old Ford when he noticed a police car behind him flashing its red-and-blue light. He immediately switched to a slower lane to let the police car pass him. But the police also switched lanes to stay behind him. He then moved back to the fast lane. The police did the same while simultaneously maneuvering his patrol car dangerously close to the rear bumper of Anatole's Ford and blaring his siren. At that point, Anatole got the message and stopped on the shoulder of the multi-lane boulevard. The arrest ensued because he didn't have a driver's license, didn't have insurance, and couldn't satisfactorily answer the policeman's query why he was sitting in the middle of the front seat while driving. The police suspected that Anatole was under the influence of drugs.

During the weeks an FBI agent was shadowing Anatole, Keith and me on campus, Anatole often invited the agent to join us at our table at Tresidder Union.

"You are welcome to join us," Anatole would say with a loony laugh. "The proximity would help you to get a clearer recording of our conversation."

The agent just stared at Anatole without a response.

Some days, Anatole would attempt to explain what we did.

"Sir, we are not plotting anything. Our motto is transparency and non-violence. If you want to know more about us, please feel free to ask questions."

Sometimes, Anatole exuded sarcasm, "Sir, I like your crewcut. It must be a vestige from your Marine Corps days."

Or, "Nice suit you are wearing!"

In reality, the trend at the time for most young people was to sport shoulder-length hair, and the agent's suit was anything but praiseworthy from a sartorial perspective.

Other times, Anatole was provocative.

"Sir, we're planning an antiwar demonstration at the Town and Village Shopping Center this weekend again. Would you like to join us?"

"Sir, are you going to pillory us in your report?" Anatole paused for a moment before continuing, "Perhaps I shouldn't use the word 'pillory.' It's a little esoteric."

Throughout all these encounters, the FBI agent remained stoically silent, unperturbed and stone-faced. He conducted himself admirably.

―――――――――――

Anatole's favorite topic of conversation was Marxism. Having read extensively in the philosophy of history and the history of ideas, he considered Marxism almost a free-standing academic discipline in its own right. In his opinion, the theoretical interpretations and expositions by such exponents of Marxism as Rosa Luxemburg, Karl Kautsky, György Lukács and V. I. Lenin were important to the understanding of Marxism, but even more important than reading the work of those authors and delving into the ideas of Karl Marx and Friedrich Engels was to explore the impact of Marxism on the thinkers, writers, artists and philosophers of the 20th century. There was hardly any worthy intellectual in the 20th century who was not affected or influenced by Marxism in one way or another.

"It's a travesty that people equate Marxism with the Communist Manifesto," Anatole would rant against anyone who conflated Marxism with communism. "The Manifesto was a political pamphlet written by Karl Marx and Friedrich Engels in a few weeks in 1848. For sure, the Manifesto summarized some of their political thought. It has had an outsized influence on world affairs during the 20th century, and the link between Marxism and communism is indelible. But Marxism is so much more than communism in the Soviet Union and China where Stalin and Mao invoked it to justify their regimes."

"I think the allure of Marxism is its sweeping prediction that all the problems of our world would be solved in one bold stroke. Not only did Marx predict the evolution of human society into utopian communism, but he argued persuasively for the historical inevitability of that ultimate utopia," I commented. "Such a prediction is appealing, romantic and hard to resist."

"But the validity of that Marxist prediction is dubious at best," Anatole responded thoughtfully. "So far, history has shown that Marx's prediction of the rise of the proletariat is wrong. The proletariat of the industrialized nations did not revolt against the capitalists in the Western world. The Bolshevik revolution was a putsch, an armed insurrection led by a handful of intellectuals against an absolute monarch, Czar Nicholas II, and the Chinese revolution was fought primarily by the neglected and starving peasants in a protracted struggle against an inept and corrupt clique led by Chiang Kai-shek in a chaotic and impoverished country where capitalism had not yet taken hold. Both revolutions ended in totalitarian regimes where the state terrorized the individual citizens. I'd like to see an end to injustice and exploitation. But I am not sure that it will ever happen."

"Perhaps we are naive and too idealistic to yearn for a society of justice and equality," I was thinking aloud.

"That makes me want to be a field anthropologist and a linguist, going to the farthest corners of the world, like the Gobi desert or the Amazon jungle or the Papuan highland, to study languages and cultures of ethnic tribes operating in stone-age technology, and find out if a materialistically primitive society might be more just and egalitarian than the post-industrial societies." Anatole said, "Colin Turnbull's description of the culture of the Mbuti (Bambuti) pygmies of Congo (The Forest People, 1961) suggests that the Mbuti people live in a much more ethical and egalitarian society than we do in post-industrial societies. Marx, of course, didn't have the faintest idea of the existence of cultures like that of the Mbuti. In his time, Western scholars thought of hunter-gatherers as "primitive" or "barbarous," not worthy of studying. But we know now that the development of wealth and technology does not entail moral advancement at either the individual or the societal level. One might even argue that the contrary is true: That is, the accumulation of wealth and the development of technology might have a corrupting impact on humans, fanning the fire of greed and avarice. At the minimum, wealth and technology have definitely made society and human life more complex and encumbering. I think as preparation, all dissidents like us should begin with reading the book *Primitive Rebels* by a young historian named Eric Hobsbawm." (I should note that at the time, Hobsbawm was far from being a world-famous, celebrated historian and intellectual. He had just published the first volume of his monumental trilogy on the long 19th century, and his superb treatise on the 20th century, The Age of Extremes, did not appear until 1994.)

"Okay, I will read Hobsbawm. But you sound like a contrarian to Karl Marx," I noted. "He predicted utopia at the end of social-political evolution, and you see utopia at the beginning of civilization."

"You are exaggerating what I said," Anatole retorted. "I never claimed that the beginning of human civilization was golden. But I do think society and human relationships were less complicated and faced fewer conflicts at the beginning of civilization. In that sense, it might be easier to maintain a more egalitarian and compassionate society. Besides, I'm making a conjecture, not an assertion."

Through that conversation, Anatole became the first person who alerted me to the study of languages and cultures of "exotic" ethnic groups unfettered by the complexity of the modern world. I thought such an undertaking would be fascinating, although I had not yet entertained the idea of specializing in linguistics.

Marxism aside, Anatole always had the uncanny ability to make me think when we discussed any topic. One could never infer his erudition and cognitive acuity from his loony laugh and outlandish behavior like driving a car while sitting in the center of the front seat. Our friend Rudy, the mathematician, in a casual gathering brought up the paradox between Anatole's thought-provoking insights and otherworldly behavior. In response, Anatole said, before unleashing his signature laugh:

"Well, I may be crazy, but I'm not stupid!"

Anatole's critical view of Marxism made him a much more interesting and attractive Marxist than all of the dissidents at Stanford in the 1960s. At a time when every leftist in America admired Herbert

Marcuse's *One Dimensional Man: Studies in the Ideology of Advanced Industrial Society*, placing it on a pedestal as if Marcuse were the new avatar of the 20th century progressive thinkers, Anatole did not think *One Dimensional Man* belonged in the pantheon of Marxist studies, even though he agreed with Marcuse's criticism of consumerism, its corrupting influence, and the stifling impact of modern technological society on individual freedom. Similarly, he dismissed Chairman Mao as a footnote in the annals of Marxism and described "On Contradiction," an article representing Mao's most significant contribution to Marxism, lightweight and sophomoric.

Aside from his erudition, Anatole struck every Stanford dissident as a living paradox. His sharp mind seemed to be reserved only for abstract intellectual inquiries. You could ask him questions on any major thinker in the history of Western civilization and you would walk away with a jewel or two. Sometimes, he could be entertaining even on serious topics.

On Bertrand Russell and Alfred North Whitehead, who collaborated for more than a decade producing Mathematica Principia, he remarked:

"Bertie thought Alfie was muddle-headed, and Alfie felt Bertie was simple-minded."

He told the story of Scottish philosopher-theologian Duns Scotus (c. 1268-1314), wined and dined by the Capetian King Philip IV, who transformed France from feudalism to a centralized state. The king paid tribute to Scotus as the most distinguished philosopher by inviting him to dinner, but being egotistical and contentious, he couldn't refrain from poking fun at the philosopher. He mockingly asked Scotus, "Please tell me, Mr. Scotus, what separates a Scot from a sot?"

"Only the dining table!" Scotus rejoined without blinking.

Yet, in practical matters of day-to-day life, Anatole was worse than incompetent or otherworldly, and could be downright frustrating to his friends and colleagues.

Many months after we became housemates in Palo Alto, he came to me for help one day, looking embarrassed and ill at ease.

"Charles, could I borrow twenty dollars from you?"

Twenty dollars in 1964-65 was not a paltry sum. I was happy to loan it to him, but I couldn't resist my curiosity.

"May I ask why you need twenty dollars?"

"Well, I can't tell you," Anatole said. "But I will give it back as soon as I get my next RA stipend."

So, I gave him twenty dollars.

Then he disappeared for two days from our house. When he resurfaced, I asked him where he had been.

"I have been sleeping in a cheap motel near the freeway," he said sheepishly.

Surprised, I asked him why.

"I couldn't stand my bedroom in our house. It smells like hell."

"Let's find out the cause of the smell." I started marching toward his bedroom.

"No, no, no, Charles!" Anatole panicked. "Don't go in there! I know the cause. The stench came from a pile of my dirty laundry on the floor. It has been there for a couple weeks."

I was dumbfounded. Not by his accumulated dirty laundry, but by his choice of escaping into a cheap motel as a way of dealing with dirty laundry.

"Anatole!" I raised my voice. "It would cost you a fraction of the motel rent if you just bring your dirty, smelly laundry to a laundry shop and ask the owner to do it for you. For three bucks or so, the employees of the shop will not only wash and dry your laundry, but also fold it. Why did you choose the clumsy, unpleasant and money-wasting way of sleeping in a cheap motel?"

Anatole shrugged and had nothing to say. He understood it was idiotic to run away from his laundry. But he simply couldn't apply his brilliant mind to such mundane matters of everyday life. His gross incompetence mystified me. Someone like him would have never survived his boyhood in China during the 1940s. As a young boy, he would have been kidnapped because of his lack of street smarts, sold into slavery and most likely killed for not performing his assigned tasks satisfactorily. After the Second World War, when I was roaming the slum of Nanjing, the capital of the Republic of China under Generalissimo Chiang Kai-shek, I always kept a watchful eye for professional kidnappers. They scared me, and, driven by my fear, I hated them. Whenever possible, my fellow street urchins and I would throw rocks at any person who fit the description of a cunning and mendacious kidnapper. Anatole represented the diametric opposite of the kidnappers of my childhood. I loved him for his honesty and his compassion in addition to his intellectual acuity. Having been schooled in the streets to survive, I wanted to help him, and, contrary to the sentiments of some of our friends, I never felt that he was a burden to me. I believe that the world desperately needs people who are decent and compassionate like Anatole, even if some of them happen to be clumsy and obtuse. To me, they are infinitely more preferable than people who are shrewd, efficient, but predatory.

Shortly after the laundry incident, Anatole lost his job as a research assistant to an entrepreneurial professor in the philosophy department who excelled at garnering huge research grants from the U.S. government by promoting a new mathematical curriculum emphasizing basic set theory instead of arithmetic in grade schools. (That set theory fad resulted in a generation of grade school children who couldn't add, subtract, multiply or divide.) The research assistantship was part of a support package awarded to Anatole upon his admission to the Ph.D. program in the philosophy department. In his letter of termination to Anatole, the professor ended it with the statement that on the basis of a number of the cited incidents, Anatole was clearly unfit to function in the modern world. When Anatole read the letter to the group of Stanford dissidents at a Tresidder Union gathering, everyone cracked up and conceded that the professor, as much as we disliked him and sympathized with Anatole, made a valid observation. Even Anatole concurred, and laughed with all of us.

During antiwar demonstrations, especially in Berkeley, I always kept an eye on Anatole, alerting him at a propitious moment to run away from the goon squads, as if he were a handicapped comrade unable to respond appropriately to his environment. But in the chaos of tear gas and panicking crowds, I was not always successful in steering Anatole away from harm. One time, a member of the San Francisco Tactical Squad caught up with him and walloped him in the cheek with a hard-wood samurai sword, then followed up with a strike on Anatole's ribcage. But Anatole didn't collapse from the assault and started running away. Amazed by Anatole's resiliency, the cop didn't give chase and moved on to attack other targets. For more than one week after the beating, Anatole nursed a blue and green swollen left cheek and a hideous bruise on his right ribcage. But he carried on with his life as if nothing had happened to him.

In 1968, Anatole miraculously earned his Ph.D. from Stanford. Miraculous not because he lacked the ability to write a good dissertation, but because none of his friends thought he could navigate the bureaucratic maze of filing for a degree. He became an assistant professor at San Francisco State University, but soon ran afoul of the radical right-wing president of SF State, S.I. Hayakawa, for directing students to engage in antiwar activities and urging the faculty union to strike against the Hayakawa administration. In 1970, Hayakawa summarily terminated Anatole's employment at SF State. Anatole then landed a faculty position at the University of Colorado at Boulder, where he taught for seven years before SF State rehired him after Hayakawa had left SF State for a seat in the U.S. Senate. Ever since his return to SF State University, Anatole has always proudly claimed to be the only professor who was fired and then rehired by the same institution. He and I kept in touch throughout the decades while he taught at SF State and I taught at UC Santa Barbara. He came down to visit with me from time to time, and I always dined with him when I went to the Bay Area.

It is our impression that since Ronald Reagan's presidency, American society has become increasingly materialistic and transactional. Ostentatious consumption has gained glamor. More and more bright young people have chosen to devote themselves to the mad pursuit of money. Sometimes, I can't help feeling that America has regressed to a state typified by Hong Kong in the 1950s, when I mischievously accused most Hong Kong people of having a brain consisting of only a limbic region and a calculator. Even worse than the people of Hong Kong of the 1950s, more and more Americans nowadays practice the scorched-earth approach in their quest for monetary reward and conventional success. Without a trace of conscience, they lie, cheat, step on anyone, do anything to claw their way ahead and stay ahead. The great Hobsbawm called the 20th century "The Age of Extremes." If he were alive today, I don't know how he would label a world dominated by America's Donald Trump, Russia's Vladimir Putin, China's Xi Jinping, England's Boris Johnson, Israel's Benjamin Netanyahu, Hungary's Viktor Orbán, and Saudi Arabia's Mohammed bin Salman.

Anatole and I often lament the fade of idealism that motivated many young people during the 1960s, even though the Women's March, Black Lives Matter and other popular movements give us hope. But the widespread and callous acceptance of indecency, mendacity, amorality and the wanton destruction of our environment distress us. Occasionally, we reminisce about our feverish activism when we were young and accept that we were wrong on many issues. One of our most uplifting memories remains the Earth Day Marches throughout American cities in spring, 1970. Anatole and I took part in San Francisco. Tens of thousands of marchers filled the streets of downtown. Everyone peacefully demonstrated their wish to save the Earth from human activities. In the entire country, an estimated twenty million marchers participated. That was one-tenth of the American population. They demanded an end to the destruction of our planet.

RUDY

A FEW WEEKS AFTER MY MOTOR SCOOTER ACCIDENT IN September 1963, I went to the Mathematics Department to find out how my academic standing would be affected by my medical leave. My head and most of my face were still wrapped in layers of white gauze that required daily dressing at the outpatient clinic of the Stanford Hospital. Only my right eye and part of my mouth were visible.

When I stepped into the elevator at the Math Department, an olive-skinned young man, mostly bald, wearing loafers, Ray Ban sunglasses, Levi jeans and a professionally ironed khaki shirt with epaulets was already in there. His left arm, resting in a black sling, was all wrapped in gauze. Short, thin, square-shouldered, his face looked as if it wore a permanent semi-sneer.

Looking at me, his semi-sneer turning into a smile, he said, "Hmm, a resurrected Mummy is visiting the math department."

"Yeah," I retorted, "to battle Frankenstein with his left arm in a sling."

He broke out in laughter. Extending his right hand, he said,

"Nice to meet you. My name's Rudy."

"Same here. I am Charles." I shook his hand.

As we stepped out of the elevator, Rudy said unexpectedly, "Come to my office if you have a minute. Let's chat."

It turned out that both of us had come to Palo Alto from the East Coast a few weeks earlier. While I got hit on my Vespa motor scooter, an equally disastrous accident happened to Rudy a few days after his arrival. Hearing a great deal about Berkeley as a preeminent intellectual center and the home of the free speech movement, he drove to Berkeley in his brand-new VW Beetle, walked around the UC campus that he admired, visited the famous bookstores, had a casual dinner, hung out at Cafe Mediterranean to take in the sights, and smoked some weed a sojourner gave him. On his return trip to Palo Alto that night, high from the weed, he cautiously cruised along the slow lane on highway 101, resting his left arm on the car door with its window rolled down. He expected the wind to counter some of the soporific effects of the marijuana. But the blowing wind from the open window wasn't sufficient to keep him alert along the drive. Near Redwood City, he failed to discern the elevated island marking an exit. When the VW beetle hit the curb of the cement island, it jumped into the air, flipped onto the driver's side, and skidded forward for more than a couple hundred feet. The skid mangled his left arm and totaled his Beetle.

We laughed at the inauspicious beginning of our lives in California. A long-lasting friendship began.

A newly minted Ph.D. from the University of Chicago, Rudy came to Stanford as an assistant professor in the Math Department in 1963, the year I entered its Ph.D. program. Although he spent five years in Chicago, he had grown up in New York City and considered himself a New Yorker. His father, an artist who retooled himself into a studio photographer, and his mother immigrated from Naples, Italy, in the early 1930s to escape Fascism and Mussolini. After graduating from Brooklyn Technical High School with distinction at age seventeen, he took a job in a Manhattan architecture firm as a draughtsman to avoid the draft and burden his penurious parents. The pay was good. In four years, having saved a good sum of money, he felt he ought to do something with his life.

Two choices emerged in his mind:

Number one: Buy a Jaguar, a car that he had always fancied whenever one passed by him in New York.

Number two: Get a college education.

It wasn't an easy decision. After mulling over the two options for a month, he took the college route, feeling that he should explore the possibilities in life while he was still young, and college seemed to be a good place to start. Many of his friends from his neighborhood in Brooklyn had gone to the City College of New York. It was a good school, but Rudy, having never ventured out of the New York metropolitan area, thought it would be edifying for him to experience a new environment. That was how he ended up at the University of Michigan at Ann Arbor.

At the University of Michigan, he was quickly recognized for his exceptional aptitude in pure mathematics. After two years, his professors guided him into the Ph.D. program at the University of Chicago, the only top-ranked program that would admit and support gifted students without an undergraduate degree.

At Chicago, Rudy specialized in differential manifolds, a trendy area in mathematics at the time, and proved a significant theorem to earn his Ph.D. degree. He was proud of the fact that, unlike his colleagues at Stanford, he had only a single academic degree to his title. No bachelor's degree and no master's degree.

One year after arriving in Chicago, he got married. But his wife abruptly left him in the third year of their marriage at a time when he was deeply immersed in his research, which meant that he behaved as if he were on an extensive space journey, deadly silent, intensely absorbed and barely communicative. For six months before his wife moved out of their apartment, Rudy was all consumed in an attempt to unknot spheres in the study of differential manifolds. He told me at Stanford, two years after his divorce, that he honestly couldn't blame his wife for abandoning him.

But abandoned, he felt! Even though he never admitted the hurt to himself or anyone else, because, in his mind, feeling hurt from being jilted was a weakness, suggesting a fear of loneliness. He considered himself a loner, a tough guy, not physically, but mentally and psychologically. But I was never fully convinced of that image he liked to project. When we were at Stanford, he was always looking for some dinner companions. There were evenings when I would have been content eating something simple like a can of tuna fish, only to end up with a change of plans because of a call from Rudy pleading with me to go to a restaurant with him.

The hurt from being abandoned by his wife unleashed Rudy's tremendous hostility, directed mostly but not exclusively at women. Yet, he was desperately attracted to them. He could never refrain from turning his head as an attractive woman passed by. Sometimes he would deliberately suck air into his mouth as if he was regretting that he had not made an attempt to befriend her or catch her attention.

The two of us often spent weekends in Carmel if there wasn't a planned antiwar demonstration that required our presence. We would drive down Saturday morning, hike around Point Lobos and Big Sur, bringing food and drinks purchased from the celebrated Mediterranean delicatessen on the first block of Ocean Avenue after the steep downhill stretch from Route 1. In the evening, we typically indulged in a hearty and inexpensive dinner at the Big Sur Inn, a ramshackle, hand-built lodge operated by an old, eccentric Norwegian sailor, who, according to legend, shipwrecked in Big Sur in the 1920s. After surviving the shipwreck, he was so enchanted by the beauty of Big Sur that he never left. With lumber collected from the mountain and the beach, he built a shack in a gully on the steep coastal mountain slope a short distance after the winding Route 1 re-emerged from the town of Big Sur onto an open vista of the Pacific Ocean. Over the years, he expanded his shack into a rustic, multi-room lodge through idiosyncratic additions, fitting perfectly into its rugged surrounding. Rudy and I often bantered with the eccentric Norwegian owner, who became an alcoholic and somewhat of a curmudgeon in his old age. But we never stayed at Big Sur Inn, preferring to sleep in our sleeping bags among the sand dunes at the end of Ocean Avenue to save money.

The main attraction for Rudy in Carmel was Kim Novak, a voluptuous Hollywood star of the 1950s. On most Sunday mornings, she could be found enjoying brunch at an alfresco bar/restaurant along lower Ocean Avenue. Rudy liked to sit at a distance and ogle her.

Rudy's ostentatious ogling always made me feel embarrassed and ill at ease. One just didn't do such things in Hong Kong or China unless one intended to pick a fight with the woman's male companion. A close friend in the Chinese culture would feel obliged, on such occasions, to admonish and warn Rudy forcefully for his benefit, and Rudy, if he were Chinese, would interpret such admonishment as a demonstration of a devoted friendship. According to Chinese social norms, it was the duty of a person to criticize and even scold a friend for aberrant behavior, as long as the criticism or scolding benefited the friend by preventing a pending disaster or improving the friend's character or situation.

This Chinese way of interaction remains valid today in my interactions with bosom friends who understand my criticism as an indication of how much I care for them. It took me a long time to put into practice the Western social rule of not being harsh on friends even if they are doing something detrimental to their own welfare, like gaining a lot of weight, smoking cigarettes, drinking too much alcohol, etc. Among friends, even casual friends, a comment like, "Oh, my God! You've gained so much weight!" is perfectly normal and acceptable in the Chinese world, but unmistakably rude and invasive in the Western world, regardless of the nature of the relationship between the interlocutors.

In the Asian world, the concept of an inviolate individual psychological space among members of a close-knit social group, whether a family or a coterie of close friends, is unknown. It doesn't mean that a person may not keep some thoughts or information secret for one reason or another. But keeping a secret is not part and parcel of observing or maintaining the cultural norm of each individual having an inviolate psychological and physical space. This difference between the East and West has profound ramifications on the psyche and well-being of a Chinese immigrant in America or Europe. It may also have a significant impact on the life of an American or European in East Asia. On the one hand, a Chinese immigrant typically feels infinitely lonely in America or Europe because she or he perceives the Western practice of respecting each other's personal space as a rejection of friendship. On the other hand, an American or European expatriate may feel socially excluded in an East Asian society because the hosts cannot comprehend what constitutes an expat's individual physical and psychological space. Consequently, the hosts keep the expat at arm's length for fear of becoming intrusive, even though they might be fond of him/her and would have loved to have him/her as a friend.

At the time of Rudy's boorish behavior, I was not fully integrated into the Western mode of human interaction, and my reaction to his antics amounted to a compromise between the Chinese way of harsh admonishment and the Western way of leaving him to his individual quirks. When he ogled, I suggested that he should get married. My suggestion inevitably elicited an instant response:

"Nope! Once was enough!"

Over the first few years I knew him, he had several affairs. But the affairs always ended with him walking away from the relationship when an attachment began to develop in earnest. For him, it was safer and easier to abandon than to risk being abandoned. Risk-taking was not in his DNA. The riskiest action he had ever taken in his life was going to Michigan to seek a college education.

Many years later, after settling into a professorship at UCLA, he started a long-term relationship with a woman who was head over heels in love with him. But he professed that he didn't love her. It was merely a convenient arrangement, according to him. They shared all expenses, living in a house he had bought in Brentwood, and she deferred to him on all issues. When Rudy and I saw each other in Los Angeles, I noticed that he continued to ogle beautiful women just as he did when we were at Stanford. Nineteen years later, in my early forties, when I fell in love and married, he told me that I was a brave soul.

During the first year of our friendship, Rudy was eager to enrich my mathematical knowledge, especially when we drove long distances to visit scenic spots in California. Explaining Lie groups, manifolds, curvatures, rings, fields, etc., he would commandeer the windshield and write furiously with his index finger as if the finger was a piece of chalk and the windshield was a blackboard. Other drivers on the road probably thought that we were engaged in some crazy games or heated arguments. It was a miracle that we never got into an accident during those tutoring sessions on the highway.

By the second year in our friendship, our conversations tended to focus more on literature and social science than on mathematics, although we continued to discuss mathematical problems. French fiction by Stendhal, Hugo, Zola, Maupassant, Gide and Camus was our favorite. (Both of us identified with Julian Sorel, the protagonist in Stendhal's *Red and Black* in terms of his lonely struggle to survive and prevail in a pitiless environment). I had been reading French fiction at the instigation of several dissidents who regularly assembled at the Tresidder Union each afternoon.

One day, during dinner in a cheap Chinese restaurant in Mountain View, Rudy blurted out without any warning, "I think you should get out of mathematics and pursue a career in humanistic studies."

Startled, I reacted very defensively.

"Why? Do you think I'm not good at mathematics?"

"No, no, no!" he protested loudly. "On the contrary, I think you are very gifted. In all our discussions, you show an uncanny ability to grasp mathematic concepts. In fact, I am very impressed. But your personality doesn't fit well in mathematics."

"I don't understand. What does it mean to have a personality unfit for mathematics?"

"Don't take offense, Charles—let me explain." He began, "Pure mathematics is detached from life and human existence, and research in pure mathematics is a solitary undertaking that transports a mathematician into an imaginary world. Mathematics does not concern itself with existential issues or the human condition or the vicissitudes of emotions or the history of civilization or the evolution of human society. The concepts and theorems in pure mathematics stand by themselves. Some of them may have applications in real-world problems. But that is not the concern of mathematicians. You, however, are deeply interested in a broad spectrum of topics related to human existence: history, politics, literature, music, art, philosophy, physics, biological sciences. I have seen how you were enthralled by Stendhal's *Red and Black*, thrilled by the intellectual history of Vienna, absorbed by the antiwar protest movement. I saw your eyes light up when Francelle talked about the paintings of Goya and Velasquez, or when she described the architecture and intellectual monuments of the Umayyad Caliphate in Andalusia during the Middle Ages. I observed you devour Robert Jungk's *Brighter than a Thousand Suns: A Personal History of Atomic Scientists* in one full day, skipping lunch and dinner to read. You have a remarkable capacity for retaining and linking information from different disciplines. It's wonderful."

He went on to explain that he wasn't denigrating mathematics. In his view, mathematics was a world in its own right. There was an unparalleled elegance and beauty in mathematical thinking. He loved it and reveled in it. But he reckoned that he also paid a price for his love of mathematics by giving up most human interactions.

At that point, he smiled and said, "Haven't you noticed how uncommunicative mathematicians are? Just look at the people in our department. Most of them are withdrawn, lost in their own mathematical world. I don't think your personality is suited for that kind of life. You like people, and you are too involved in the real affairs of the world."

"Are you telling me that mathematics is not real?" I asked.

"Well, I'm not sure if there's a definitive answer to your question. Take a number, say, five. Is it a real entity or is it merely a mathematical invention? I don't know."

Rudy became pensive, which was uncommon. He tended to be exuberant most of the time. Then, he said, "Perhaps Kurt Gödel can give you an answer."

Gödel, a titan in mathematical logic, proved the *Incompleteness Theorem* in 1931 that shook the mathematical world. That theorem showed conclusively that "mathematical truth" is NOT the same as "provability." In other words, there are TRUE mathematical statements that cannot be PROVED.

"Yes, I agree with you." I felt Rudy had touched a delicate nerve in my life. "I have not thought of how mathematics is detached from everything in life. But I'm very much affected by the insecurity of doing mathematics. I'm never sure that I can solve a chosen problem. In addition, at my stage of development, I have absolutely no way to assess my potential. Am I going to be a good or mediocre or lousy mathematician? I don't have the faintest idea. Yet, in all other domains of intellectual endeavor, I feel relatively at ease with my ability and relatively confident that I could do well. You are right. I tend to be dilettantish, eager to get my hands on every branch of knowledge, trying to learn everything, dabble in every subject. For me, the quest for knowledge, which confers great pleasure, is like going to a See's Candy store, where I can never be content with eating only one piece of truffle. I want to taste all the other truffles, perhaps not at one time, and I don't feel like leaving the shop until I have acquired at least a box of them. They all look tempting and delicious."

Rudy tried to reassure me that if I wanted to remain in mathematics, I would do well. His generous assessment didn't assuage my insecurity, but he had successfully planted the idea in me to switch from mathematics to some other discipline. What that other discipline would be, I didn't know at the time. When Anatole brought up anthropology and linguistics in one of our conversations and induced me to read Colin Turnbull's *The Forest People*, I did get a hunch on what that other discipline might be because the book was captivating.

That evening in my bedroom, as I mulled over what Rudy said about mathematics, the images of the Friday afternoon tea party at Stanford's Math Department surfaced in my mind.

The weekly afternoon tea party was designed to facilitate faculty and graduate student interaction. At the party, people stood around in a spacious lounge, sipping tea or coffee while munching cookies. Quietness prevailed the gathering, even though it was a social event. A Hi-Fi system purred classical music, typically Mozart if not J. S. Bach. A favorite piece was Mozart's clarinet quintet, K. 581, a subdued elegy that was at once plaintive and beautiful as the clarinet wailed softly. J. S. Bach's *Well-Tempered Clavier* and Domenico Scarlatti's harpsichord sonatas were the other frequently played pieces, as if the elegance of the preludes and fugues in the *Well-Tempered Clavier* and the lyricism of Scarlatti's sonatas reflected the essence and beauty of pure mathematics. As a rule, the departmental staff always selected music that was subtle, intricate, gentle and of course, classical. Even Mozart's *Eine kleine Nachtmusik* would be too bombastic. Most of the attendees of the party, however, were silent. Only a few engaged in conversations. Many stared at their feet as if they suffered from Asperger's Syndrome. When I walked into the tea party, I always felt as if I had entered an archaic necropolis, eerie and spooky, especially if the background music happened to be the Gregorian chant.

One exception to the norm at the party was Professor Kai-lai Chung, a distinguished probability theorist. Incapable of suffering fools or moderating the amplitude of his voice, he would occasionally shake up the party with his favorite rejoinder delivered in a deafening voice with a thick accent:

"You have no taste in mathematics, just like you have no taste in Chinese food!"

No one ever took offense from Professor Chung because he never intended harm when he barked. In fact, he always acted generously to those who sought advice from him on mathematical problems.

At the tea party on November 6, 1964, three days after the presidential election, Professor Chung burst in and asked the assembled people there in his usual loud voice, "Who did you vote for, Goldwater or Johnson?"

Everyone was surprised. No one among the department, faculty and graduate students espoused conservative or right-wing ideology. Why would anyone vote for Goldwater? He had said that he would seek victory in Vietnam at any cost and prosecute the war even if America had to bomb Vietnam back to the stone age, whereas Johnson campaigned on the promise to end the Vietnam war. Most of the people looked at Chung and wondered what he was up to when he posed such a stupid question, even though a few did meekly respond with "Johnson."

"I knew it! I knew it!" Chung hollered. "You all voted for Johnson. Now you have given him a mandate, and he will do the opposite of what he promised to do in Vietnam during his campaign. You are fools!"

A few months later, everyone came to appreciate the brilliance of Professor Chung's prescience.

After that initial conversation about my fitness for mathematical research, Rudy never gave up urging me to move into humanistic studies. When I did end up studying linguistics at UC Berkeley, he was delighted and congratulated me for my courage in making the switch.

At UCLA, where he spent his entire career after Stanford and a two-year interlude at the Institute for Advanced Study at Princeton, he became an avid long-distance runner. Some days, when I drove to UCLA to attend a linguistic seminar, I would find him jogging along the wide grassy median studded with coral trees on San Vicente Boulevard between UCLA and the Pacific Ocean. Occasionally we would have dinner together. He remained a loner all his life, even though for twenty-some years, he had a woman as a housemate who adored him and yearned for his love.

In 2017, at age 81, he was diagnosed with prostate cancer. Refusing medical treatment, he died five months later, a loner as he wished, in the UCLA hospital, his female housemate having already passed away two years earlier from a sudden massive heart attack. In the hospital, he had instructed his lawyer who handled his estate to notify me and the UCLA Department of Mathematics of his death after it happened.

FRANCELLE

IN FALL 1964, EVERY MALE DISSIDENT AT STANFORD WAS IN LOVE with Francelle.

Well, almost every male dissident.

I didn't think I was.

Rudy was not. He wouldn't have fallen in love with anyone, not even if Aphrodite materialized in front of him with a beckoning smile. He would've stared at her lustily and tried to get her into bed. But falling in love? Not a chance! His heart had been sheathed in cast iron, never to face the risk of being broken again. In fact, he was disturbed by the obsequious behavior of those who were awed by Francelle.

One afternoon, as a good number of dissidents congregated at Tresidder Union, Francelle approached. When she drew near, Rudy announced loudly with a sneer, "Ah! The Queen Bee is here. Everyone gets up!"

Much to my surprise, everyone did rise to offer his chair to Francelle, as if they were members of an infantry platoon responding to an order from their commander. When Francelle took her seat, Rudy and I chuckled at the expense of everyone else who suffered a brief moment of embarrassment.

Besides having a steady girlfriend in Berkeley, Anatole thought it would be foolish to pine for a woman like Francelle.

"I'm not in her league," Anatole conceded one day when we were alone.

In spite of the passion Francelle stirred up among the male dissidents at Stanford, her face did not carry the picture-perfect beauty like that of Elizabeth Taylor; her figure was not voluptuous like that of Kim Novak; in fact, she was relatively flat-chested, and she did not project the image of a provocatively attractive woman like Ava Gardner. What she did have, as everyone could see, was that feminine mystique so exquisitely portrayed by Jeanne Moreau as Catherine in François Truffaut's film, *Jules et Jim*. Catherine was formidable yet irresistible, strong and unyielding yet tender and kind-hearted, intelligent and analytical yet passionate and capricious.

Tall, lanky and full of energy, her face chiseled and adorned with eyes like a doe, a Roman nose hinting a Mediterranean lineage, and sensuous lips, Francelle always tied her auburn hair in a loose ponytail that bounced cheerfully when she walked in her casual clothes. I never saw her dressed up during the two years I knew her. But one could hardly be in her presence without being mindful of her magnetism.

She hailed from England in 1964. Before matriculating in Romance languages and literature at Oxford University, she received an elite education at a private boarding school in Switzerland where she acquired fluency in five languages. She was a Marxist, a dedicated fighter for the underprivileged. There would've been a theatrical competition among the male Stanford dissidents for her hand, worthy of a thrilling novel, if it were not for the fact that she came from England to be with her boyfriend, Ken Mills.

Ken projected a large presence in his own right. Born and brought up in Trinidad, he earned his D. Phil degree in philosophy from New College at Oxford, where John Austin, Peter Strawson, et al. developed the school of ordinary language philosophy during the 1950s and 1960s. Among other scholastic contributions, the school of ordinary language philosophy was known for the elucidation of speech acts: predicates such as "thank," "regret," "forgive," "be sorry," "order," "condemn," "ordain," "sentence" (as in the judiciary domain), and "declare" constitute speech acts when they are cast in present tense with a first person subject and a second person object (if the predicate is transitive) in ordinary speech. Phrases such as:

"I forgive you."

"I order you to leave."

"I am sorry."

"I sentence you to life imprisonment."

differ from declarative statements in that they perform the act of forgiving, the act of ordering, the act of regretting, the act of sentencing in addition to having a communicative function as all expressions in speech do. Speech acts like those occur in every language of the world. They involve a class of predicates that stands apart from all other predicates. Ken taught a popular course at Stanford on speech acts after joining the faculty of philosophy in fall, 1963.

Light-skinned, Ken combed his kinky hair straight up to further enhance his six-foot-four stature. He had a mellifluous voice and spoke perfect Queen's English better than anyone I had ever met, and certainly more eloquently than most Englishmen, including the Oxbridge elite. Effeminate and cool, he was a serial womanizer, seducing most undergraduate females who attended his classes with wit, charm and erudition. By the time Francelle arrived at Stanford during the Fall quarter of 1964 to continue their relationship, he was already well-known throughout the campus for his sexual conquests. But he was unfailingly gentle and kind to every one of his past sexual partners, although some complained to their confidants that he had misled them with false promises. No one knew the details of his relationships. But I heard rumors that he had promised to marry several of his liaisons. His presence gave cold feet to those who were secretly in love with Francelle. But Francelle's arrival at Stanford had no inhibitive effect on his philandering. Everyone was mystified by their skewed relationship. Some expressed dismay at Francelle's acquiescence in Ken's unfaithfulness.

As someone whose physical contact with females stopped at hand-holding in Hong Kong, I found Francelle and Ken's relationship beyond comprehension. In fact, I made no attempt to understand it.

When other dissidents gossiped about the relationship between Francelle and Ken in their absence at our Tresidder Union gatherings, I never participated. The topic was simply too strange, complex and incomprehensible for me.

Of course, in traditional China, a well-to-do man would keep concubines in his home together with his wife. (The fabulous 1991 movie *Raise the Red Lantern* by Zhang Yimou tells a gripping story about the lives of a rich merchant's concubines and wife in a changing era in China.) But that was the tradition of feudal China, which the intellectuals of my parent's generation had already denounced and abandoned. In addition, that tradition had its own rules and code of conduct, none of which applied to America in the mid-1960s. I only knew of that tradition as part of Chinese socio-history.

The way I grew up entailed absolutely no education about man-and-woman relationships. I had a very romantic ideal of love and marriage that couldn't be more alien and outlandish to the liberated and free-wheeling young Americans in the 1960s. One evening in 1965 at a party, a young woman taking an interest in me offered me some weed, which I declined—it wasn't my moral principles but my instinct for self-preservation that instructed me to stay clear of all recreational drugs. She then asked if I would like something stronger, like hashish, cocaine or opium.

Horrified, I responded with an emphatic NO, at which point she said in an accusatory tone, "Are you some kind of a square?"

"No, much worse than that," I responded. "I'm a polygon."

She didn't think I was funny at all and lost interest in me immediately.

Francelle was a steadfast and industrious participant in all antiwar activities at Stanford, making picket signs, designing leaflets, milling around with fellow protestors at different locations. Ironically, she held a research job at the Hoover Institution, a well-known right-wing national think tank which the Stanford faculty repeatedly tried to dislodge from the campus. When she worked at the Hoover Institution, among the permanent Hoover fellows was Alexander Kerensky, a key politician in the 1917 February Bourgeois Democratic Revolution, also known as the March Revolution in Russia. For a brief few months, Kerensky served as the Minister-Chairman, i.e., Prime Minister, of the Socialist government of Russia until the October Bolshevik Revolution led by Lenin. Because of Kerensky's role in overturning the Romanov Czar dynasty and my interest in modern Russian history, I was curious to meet the man. Francelle did me a favor by securing an appointment for me to meet him. Unfortunately, Kerensky was already a broken old man by then, stuck in exile since the Bolsheviks came to power nearly fifty years earlier. He was neither mentally sharp nor coherent during our conversation. Nevertheless, I was glad to have met a historical figure like him after having read several books on 20th century Russia.

In the eyes of some dissidents, Francelle's research assistantship at Hoover Institution amounted to a blemish in her credentials. But to her, even though the Hoover Institution accommodated many rightwing politicians, it offered her a job with a decent salary. I always defended her when someone disparaged her job behind her back. In my view, 1960s America, its imperialistic foreign policies and domestic racism notwith-standing, bore no resemblance to Germany of the 1930s when the Nazis were laying the foundation for a scheme to foist their evil on the world. I did not consider living and working in America, including working in a conservative think tank, equivalent to complicity in an evil empire.

Some dissidents in Berkeley and Stanford did raise the thorny issue of when and at what point an ordinary citizen became complicit in a nation's unethical policies, such as the U.S. government's bombing and killing of Vietnamese. I knew a number of brilliant young men and women who felt so despondent over the antiwar movement's impotence that they emigrated to western rural Canada and joined agricultural communes. A fellow student of Keith's in the English department gave up an offer of a tenure track professorship from Columbia University and left America permanently to become a farmer. The best student in my program abandoned his pursuit of his doctoral degree and disap-peared. Many more, who might not have been brilliant with the promise of successful academic careers, succumbed to drug culture to escape the depression caused by the political climate in America. Some fell into the ranks of the so-called "drop-out" movement. Many of them became "hippies." Rudy had no patience with them, defining a hippie as a person who considered "everything that belonged to him was his, and everything that belonged to you was also his." I viewed hippies as hedonists who, with minimal social or political awareness, detested hard work.

One day, Rudy, who tended to drape in sartorial elegance with his tailored shirt and Italian blazer tightly hugging his torso, and I walked by a bearded, unkempt young man on Telegraph Avenue in Berkeley. He was panhandling.

"Spare change," he called out as he stretched his right arm toward us.

We ignored him and kept walking. But he refused to accept our rejection. Following us, he persisted in his begging for "spare change," probably because Rudy fit the bill of a wealthy square, even though he was far from being wealthy, and I, in no way, resembled a hippie.

Suddenly, Rudy wheeled around and barked, "Yeah! Not for you!"

The panhandler was startled. So was I. But I didn't admonish Rudy because by then I harbored my own resentment against hippies. They destroyed the free universities I had helped establish in Berkeley and Palo Alto by voting my friends and me out of the steering committees.

On the Saturday afternoon of Thanksgiving weekend of 1964, Francelle, Anatole, Keith, Rudy, I and a few others were sitting outside of the Tresidder Union anticipating a dramatic event. The campus was relatively deserted. Most undergraduate students had gone to the "Big Game" held at the Stanford Stadium, the annual football contest between UC Berkeley and Stanford.

A couple of weeks earlier, two undergraduate dissidents had announced to us confidentially that they intended to "bomb" the Big Game with antiwar leaflets from an airplane. Scions of wealthy families, they had pilot's licenses and the funds to print tens of thousands of leaflets they had designed. On one side of the leaflet was the iconic photo of a naked young Vietnamese girl with napalm burns on her body, running on a wide thoroughfare, mouth agape, tears streaming down her cheeks. The other side of the leaflet contained four large bold-lettered words, **STOP THE VIETNAM WAR.**

The two of them conceived and financed the project all by themselves. They informed my friends and me. We were supposed to keep it a secret.

On that fateful afternoon at about 3 p.m., as we were anxiously expecting the event while sitting outside of the Tresidder Union, we could hear the roar of the fans at the stadium about half a mile away. Then, a small single-engine plane appeared in the sky. It circled the Stanford campus. We all tensed up.

After the plane completed a triangular flight path over the stadium, we heard the sudden roar of a revved-up engine, and the plane seemed to dive toward the ground before disappearing. Even though we didn't hear any explosion, everyone was distraught, believing that the plane had crashed.

Rudy cried out, "Jesus!" He got up and left.

Without a loony laugh, Anatole cupped his cheeks and swore, "Shit! Anyone have a bottle of Old Bushmills? Please!"

Keith, wordless, was pulling his kinky hair with both hands.

Francelle was in tears. Sitting next to me, she reached out with her left arm and held my right hand tightly.

I got up and walked Francelle to her campus apartment, a loft in an old army barrack building. It was the first time I felt something for Francelle. But I didn't know what it was and didn't dwell on it.

The next day, I found out that the "bombing" attempt, although failed, did not end in tragedy. Our friends' plane carrying tens of thousands of leaflets did not crash. As the "bomber" (the other fellow being the pilot) released the leaflets, many of them were caught on the rudder on the tail of the plane. None floated down into the football stadium. As the leaflet caused the rudder to jam, the pilot had difficulty navigating the plane. In desperation, he dropped the plane to tree-top level, gunned the engine at full throttle, sent out an SOS signal, and aimed for an emergency landing at San Carlos Airport, the nearest airport, about ten miles directly north of Palo Alto. When it landed, FBI agents carrying submachine guns were waiting for the two young antiwar protestors. As they were handcuffed and being led away, one FBI agent prodded the blond, blue-eyed pilot with the muzzle of his submachine gun and asked, in all seriousness:

"Do you eat with chopsticks?"

The entire incident ended rather comically. The Big Game was not affected. The spectators of the game never got wind of what transpired in the sky above them. When the FBI agents took the two antiwar protestors to the San Mateo police station to book them in prison, the authority didn't know what crime to charge them with. They didn't endanger anyone's life other than their own. They didn't hurt anyone or damage any property. They didn't trespass on forbidden air space. They didn't cause a public disturbance. They didn't threaten anyone with violence. After hours of delay, during which the FBI officials were presumably consulting their superiors and attorneys in various departments under different jurisdictions, it was decided that the Santa Clara County Sheriff would charge our two friends with a misdemeanor of littering. After signing some papers and posting bail, our friends were released.

The two "litter bugs" told me the whole story the next day.

They laughed hysterically when they repeated the FBI agent's question about eating with chopsticks.

"The question came from nowhere. It was so absurd!" one of them commented.

I took it as an ominous sign of forthcoming repression and harassment in my direction because of my ethnicity. Indeed, a few months later, an FBI agent and an INS agent, with guns drawn, broke into my house in the wee hours of one morning, and two years later, INS revoked my student visa to initiate my deportation.

———————————

As the summer of 1965 drew near, Francelle and I often spent time alone talking about life as well as politics, art, literature and biological science (which began to draw my interest because of the ramifications of molecular genetics that would elucidate the inheritance of phenotypic traits). I learned that her father was a fiercely independent scholar and musician of Armenian ethnicity and her mother, an equally learned American beauty. They chose to make their home in Andalusia, Spain, after their marriage in Boston, where he earned his doctoral degree in philosophy from Harvard while generating an income as a professional violinist. In post-war Europe, which was poor and chaotic, they managed to corral the copyrights and monopolize the publication of most pre-Baroque music, as they unearthed and purchased early music scores hidden in remote monasteries, nondescript churches and obscure libraries all over the continent before the resurgence of interest in Medieval and Renaissance music in the late 1950s.

Living with her parents in Andalusia, a region known for its strong identity, rich culture and tumultuous history involving the adherents of the world's three monotheistic religions, Judaism, Islam and Christianity, Francelle was American by birth but Andalusian in her upbringing. She carried with her that Andalusian enchantment marked by verve, vitality and passion with a tragic submission to fate. That enchantment manifested itself dramatically in copla and flamenco, the two musical genres originated in Al-Andalus and epitomized by the songs of Antonio Quintero, Rafael de León and others. Among Francelle's meager belongings in her loft in a former army barrack on Stanford campus were several flamenco records of those haunting and dramatic songs rendered by a Spanish singer with a rich, dark, beautiful mezzo-soprano voice, and a record of the same singer reciting Federico García Lorca's lamentation of death, *A las cinco de la tarde*. The poem's cadence and prosody were dramatically rendered in the singer's low, resonant voice. It invoked an image from Mozart's grand opera *Don Giovanni*, where the Commendatore statue's pounding steps accompanied its ominous calling for Don Giovanni as it approached to take the womanizer to hell.

On the coffee table in Francelle's loft laid two art books of Moorish architecture in Al-Andalus and Morocco, obviously treasures to her, because she brought them with her all the way from England. Looking at the photographs of the Great Mosque of Córdoba, built by the order of Abd al-Rahman, the Umayyad founder of the Muslim dynasty in Andalusia, and the photographs of Alhambra in Granada, the opulent palace of the Nasrids caliph, the last Moorish Muslim dynasty in Spain, I was awestruck by their exquisite beauty—soaring geometric designs imbued with rich colors and shapes.

As a little girl, Francelle used to play hide-and-seek with her younger brother in the forest of columns in the enormous main prayer hall of the Great Mosque. The columns varied in design: spotless ivory white, wine-colored marble, polished granite with glittering quartz and mica, onyx with parallel bands of alternating colors, pure red jasper with intricate veins. Each column stood as an exquisite piece of art crowned with an ornate capital, and every two columns were conjoined by a double-layered arch made of alternating red and white wedge-shaped stones (voussoirs). The lower arch was shaped like a horseshoe while the upper arch was almost semicircular. Together they framed an open space that looked like the maw of a gigantic great white shark. These double arches, while serving a dazzling decorative function, enabled the architect to raise the ceiling of the prayer hall to an imposing height. The cornucopia of color and geometric patterns of structures in this enormous prayer hall was breathtaking.

Francelle pointed out to me that the focus of the great prayer hall was the gilded prayer niche called mihrab.

"It's arguably the most exquisitely decorated mihrab in the Islamic world," she said.

High above it, a beautiful dome with crisscrossing ribs covered by gold mosaic reflected ambient light onto the mihrab. Never tired of wandering inside and outside the mosque, Francelle, as a grown-up visiting her parents, would spend days examining the mosaics and azulejos.

Her description of the Great Mosque and the Alhambra fueled my wanderlust.

"Someday I will visit Al-Andalus," I promised myself.

The visit occurred decades later in the company of my wife, my daughter and my son. In Córdoba, as I stood in front of a bronze statue of Maimonides (Moses ben Maimon), decked in Arabic robes and replete with a turban, the preeminent physician, scientist, philosopher in both the Jewish and Islamic world during the Middle Ages, images of Francelle expounding all of the splendor of Al-Andalus flickered through my mind. She loved Talmudic studies and revered Maimonides.

"I've always wanted to be a rabbi. If I were a Jewish man, that would have been my calling!"

Those were her words. But she was born long before women were admitted into the rabbinical profession.

The summer of 1965 began uneventfully. Most Stanford dissidents went home to visit their families. Francelle's boyfriend, Ken, returned to England to take care of his remaining affairs. The free universities were taken out of my hands, and antiwar activities at Stanford slowed to a halt. One balmy evening, after Francelle, Rudy and I finished a late dinner in a restaurant, she and I decided to take a stroll on the 18-hole Stanford golf course in the foothills west of the campus.

The soft, rolling fairways, surrounded by eucalyptus and conifers, were partitioned by several wooded groves. I had always thought it was the most enchanting place for a promenade, especially in the night when it appeared to be a world unto itself, peaceful and idyllic, quiet and still, barricaded from its dull surroundings. It evoked the rolling hills of England's Lake District where Wordsworth, Coleridge and Southey strolled and sought their muse.

When Francelle and I arrived at the golf course, it was absolutely still and silent. A starry sky glittering above our head, a new moon rising just beyond the horizon, casting a silver sheen over the soft grass on the fairways. Shadows of trees added a mystic and primal dimension because of their darkness. Occasionally the silence was broken by an owl hooting, perhaps calling for a mate, perhaps declaring its territory. But Francelle and I did not feel we were intruders. Immersed in the bucolic beauty, we felt we were part of the environment as we walked. Holding hands, neither of us uttered a word.

Suddenly she stopped, pulled me toward her and embraced me in her arms.

That was my first encounter with love, not just romantic love, but LOVE, period. The journal I kept at the time was filled with the sort of rapturous writing typical of a wide-eyed teenager in love, even though I was already in my mid-twenties:

"Her auburn hair, her hazel eyes, her velvety skin and enticing scent, her voluptuous lips seeking kisses, her soft and caressing hands, ah, the beautiful contour of her long legs, her buttocks like the golden peach of Samarkand . . ."

In my teens, I was perpetually searching for love, in vain, without any awareness of what love was or could be. Was I yearning for familial love, brotherly love, or romantic love?

Even today, I'm not sure of an answer.

I knew only that I wanted someone to snuggle with, someone I could trust, someone who thought well of me, someone who would hold my hand and back me up in a world which, I thought, was hostile and unforgiving.

In hindsight, what I wanted as a teenager seemed to be a fusion of everything spiritual, platonic as well as carnal. Carnal desire was a latent feeling that I had never dared admit to myself. Sex was taboo in my upbringing. My yearning for love at that time probably stemmed from a tangled web of emotions, intense yet unfulfilled, pitiful yet genuine, fearful yet romantic.

When I was smitten with Francelle, love brought ecstasy, a sense of fulfillment and wholesomeness, as if my world had been transformed, magically, from infinite loneliness into a warm cocoon suffused with happiness, goodwill and benevolence.

That summer, I put aside everything that was important: antiwar protests, mathematics, my quest for knowledge, the free universities, the dissident organizations. Francelle, on her part, took an unpaid leave from Hoover Institution. We spent every day and night together, taking trips to Mendocino, Big Sur, the Sierras, the Oregon coast, hiking in the mountains of the Sierra Madre, strolling on the beaches along Big Sur, reveling in the grandeur and beauty of nature. We picnicked at secluded meadows and isolated sea coves to ensure our privacy. We told each other stories of our youth: hers mostly bright and cheerful; mine, often dark and grief-stricken. We read short stories and novels to each other when we felt lazy, cozying up in front of a fireplace in our hotel room on the wind-swept Oregon coast, or simply in her loft on campus.

She introduced me to the Beatles, whose simple lyrics and rhapsodic music astonished me with their beauty. I was sorry for preemptively dismissing them as part of the loud and deafening rock and roll genre I called "hippie music" without ever listening to their records. Thankfully, Francelle corrected my unfounded prejudice.

I took her to the Jazz Workshop on Broadway in San Francisco to hear Charles Mingus, John Coltrane, Miles Davis, Thelonious Monk, Dizzy Gillespie, Cannonball Adderley, John Lewis and other great jazz musicians perform stirring melodies with intricate polyrhythms and mind-boggling improvisations in small combos. She had heard their music but never seen them in live performance, and she was thrilled.

We attended the Bach Music Festival in Carmel, where early music discovered by her father played a prominent role. When we chatted with some festival musicians at an open gathering after a concert, they talked about her father as the "king of early music."

"If you want to play early music, you have to buy the scores from him," one of them said.

When her father came up in our conversation at the festival, Francelle told me unexpectedly that her parents refused to meet Ken because he was Black, but they might consider a Chinese an acceptable partner for their daughter. That was the only occasion that Ken came up in our conversation. For a brief movement, he cast a shadow in my mind, but vanished quickly, swept away by the brisk activities of our newly minted life.

For three months, Francelle and I, oblivious to the rest of the world, lived, loved, laughed, sang, shared our thoughts and hearts by ourselves. It was a magical time, as if we had serendipitously landed on an unknown island of bounty in the south seas.

We were in heaven!

We also encountered some unbelievably bizarre vestiges of pre-World War II America that defied common sense. The first time we checked into a hotel on our trips, I signed for us at the check-in desk as "Charles Li and Francelle Karapetyan."

The proprietor looked at me and asked, "Are you married?"

"No," I said.

"Well, I didn't hear that," he said. "Please sign in as Mr. and Mrs."

Mystified, I enquired, "Why?"

"The law of the land says male and female guests checking into the same hotel room must be husband and wife," he informed me. "Fortunately the California government no longer takes the trouble to enforce the law. But it remains valid. As the manager of this hotel, I don't want to get into any legal trouble. Please sign in as a married couple."

Francelle and I were aghast. Why would any government enact a law prohibiting unmarried couples from occupying the same hotel room? What purpose did such a law serve? If the legislators had intended to enforce Puritanism, such a law would be completely futile, if not frivolous and hypocritical. After all, hotel rooms were not the only places where men and women could engage in sexual liaisons or illicit relationships.

But I followed the hotel proprietor's advice and signed in as Mr. and Mrs. Charles Li.

Noticing my ill-concealed contempt, the proprietor decided to enlighten me with some related information. "Many states in the Union still enforce anti-miscegenation laws. The California anti-miscegenation statute was declared unconstitutional seventeen years ago in 1948. If that statue remained today, I would not be able to accept you as guests at this hotel."

"Well," I turned to Francelle. "We learn some unbelievable feature about America every day, don't we!"

After that incident, in order to avoid unnecessary fuss, I always signed into a hotel with Francelle as Mr. and Mrs. The name depended on what struck my fancy at the moment. I used, among other celebrated names, Mr. and Mrs. Kublai Khan, Mr. and Mrs. Akira Kurosawa, Mr. and Mrs. Toshiro Mifune—the main actor in almost all of Kurosawa's samurai movies—Mr. and Mrs. Minamoto (Members of the Minamoto clan reigned as Japan's Shoguns during the Kamakura Period from the 12th to the 14th century). None of the celebrity names I borrowed ever raised an eyebrow.

One day, as Francelle and I were checking into a hotel near Mount Shasta, California, I signed as Mr. and Mrs. Karl von Lie, probably because at that moment, I was thinking about a mathematical construct, the Lie group, named after the Norwegian mathematician, Sophus Lie.

Observing my full head of pitch-black straight hair, my quintessential Chinese face, and my borrowed name, Karl von Lie, the proprietress humorously quipped, "German, eh?"

"No, no, no." I wagged my index finger. "Austrian."

She broke into laughter. So did I.

———————————————

The summer of 1965 was blissful but short. As Fall approached, Francelle and I knew we could no longer ignore the fact that Ken was returning from England.

Throughout the summer, I never asked about Ken or Francelle's relationship with him. Absorbed in the present, Francelle and I pursued our dreams and activities as if he never existed.

The day before Ken's return, Francelle broached the forbidden subject. She said that she needed to talk to him about us, and I'd better clear out my belongings in her loft. I didn't know what she meant by "talking to him" and didn't have the heart to ask her for an explanation. To me, her announcement spelled the end of our relationship, no matter how desperately I wanted to win her from Ken. Deeply hurt and nearly despondent, I left her loft and never spoke to her again.

During my remaining three quarters at Stanford, I did my best to avoid Francelle and Ken, never showing up at the afternoon gathering of dissidents at Tresidder Union, preferring to protest the Vietnam War in Berkeley rather than Stanford. On the whole, the 1965-66 academic year was an uneventful time except for a bout of gastric ulcer, which caused me to vomit blood. I had to be hospitalized for five days and given a blood transfusion. By the time I moved to Berkeley to start my new pursuit in linguistics during the summer of 1966, I had reached a closure of my relationship with Francelle. She no longer lingered in my mind.

Keith later wrote me in a letter, when he and I were facing deportation, that Francelle and Ken moved to New York City shortly after I went to Berkeley. Ken took a position at Yale University. In spring, 1968, walking down Telegraph Avenue one day, I saw the name Kenneth Mills in a front-page headline of *The New York Times* at a corner magazine store. Surprised, I bought the paper and read the story. It turned out that he was involved in a legal dispute with Yale University because, while teaching full-time there, he accepted another full-time professorial appointment at the Stony Brook campus of the New York State University without informing either of his two employers of his other position. When Yale discovered his dual appointment, the administration issued an ultimatum requiring him to resign from one of the two professorships. Ken then challenged Yale's ultimatum in court, claiming that he had faithfully and diligently fulfilled all of his duties and responsibilities at both institutions and therefore, Yale's demand had no substantive legal standing. *The New York Times* article raised the possibility that Ken's argument might be meritorious if Yale could not prove that he had been derelict in fulfilling his professorial duties there. The case was being argued in court at the time. The novelty of the dispute between Ken and Yale caught the interest of the news media, because presumably no one had tried to hold two full-time professorships simultaneously at two universities before Ken. I never bothered to find out the verdict of the trial. It didn't interest me enough to warrant my time and effort.

Decades later, Keith told me in Toronto that Ken had died tragically of a sudden heart attack a few years after he went to Yale, and Francelle, after earning a Ph.D. in Romance languages and literature from Yale, became the headmistress of a boarding school for girls in Vermont.

DAVID

ONE EVENING IN 1969, I STEPPED INTO LARRY BLAKE, THE ONLY restaurant on the four blocks of Telegraph Avenue south of the campus that was quasi-formal in the sense that, unlike the other eateries in the area, it had waiters, a bar and well-furnished booths for customers to sit in. I never ate there precisely because it was quasi-formal and relatively expensive for my budget. That evening, I was famished and decided to splurge.

In the restaurant, I was startled to find David, an old friend from Hong Kong. He was a friend, not a bosom friend, mostly because he came from a close-knit and well-to-do family, which meant that he was properly supported and didn't behave like a rebel. My close friends in Hong Kong were like me after I left China in 1958—poor and deprived of the comfort of a family. Unlike well-supported young people, we tended to be irreverent, non-conforming and occasionally mischievous troublemakers. But David was definitely a friend. Sometimes, we played bridge at his girlfriend's family apartment. We also saw each other in track meets. He ran the 400-meter event, and I ran the 100-meter and the 200-meter events.

At the time we ran into each other in Berkeley, David was working as a waiter at Larry Blake's restaurant. Both of us were overjoyed to see each other, and naturally, after so many years, we wanted to catch up.

"Meet me here at 11 p.m. The restaurant will be closed by then," he told me.

It turned out that he had an apartment right around Telegraph Avenue on Dwight Way. We walked over to his place. Getting a lift from the caffeine of the green tea he brewed, we started talking, sometimes in Cantonese, sometimes in English, depending on the topic.

He was enrolled in a Ph.D. program in biophysics at Berkeley and had taken on the waiter job to earn some extra money. He projected confidence and optimism. Anyone with a Ph.D. in biophysics, a newly minted area of research with a wide range of application in bio-medical technology, could expect a well-paid position in the pharmaceutical industry. He was expecting his Hong Kong girlfriend to join him in a couple of months, and then they would get married, start a family, live in a nice suburban home and enjoy an upper middle-class life. He had a blueprint for his whole life all mapped out, a life of security, comfort and routines.

Surprised that I was studying an esoteric humanistic discipline called linguistics, he asked, "I thought you were a mathematician."

"I was, but I switched fields three years ago."

"So, what is linguistics?"

"Well, as you can infer from the word, it's the study of language, all aspects of language—its structure, its dynamism, its relations with culture and society, its psychological and neurological bases," I tried to explain.

"Is it a scientific discipline or does it belong to some non-scientific domain?" He went straight to the heart of the matter. In our time, every smart young Chinese chose a career in science and technology.

"Well, linguistics is hard to pinpoint in the classification of knowledge. I would say it's highly interdisciplinary."

Before I could finish my answer, he said, "My research area, biophysics, is also highly interdisciplinary. But it remains a scientific discipline. Where does linguistics fall?"

"Well, I would say that language is first and foremost a human behavior. It's definitely not a physical entity like an atom or a phenomenon like gravity. To the extent that all behaviors are biological, linguists seek to understand the biological foundations of language: How is it produced? How is it perceived? What are the neurological underpinnings of the production and perception of language? What is the nature of the relation between meaning and structure in language? How did human communication evolve into what we now call 'language' today? Language also reflects culture and society. Different cultures typically have different languages, and different languages have different ways of saying the same thing. The study of language, therefore, includes the discovery of its cultural and social underpinning."

"Gee, it sounds really complicated," David interjected. "Is linguistics a science?"

"No, I wouldn't say so. Some linguists like to claim that linguistics is a science. In fact, some go so far as to think the human language is fundamentally similar to logic or formal languages that we devise for harnessing computers. But I came from math and spent two months in software design at Burroughs Corporation, which had the largest computer (B5500) at the time, and I don't think natural language is similar to mathematical logic or formal language. If there is any similarity between natural language and formal language or logic, it's confined to a very general statement that both natural language and formal language exhibit regularities, but the regularities of natural language are fuzzy and full of exceptions, whereas the regularities of logic and formal language are air-tight and strictly rule-governed."

I could tell he was listening intently, so I pressed on, "If you think for a moment, the decoupling of logic and formal language from natural language is not surprising at all. Logic and formal language are for machines. Machines are fixtures, and their performances or operations are prescribed by a priori rules and constraints laid out by designers. Natural language is the tool for human communication and human thought. A critical feature of human communication and thought, in contrast with the functions of a machine, is flexibility, creativity, and sometimes, unpredictability. Humans are NOT machines, and machines, thankfully, are not humans. Our behavior and thoughts change at all times, depending on our culture and environment. The structure of language must have fuzzy edges to accommodate the continuous change and demands of a particular culture and society. In the end, a language is inextricably linked to its speakers—their culture, tradition, psychological and physical environments. I think those who believe natural language is similar to logic and formal language suffer from science envy."

"Why did you leave mathematics to get involved in something like that?" David finally got the hang of what I was saying. "Especially if it's not a scientific discipline?"

"I like linguistics precisely because it concerns human behavior, cultures and societies. Actually, I like all disciplines including mathematics, but prefer to specialize in an area that deals with a broad spectrum of human knowledge like: How do we think? How do we communicate? How are we conditioned by the culture and society in which we are brought up? What are the substantive and structural differences or similarities between the thousands of languages in the world? How did language originate in hominid evolution? What distinguishes human language from animal communication? How do children acquire their native language? Exploring these questions gives me a bird's-eye view of the human mental world. Don't you think those are fascinating questions? They induce linguists to seek an expansive view of the human intellect taking into consideration all of the fields of human knowledge."

"Well," David thought for a while, "Perhaps. But that is unrelated to the central issue of life, which is money. What is the job prospect in linguistics?"

"It's not bad, but not as good as the job prospects in science and technology." My assessment was honest, "If I am lucky, I will land a faculty position."

"That would be nice," David commented, "except academic salary is terrible. I don't understand why you give up the opportunity to work in industry."

"Money is not the most important thing to me." I wanted to elaborate but thought I'd better stop.

At this point, our conversation almost reached a dead end. Both of us had come to understand that there wasn't much common ground between us. Adroitly, he switched topics and wanted to know what I had been doing outside of pursuing graduate studies. As for himself, he had been scrupulously saving money to purchase the amenities of life like furniture, household appliances, a new automobile, in anticipation of the arrival of his fiancée from Hong Kong. To make those purchases, he took on the job of a waiter at Larry Blake three evenings per week even though he enjoyed full financial support from his department at UC Berkeley. When I told him my preoccupation with the antiwar protest and the civil rights movement, he was aghast.

"You have become strange and crazy!" he said in Cantonese. "Why do you get involved in stuff like that?"

I didn't venture to offer an explanation, mostly because I didn't think I could come up with an explanation that would satisfy him.

Later he found out that I practically had no material belongings other than scores of books and an old Chevy in disrepair. Filled with pity for me, he was dismayed.

He then switched the conversation to query about my Hong Kong connections, in particular, Kim, my girlfriend in Hong Kong, a track and field athlete like David and myself. When we played bridge at the home of David's girlfriend in downtown Kowloon, Kim was always my partner. She knitted a dark green sweater for me as a farewell present when I left Hong Kong for America. I was sure that David had known about it. Now, he wanted to find out what had happened between Kim and me.

"Nothing happened," I said dreamily. "It was a long time ago."

In objective time, it was eight years ago. In the subjective time of my emotional world, it was so remote that it seemed to belong to a different era or a previous life. Retrieving that memory induced pangs of guilt. At some point in my struggle to cope with life at the Kappa Sigma fraternity of Bowdoin College, I stopped writing letters to Kim and all of my friends in Hong Kong.

In China and Hong Kong, my preoccupation was physical survival, earning enough money to purchase food and the daily necessities. At Bowdoin, I struggled for psychological survival, striving not to succumb to a hostile, alien world. It was not a struggle that I could understand or explain at the time, even though it was so harrowing and eviscerating that I often entertained the thought of abandoning my education and returning to the emotional and psychological wholesomeness of the physically harsh environment of Hong Kong. Writing to Kim or my friends to tell them my unending anguish seemed pointless. I did at the beginning. Then I stopped because it was futile to describe repeatedly my difficult experience at Bowdoin. My friends in Hong Kong couldn't help me. It would only reveal my weakness.

If I had told them that I felt infinitely lonely, they would've said that I was suffering from the inevitable malady that afflicted every Chinese who went to America or Europe to forge a new life. They understood that it was an American tradition to extoll self-reliant individualism and eschew, if not disdain, any form of dependency in adult rela-tionships, whereas the Chinese motto of life advocated the opposite: cultivate and cherish devoted and emotionally dependent human relationships. This Chinese motto of life could very well explain why few Chinese people suffer from existential quandaries. I still remember vividly my own startled reaction during a visit to Hong Kong in the 1970s when I heard my father proudly telling his friends that I sent him money every month to support him. By then he was proud of me for having become a professor. When he announced to his friend my monetary support of him, he was showing off his close-knit, mutually **dependent** relationship with his "accomplished" son, even though by my reckoning, our checkered relationship had never come close to mutual devotion. Furthermore, in my world in California, teaching and research in a major university stood as a respectable profession, but not a spectacular achievement as it was in my father's antiquated worldview.

My imperative at Bowdoin College was the pursuit of conventional success. In the madness of that pursuit, I inadvertently severed the tether to the world in which I was born.

After I left David's apartment, walking through the empty streets south of the Berkeley campus deep in the night, wafts of tear gas odor still lingering here and there from the antiwar demonstration of the previous afternoon, I felt rattled by a strange sense of isolation coupled with some nonspecific nostalgia.

Like a mirror, David had enabled me to see my metamorphosis that took place during the years at Stanford and Berkeley. It had never been my intention to undergo a metamorphosis. Unlike my good friend Keith, I almost never reflected on my identity. It was not an important issue for me. If I had changed during the 1960s, I would have been unaware of the transformation. That was true until my meeting with David.

Was the metamorphosis good?

Was it bad?

I didn't have a clue.

Only the mixed feeling of nostalgia and isolation was unmistakable at the time. That feeling stirred up my desire to re-establish a link to my past. I decided to compensate for the loss of human connection I had in Hong Kong by learning about the people, culture and history of China.

Since then, I have become as eager to learn about the Chinese and East Asian civilizations as I have been keen in familiarizing myself with the Greco-Roman civilizations. Serendipitously, not long after meeting David, I stumbled upon a book by Owen Lattimore while browsing in the East Asian library at UC Berkeley. The book was *Studies in Frontier History: Collected Papers, 1928-1958*, Oxford University Press, 1962. It opened my eyes to a China from the perspective of her multi-ethnic population and the history, geography, civilizations of China's frontiers in the west, north and south. For the first time, I learned that China, far from having a monolithic culture and a homogenous population, was forged and shaped by the confluence of scores of ethnic groups and four great civilizations: the pastoral civilization, the Islamic civilization, the Buddhist civilization and the Confucian civilization. The confluence of these four civilizations remains vividly preserved in the forms of cave painting, sculptures, steles and ruins along the thousand miles of the silk route east of Afghanistan, within the border of China.

Lattimore's book showed that my former understanding of China sprang exclusively from the perspective of the Han ethnic group. It is a perspective that has dominated sinology in China as well as overseas.

During the past fifty years, I have learned that my early conception of the country in which I grew up represented a particular point of view, valid and useful in some ways but false and misleading in others. Lattimore's work was pioneering and trail-blazing in sinology. Sadly, he was persecuted during the McCarthy era for his socialist leanings and hounded out of the country—one of the many brilliant minds driven out of the United States by McCarthy and his enablers.

It is true that the Han ethnic group has been the dominant component of China's population for more than two thousand years. China's early philosophers, from Confucius, Mencius to Laozi, Zhuangzi, Mozi, Xunzi, who laid the foundation of the Chinese civilization, belonged to the Han ethnic group. Throughout the history of China, the literati, the historians, the record keepers, the scholars, the ministers of the imperial court of China were overwhelmingly members of the Han ethnic group. They created a paradigm in sinology portraying China as a homogenous, xenophobic and inward-looking nation, philosophically steeped in the Confucian civilization and economically based on labor-intensive agriculture. To them, the fact that many dynasties were founded by warriors from non-Han ethnic groups was not an important factor. (In the Western world, the best-known example of non-Han dynasties was the Yuan Dynasty founded by Kublai Khan, a grandson of Genghis Khan). In the opinion of the traditional Han Chinese historians, scholars and court officials, the non-Han origin of each imperial household in Chinese history amounted to a mere trifle. In time, according to the lore created by the Han people, every "foreign" imperial household became culturally assimilated, and the "foreigners" were absorbed into a sea of Han Chinese.

Over the years, I have learned that the traditional account of Chinese history is far from the truth. The Liao Dynasty (916-1125 A.D.), for example, also known as the Khitan Kingdom (The word "Khitan" might be the etymological origin of the English word, "China") and founded by Yelü Abaoji (Emperor Taizu of the Liao Dynasty in Han Chinese historiography), was so culturally independent of the Han ethnic group that they had created their own written language which, to this day, remains not fully deciphered.

286

Even the most glorious dynasty, the Tang (618 – 907 A.D.), known as the Golden Age in Chinese history, was not created by full-blooded Han Chinese leaders at the head of a Han Chinese army. (In the Cantonese language, indigenous to the southeastern coast of China, the term signifying "Chinese" is *tong-jen*, which literally means "people of Tang Dynasty.") A father-and-son team, Li Yuan and Li Shimin, founded that great dynasty. They conquered China with the help of Uighur and other pastoralist warriors, amassed through their maternal connections with the pastoralists in the northwest of present-day China.

During the early stage of Tang Dynasty, its capital, today's Xian, was a prosperous and sophisticated metropolis with a diverse population including Hans, Uighurs, Kazakhs, Kyrgyzs, Uzbeks, Arabs, Jews, Tibetans, Indians, Persians and Europeans, all of whom enjoyed equal rights under an enlightened imperial rule. Their religions included Buddhism, Taoism, Nestorianism, Judaism, Christianity, Manichaeism, Zoroastrianism, folk beliefs and tribal rituals. According to some demographic studies, this diverse population of Xian in the seventh century exceeded three quarter million. The Tang people adored and yearned for everything exotic. That curiosity and yearning of the people was facilitated by Xian being an eastern terminal of the silk route that served as a mercantile highway linking China to the Fergana valley, India, Persia, the Mediterranean basin and Europe. The exotica in Xian ranged from European dances, Persian rugs, Mediterranean fashions, Central Asian music to the vermillion birds and wild animals of the equatorial jungles. Supposedly, Xian even had a Parisian brothel. In short, the Tang people's mentality was diametrically opposed to that of an inward-looking and xenophobic nation. Perhaps the blossoming of arts and literature during the Tang Dynasty was partly engendered by the diversity and interface of the cultures promoted by Li Yuan and his son, Li Shimin, the first two Tang emperors.

At the time I learned about the ethnic and cultural diversity of Xian during the early period of the Tang Dynasty, I was familiar with Vienna's fin-de-ciècle cultural blossoming, a frequent topic of conversation among my friends at Stanford. It is astonishing to see that ethnic and cultural diversity was at the foundation of the cultural bloom in Vienna toward the end of the 19th century as it was at the heart of the expansion of China's civilization centered in Xian of the 7th and 8th century.

Since meeting David, learning about China and East Asia has become a life-long interest. Sometimes, the learning makes me feel as if I have become a kind of reborn Chinese who is physically removed and psychologically detached from China, yet intellectually glued to its cultures and history. I have been fortunate in that my interest in the Chinese civilization has been facilitated by my profession as a linguist. For the inception of my pursuit to understand the civilization in my country of birth, I am grateful to David.

Arendt, Hannah. *The Human Condition*. Chicago: University of Chicago Press, 1958.

Arendt, Hannah. *Eichmann in Jerusalem: A Report on the Banality of Evil*. New York: Viking Press, 1963.

Arendt, Hannah. "Lying in Politics: Reflections on the Pentagon Papers." In *The New York Review of Books*, November 18th issue, 1971.

Arendt, Hannah. *The Life of the Mind*. New York: Harcourt Brace, 1977.

Ariosto, Ludovico. *Orlando Furioso*. Translated by A. H. Gilbert, 1954. Durham: Duke University Press, 1516.

Beard, Yolande. *The Wappo: A Report*. Morongo Indian Reservation: Malki Museum Press, 1979.

Brontë, Emily. *Wuthering Heights*. 2nd ed. (vintage paperback). New York: Dodd, Mead & Co., 1960.

Carson, Rachel. *Silent Spring*. Originally serialized in *The New Yorker*. Boston: Houghton Mifflin, 1962.

Cervantes (Miguel de Cervantes Saavedra). *Don Quixote*. Translated by J. M. Cohen, 1950. Penguin Books, 2001.

Deutscher, Isaac. *The Prophet Armed: Trotsky, 1879-1921*. New York: Oxford University Press, 1954.

Deutscher, Isaac. *The Prophet Unarmed: Trotsky, 1921-1929*. New York: Oxford University Press, 1959.

Deutscher, Isaac. *The Prophet Outcast: Trotsky, 1920-1940*. New York: Oxford University Press, 1963.

Dickens, Charles. *David Copperfield*. Originally published as a serial in 1849-1850. Penguin Books, 2004.

Galois, Évariste (1811-1832). A French mathematician who died from injuries suffered in a duel at age 21. His notes on the conditions for solvability of certain algebraic equations (polynomials) led to group theory and field theory, two of the most important branches of pure mathematics. Joseph Liouville edited and published Galois's theory in 1846, fourteen years after Galois's death. But the significance and ramifications of his theory was not recognized until the late 19th century. See *Galois Theory* by Emil Artin, Dover Publishers, 1944, and *Galois Theory for Beginners: A Historical Perspective* by Jörg Bewersdorff, 2006, published by the American Mathematical Society.

Gödel, Kurt. "On Formally Undecidable Propositions of Principia Mathematica and Related Systems." In *From Frege to Gödel: A Source Book on Mathematical Logic 1879–1931*, translated by Jean van Heijenoort. Cambridge, MA: Harvard University Press, 1967.

Hammett, Dashiell. *The Maltese Falcon*. New York: Alfred A. Knopf, Inc., 1930.

Harrington, Michael. *The Other America: Poverty in the United States*. New York: Macmillan Publishers, 1962.

Hauser, Arnold. *The Social History of Art*. New York: A. Knopf, Inc., 1951.

Hawthorne, Nathaniel. *The Scarlet Letter*. Boston: Ticknor and Fields, 1850.

Hersey, John. *The Wall*. New York: A. Knopf, Inc., 1950.

Hesiod. *Theogony*. Translated by A. Athanassakis, 1983. Baltimore: Johns Hopkins University Press, 8th-7th century BC.

Hobsbawm, Eric. *Primitive Rebels: Studies in Archaic Forms of Social Movement in the 19th and 20th Centuries*. Manchester, England: University of Manchester Press, 1959.

Hobsbawm, Eric. *The Age of Extremes: The Short Twentieth Century, 1914-1991*. Vintage Books, New York: A. Knopf Inc., 1994.

Ibsen, Henrik. *Complete Works of Henrik Ibsen*. Oxford: Oxford University Press, 1928.

Jackson, Helen. *A Century of Dishonor*. Reprinted in 1964 by Ross &Haines, Minneapolis. 1881.

James, Henry. *The Portrait of a Lady*. New York: Oxford University Press, 2009.

Jungk, Robert. *Brighter than a Thousand Suns: A Personal History of the Atomic Scientists*. Translated by J. Cleugh. New York: A Harvest Book, Harcourt, Inc., 1958.

Lattimore, Owen. *Studies in Frontier History: Collected Papers, 1928-1958*. New York: Oxford University Press, 1962.

Lee, Harper. *To Kill a Mockingbird*. Philadelphia: J. B. Lippincott, 1960.

Lucretius. *The Way Things Are: De Rerum Natura*. Translated by Rolfe Humphries. Bloomington, Indiana: Indiana University Press, 1968.

Luo, Guan Zhong. *San Guo Yanyi*. Translated by Luo Guanzhong in *Romance of the Three Kingdoms*. 14th century.

Mailer, Norman. *The Naked and the Dead*. New York: Rinehart & Company, 1948.

Marcuse, Herbert. *One Dimensional Man: Studies in the Ideology of Advanced Industrial Society*. Boston: Beacon Press, 1964.

Marquez, Gabriel Garcia. *One Hundred Years of Solitude*. Translated by G. Rabassa. New York: Harper & Row, 1967.

Said, Edward. *Orientalism*. New York: Pantheon Books, 1978.

Scott, Walter. *Ivanhoe*. A modern edition appeared as Volume 8 of the *Edinburgh Edition of the Waverley Novels*. Edinburgh: Edinburgh University Press, 1820.

Shi, Nai-an. *Shui Hu Zhuan*. (English translation: *Water Margin* or *All Men Are Brothers*.) 14th century.

Stendhal, Henri. *The Red and the Black*. Translated by L. Blair, 1959. New York: Bantam Books, 1830.

Stowe, Harriet Beecher. *Uncle Tom's Cabin*. Boston: John P. Jewett and Company, 1852.

Turnbull, Colin. *The Forest People: A Study of the Pygmies of the Congo*. New York: Simon & Schuster, 1961.

Williams, Tennessee. "The Catastrophe of Success." In *The New York Times*, November 30, 1947.